ETHICS IN POLICING

Misconduct AND Integrity

JULIE B. RAINES, JD, PhD

Assistant Professor
Department of Political Science and Criminal Justice
Northern Kentucky University

JONES AND BARTLETT PUBLISHERS
Sudbury, Massachusetts
BOSTON   TORONTO   LONDON   SINGAPORE

World Headquarters

Jones and Bartlett Publishers
40 Tall Pine Drive
Sudbury, MA 01776
978-443-5000
info@jbpub.com
www.jbpub.com

Jones and Bartlett Publishers
Canada
6339 Ormindale Way
Mississauga, Ontario L5V 1J2
Canada

Jones and Bartlett Publishers
International
Barb House, Barb Mews
London W6 7PA
United Kingdom

Jones and Bartlett's books and products are available through most bookstores and online book-sellers. To contact Jones and Bartlett Publishers directly, call 800-832-0034, fax 978-443-8000, or visit our website www.jbpub.com.

Substantial discounts on bulk quantities of Jones and Bartlett's publications are available to corporations, professional associations, and other qualified organizations. For details and specific discount information, contact the special sales department at Jones and Bartlett via the above contact information or send an email to specialsales@jbpub.com.

Production Credits

Publisher, Higher Education:
  Cathleen Sether
Associate Editor: Megan R. Turner
Production Director: Amy Rose
Senior Production Editor: Renée Sekerak
Production Assistant: Jill Morton
Associate Marketing Manager: Jessica Cormier
Manufacturing and Inventory Control
  Supervisor: Amy Bacus

Composition: Arlene Apone
Cover Design: Scott Moden
Photo Research and Permissions Manager:
  Kimberly Potvin
Cover Image: © UpperCut Images/
  age fotostock
Printing and Binding: Malloy Incorporated
Cover Printing: Malloy Incorporated

Library of Congress Cataloging-in-Publication Data
Raines, Julie B.
  Ethics in policing : misconduct and integrity / by Julie B. Raines.
     p. cm.
  Includes bibliographical references and index.
  ISBN-13: 978-0-7637-5530-0
  ISBN-10: 0-7637-5530-3
  1. Police ethics. 2. Police misconduct. I. Title.
  HV7924.R35 2010
  172'.2--dc22
                                    2009017086
6048

Printed in the United States of America
13 12 11 10 09   10 9 8 7 6 5 4 3 2 1

Contents

Preface

The ethical behavior of public officials is critical to the performance of public agencies. Yet, it is rarely the subject of quantitative research. This text contributes to our understanding of the norms followed by police officers regarding misconduct that are shaped among street-level bureaucrats who, regularly and without warning, confront important value choices. A complete investigation of police ethics would need to consider both the factors that contribute to unethical behavior as well as ethical behavior. The literature focuses on the former. This text focuses on those factors that contribute to unethical, as well as ethical behavior. This text examines one type of street-level bureaucrat, namely police officers, and their attitudes toward misconduct using existing data from police officers in thirty police agencies. The specific issue examined is whether a police officer's tendency to report peer misconduct is influenced primarily by attitudes regarding misconduct or individual characteristics, peer behavior, the nature of the misconduct, or organizational characteristics. Using descriptive statistics and regression models, this text explores an officer's willingness to report misconduct as it is influenced by attitudes, as well as the nature of police misconduct.

This text is designed to expose students to police integrity in the United States. Relevant literature in administrative ethics, social deviance theory, organizational culture, and street-level bureaucrats are explored in an effort to better understand what officers face in their day-to-day interactions with citizens. Within this text, there is a recurrent application of data from a National Institute of Justice (NIJ) study. The NIJ study contains realistic scenarios of ethical issues and this text attempts to apply this data to various theoretical frameworks in order to derive an understanding of police integrity.

Students will benefit not only from the background information presented here, but also from exposure to advanced data analysis. Correlation, regression, and structural equation modeling are each presented several times giving the student and the instructor an opportunity to discuss the difference between strength of relationships and predictability. As students will have little exposure to these concepts, it is presented in a way that should be easier to follow given the subject matter—most students are interested in ethics, integrity, and the implications of unethical behavior.

This text has been a long journey for me, beginning as a dissertation topic. I have learned far more than I can relate in this one text. I hope you enjoy using this text as a springboard for discussing ethical issues as much as I have enjoyed researching these issues over the years.

Acknowledgments

I would like to express my deepest appreciation to Dr. James Svara for his advice and seemingly limitless patience. Dr. Dennis Daley, Dr. Michael Vasu, and Dr. James Brunet gave invaluable assistance in the completion of this study. Dr. Swiss has also given me advice from time to time that has greatly enhanced my PhD experience. I would also like to thank Steven Klingaman for allowing me to include his article in this text, the subject of his Master's thesis—it was an honor working with Steven. Without the time and loving support of my husband and parents, I would never have completed this journey. A special thanks to my daughters, Leila and Sarah, who constantly remind me that there is always time to play.

Biography

Julie Raines is an Assistant Professor at Northern Kentucky University. Dr. Raines received her JD from The Catholic University of America, Columbus School of Law, where she was Senior Lead Article Editor for *ComLaw Conspectus*. She received her undergraduate degree from North Carolina State University. Dr. Raines worked for American Airlines for five years after graduation as an International Security Agent, a reservation agent, and finally a ticket counter agent in Washington, D.C. Upon graduation from law school, she was an Associate with Sandman & Strickland practicing a mixture of litigation and corporate law. She opened her own practice one year later specializing in entertainment law. Dr. Raines' dissertation topic addresses ethical awareness, standards, and action of police officers in the United States. Currently, she has published three articles, which include *The Gender Card v. The First Amendment*, Dicta, Fall 1995 and *The Fairness in Musical Licensing Act: The Tavern Bill Casts a Shadow*, University of California, Hastings College of Law, Communications & Entertainment Law Journal, Fall, 1997, and *Law Enforcement Policy: Use of Force*, Law Enforcement Executive Forum, 5(4) 2005. She has also published a teaching supplement for a Cyberlaw text. Courses she has taught include Intro to American Government, Legal and Regulatory Environments, Communication Law and Ethics, and Intro to Criminal Law.

CHAPTER 1

Introduction to a Street-Level Bureaucrat: The Police Officer

OBJECTIVES

- Summarize some of the reasons why police officers might commit unethical acts
- Introduce some of the ethical issues that arise within public administration, particularly for police officers
- Provide historical background regarding the role of the police officer in the United States
- Point out some of the benefits and drawbacks with respect to discretion in policing
- Briefly describe the National Institute of Justice police officer survey that is discussed at length in this text

Spectacular scandals illustrate the underlying issue of the performance and accountability of public servants. The video-taped Rodney King beating in Los Angeles, the torture of a Haitian immigrant with a plunger in New York, and the widespread corruption in the New Orleans police force are just a few of the examples found within law enforcement. In North Carolina, police officers struck up e-mail friendships with a 17-year-old Chicago girl that quickly escalated into sexually explicit conversations (Anonymous, 1998). In Wake County, eight deputies were disciplined for exchanging sexually suggestive messages with the girl while they were on duty. The girl's mother said that one deputy sent her daughter a photo of his genitals. Wake County Sheriff John H. Baker Jr. demoted one deputy and suspended seven for 2 to 4 days (Anonymous, 1998). The most compelling stories are those of officers who are willing to break the "code of silence" and report fellow officers for engaging in misconduct.

These incidents highlight the need for empirical research that will explain why some officers commit these acts and what might prompt other officers to report such examples of misconduct. In light of the heightened sensitivity to ethical decision making, there is growing research interest in the areas of misconduct, corruption, ethics, and moral reasoning within government. In particular, attention has been placed on police ethics. Understanding police officers' attitudes about misconduct is an important step toward understanding ethical and unethical behavior within the ranks.

Police are a unique group of individuals because they seek to prevent crime as their career. Officers are entrusted with a somewhat unique responsibility in our society—to protect other members of society, much like fire fighters and security guards. Officers are required to safeguard property and lives fairly, avoid use of excessive force, avoid corruption, use consistent and wise discretion, keep confidences when appropriate, cooperate with other law enforcement agencies, exhibit exemplary behavior off duty, and balance the ultimate authority—the taking of a life. The vast majority of officers accomplish these goals effectively, serving their communities honorably.

Only a very small percentage of officers are disciplined annually for misconduct in the United States. For example, approximately 3,104 officers, of the over 600,000 sworn officers in state and local departments, were disciplined for unethical behavior from 1990 to 1995 in the United States (Trautman, 1997). Although this is a quite small proportion of the total, the nature of the police task makes even these few a matter of concern. When one officer commits a transgression, the entire agency suffers, particularly when the news media reports the incident.

Steinberg and Austern (1990) summarize some of the reasons why officers might commit unethical acts. Some claim that they did not realize it was against the law, policy, or procedure. Some officers admitted that unethical conduct can be the result of basic stupidity. There are those police officers who believe corruption is a part of the job, that it is required in order to survive their job, or that it is a game. Some of the most destructive reasons in history center around those individuals who believe that he or she is doing the right thing, going along with what the agency requires, or simply just following orders. Other officers admitted that it was a way to speed up the way the system processes clients, to help out a friend, to abuse the system, to feed their ego, to satisfy their greedy nature, for personal gain, as a type of revenge, or to solve a financial problem (Steinberg & Austern, 1990, pp. 33–55).

Actual misconduct is hard to investigate because of unwillingness on the part of public officials to admit wrongdoing (Klockars et al., 2000). Because answering questions regarding the behavior of others is less threatening, officers may be more willing to answer questions regarding whether they are willing to report others for misconduct as well as their attitudes regarding peer misconduct. Several chapters in this book analyze a large existing data set to measure more precisely officer attitudes regarding peer misconduct and the propensity for those who would report the misconduct of peers. Chapter 1 begins with a thorough examination of variations in behavior among police officers.

Individuals respond in a variety of ways to inefficient and/or inferior working conditions. According to Hirschman (1970), employees who face undesirable work environments can exit the organization, voice their discontent, remain loyal to the organization and ignore the situation, or neglect their work as a passive aggressive response (Farrell, 1983; Rusbult et al., 1982; Rusbult et al., 1988; Withey & Cooper, 1989). Police officers may accept misconduct in their personal values as a passive aggressive response to undesirable working conditions. Officers may tolerate the misconduct of other officers and not report those officers out of loyalty. Some officers, however, may report the misconduct of fellow officers, an act more commonly called whistle-blowing behavior in public service.

Whistle blowers are not disgruntled employees. According to Brewer and Selden (1998), they rank among the most productive, valued, and committed members of their organizations. Whistle blowers are normal people who have a strong conscience, are high performers committed to the formal goals of their organization, and have a strong sense of professional responsibility. Whistle blowers are less motivated by job security and are more motivated by regard for the public interest. They report high levels of job commitment and job satisfaction (Brewer & Selden, 1998).

Police officers, however, are not typically prone to reporting fellow officers for misconduct. The code of silence is well documented within the police culture literature (Human Rights Watch, 1998; Klockars et al., 2004; Skolnick & Bayley, 1986; Skolnick & Fyfe, 1993; Vila & Morris, 1999). Officers who violate the code of silence by reporting fellow officers are shunned, and any transgressions committed by the reporting officer are exposed (Cancino & Enriquez, 2004; Skolnick & Fyfe, 1993). According to Klockars et al. (2006), agencies weaken the code of silence if they strongly adhere to specific policies that encourage reporting misconduct and policies that impact both officers and supervisors.

The code of silence is just one of several factors influencing the ethical conduct of police officers. Other factors include hiring practices, the demands of the profession, socialization, personal morality, character, and supervision. The following section briefly explores these factors and the conditions under which they arise.

THEORETICAL FRAMEWORK: ADMINISTRATIVE ETHICS

The questions analyzed by this study are fundamental to administrative ethics.

1. What are the differences in ethical attitudes and behavior in street-level bureaucrats and what causes these differences?
2. Do police officers come to public service with strong public service values?
3. Are officers socialized within their agency to commit unethical acts or to uphold ethical standards?
4. Are officers exposed to such stressful and/or unusual working conditions that it leads inevitably to erosion of their commitment to ethical behavior or do officers choose to remain more committed in their ethical values?
5. Is the ethical behavior of officers shaped by the attitudes of peers and the police and actions of their agency?
6. Which of these issues has the greatest impact on the ethical behavior of police officers?

That small percentage of officers who do commit unethical acts during their careers may not be screened during recruitment. Another possibility is that the job itself attracts officers of a certain personality type and/or disposition that are conducive to abandoning public service values when the right conditions exist. The minimum requirements for hiring new recruits may be inadequate by allowing inexperienced, young individuals into a career at a stage of moral development that is not appropriate to a job that demands the highest moral character. Police officers, in fact, all adults, have a level of moral development that reflects in part their experience. The majority of the population has moral reasoning based on conventional stages of moral development that are guided by moral values, understanding the difference between what is right and what is wrong, and maintaining social order and a sense of duty to others (Kohlberg, 1984).

An alternative possibility is that young recruits have good intentions but have weakly formed ethical attitudes and a naive view of police work. They may be subject to the influence of peers and become disillusioned and "hardened" by conditions they encounter on the force. The police officer's level of moral development before joining the police force will affect how they respond to ethical challenges. Socialization on the force, the process by which officers learn group values and established behaviors, will affect their level of moral development after joining the police force and will alter how they respond to ethical challenges (Lundman, 1980).

Officers who come to the public service with strong public service values may still be ultimately socialized to commit unethical acts through training, peers, and supervisors. Police officers, like public administrators generally, are greatly impacted by peers and supervisors with respect to their attitudes toward misconduct. Their values may be reinforced with professional ethical norms and organizational practices. If the organizational norms of an agency support unethical behavior, then eventually officers will either quit the force out of frustration, join in the undesirable behavior, or alienate themselves from their fellow peers who may be engaging in unethical conduct (Hirschman, 1970). The individual officer's relationship with his or her peers and supervisors will greatly impact which direction the officer chooses.

The demands of the job may be in itself too much for some officers. Facing danger constantly, having unusual working hours and sleep habits, and being continually surrounded by criminals may be too much stress, particularly when experienced over a period of several years (Kenney & McNamara, 1999; Lundman, 1980; Paoline, 2001; Wilson, 1968).

This book also takes into consideration the factors that contribute to an officer's ability to commit unethical acts. Officers, in particular patrol officers, are difficult, if not impossible, to monitor on a daily basis as they work outside the normal confines of an office setting (Walker, 2004). Police officers, like most street-level bureaucrats, enjoy a great deal of autonomy in their jobs. Discretion does not automatically lead to unethical acts and is necessary in order for bureaucrats to carry out their jobs effectively; however, it does allow the opportunity for unethical acts to occur.

Those who can report misbehavior—the citizens who perceive that they have been mistreated by police officers—are at a disadvantage on several levels. Because most of the citizens who would be prone to complaining are in the process of being arrested, the veracity of their claims is suspect at best. Those that might complain are faced with the fear of reprisal. There is also some skepticism on the part of the citizen who feels that such complaints will fall on deaf ears (Maynard-Moody & Musheno, 2000). In some instances, supervisors who wish to protect their employees do in fact ignore such complaints (Raines, 2005).

There are two primary factors that contribute to the police officer's opportunity to commit unethical and/or criminal acts (Lipsky, 1980; Maynard-Moody & Musheno, 2000; Vila & Morris, 1999). First, the role the police officer plays in society shapes the job he or she performs. The police officer's role also impacts attitudes toward that work. The role an officer plays contributes to the second factor—autonomy on the job. The complaint process and lack of adequate monitoring allow an officer autonomy and wide discretion on the job. Discretion will be covered more extensively in Chapter 2. The section that follows briefly describes the evolution of the police officer's role in society.

THE ROLE OF THE POLICE OFFICER

The Political, Professional, and Community Policing Eras

The role of the police officer has changed dramatically over time. Initially, the police in the United States were merely average citizens without formal training who stood as night watchmen, collected taxes, caught and punished criminals, and enforced the law. As territories were settled and the railroads expanded westward, private police forces and elected governments kept the peace between 1840–1920, but some private citizens in smaller communities became involved in vigilante justice. During this time, however, with the growth of cities and the influx of immigrants, modern policing modeled after the London Metropolitan police force was born. The American version was highly politicized and corrupt, however, relying heavily on favoritism. This was known as the Political Era (Vila & Morris, 1999).

The merit-based system reformed the organizational structure of the police in the early 1900s, beginning what is known as the Professional Era of policing that lasted until the 1970s. By the Depression, the role of the police was to protect the general public from crime, enforce the law, maintain order, and keep the peace; however, diversity was nonexistent, and corruption was still widespread. Many laws were passed improving how officers were chosen and how police organizations were managed, but crime rates continued to increase because of growth in population and urbanization.

With the advent of new technologies in the 1970s, the Professional Era ended, leading to the beginning of Community Policing. Ultimately, the role of the police changed in the 1990s to reflect a growing need for officers to do more than simply respond to criminal activity, but to also work with communities in solving other crime-related problems. Thus, the concept of community policing was born. Community policing not only demands more interaction of the police with members of the community, it also gives members of the community more control over how crime is controlled within their neighborhoods (Vila & Morris, 1999).

Community policing has some drawbacks in that it produces "conflicting demands on police officers and police organizations" (Vila & Morris, 1999, p. xxix). Officers are required to perform multiple roles within a community including counseling, mediating, and enforcing the law. This requires a great deal of autonomy, which can lead to the rise of corruption and/or misconduct (Vila & Morris, 1999). Discretion becomes necessary, allowing both good and harm within the community.

Today, officers are working within the Homeland Security era initiated by the September 11th attacks. This era is characterized by mass hirings in law enforcement, as well as the need for officers to understand terrorism, technology, and weapons of mass destruction. This era focuses on the crime control and prevention model using highly centralized management and organization (Oliver, 2006).

Discretion in Policing

Discretion is inevitable for the street-level bureaucrat (Maynard-Moody et al., 1990). Police officers, in particular, enjoy high levels of discretion given the nature of their job. Does discretion automatically lead to abuse? Are tighter controls and supervision the answer? One problem with tighter controls is that it causes abuse to become more secretive and harder to find. There are existing controls that street-level workers self-monitor. They also rely on peers, supervisors, and clients to keep themselves in check (Maynard-Moody & Musheno 2000). As Lipsky (1980, p. 23) pointed out, "Discretion provides opportunity to intervene on behalf of clients as well as to discriminate among them." Discretion, then, can provide flexibility for bureaucrats, and limiting discretion can create as many problems as it solves.

Within the police force it is difficult, if not impossible, given the nature of the work to increase supervision significantly in as much as the officer works alone (Lipsky, 1980). In addition to self-controls, officers rely on peers and the complaints from the public to keep them in check. Relying on these resources, however, raises further problems. For example, citizens have difficulty reporting police misconduct (Maynard-Moody et al., 2000). Furthermore, peers can also be corrupt, leading to the corrupt socialization of officers on-the-job (Lundman, 1980).

A 2000 survey reveals that approximately 95% of police departments in the United States have currently adopted community policing (Law Enforcement Management and Administrative Statistics, 2000). Community policing allows policing to retain its autonomous characteristics. This autonomy, in turn, allows officers the opportunity to commit deviant acts; however, discretion alone does not mean that an officer will automatically turn to deviant behavior. The following section takes a more in-depth look at how unethical behavior can arise within an agency.

Given these circumstances, how can misconduct be detected in agencies? One possibility is to examine complaints, but these reports are incomplete and difficult to acquire. An alternative approach is to examine an employee's attitudes toward work, work environment, peers, supervisors, and the unethical behavior of peers and supervisors. The National Institute of Justice (NIJ) has collected data regarding police officer attitudes toward misconduct, officer behavior, and the officer's perception of peer attitudes and behavior.

NIJ POLICE SURVEY

There are several ways to answer these questions regarding whether and how some officers turn to unethical behavior in their careers. These questions can be at least partially answered by looking at officer attitudes and those of their peers and by examining factors that might impact officer behavior. The NIJ conducted a study in 1997 that offers a rare opportunity to analyze police officer attitudes and behavior (Klockars et al., 2004).

The NIJ is an agency under the U.S. Department of Justice whose mission includes conducting research on crime control and justice issues. The NIJ funds millions of dollars annually to individuals and institutions for research and evaluation within the criminal justice system. The 1997 study was funded by the NIJ and conducted by several scholars from different universities. To date, the data have not been analyzed using advanced statistical methods to examine multiple explanations for variations in attitude and behavior, nor have the data been analyzed regarding the impact socialization has on police attitudes and behavior.

The NIJ study measures the attitudes of police officers with experience ranging from 1 to more than 20 years of service in 30 different agencies within the United States. The researchers chose agencies with which they had existing relationships, making the sample one of convenience (Klockars et al., 2004). The NIJ study includes responses from over 3,200 officers in the United States, with an overall response rate of 55.5% (Klockars et al., 2000). The NIJ study has been replicated internationally to over 10,000 officers worldwide. Observational studies of three police agencies in the United States have also been added to this body of work. The NIJ work is primarily used as research in the field of police integrity. The NIJ study has been used by its researchers to measure integrity at the organizational level and to generate practical advice aimed at advising police administrators what they can do to improve organizational integrity through policy (Klockars et al., 2004).

This study begins in Chapter 2 by examining the institutional norms of the law enforcement profession. This is followed by a thorough review of the causes of unethical behavior in street-level bureaucrats, with an emphasis on the police officer, police culture, police ethics, and police use of discretion. Organizational deviance within law enforcement is reviewed in Chapter 3, including those issues raised previously here. Chapter 4 reports on law enforcement ethics training in the United States. Chapter 5 explores the NIJ study, including the survey instrument, the variables, and the data collected. Chapters 6, 7, and 8 analyze that data using descriptive statistics and regression models. The focus of the analysis is on ethical awareness, standards, and action of police officers. The reprint of a published article regarding supervisor behavior can be found in Chapter 9. The final chapter makes recommendations to law enforcement agencies striving to encourage ethical decision making.

DISCUSSION QUESTIONS

1. Are there ever circumstances under which a police officer should violate ethical norms?
2. Can you think of any other ethical issues not mentioned in this chapter that police officers face?
3. Do you agree with Oliver that we are in a Homeland Security era? How is this era similar, and how is it different from the Community Policing era? Does this mean that community policing no longer exists?
4. How can police discretion be effectively and reasonably supervised without interfering with the benefits of discretion on the job?
5. The NIJ study attempts to measure integrity of police officers. Do you think it is possible to measure someone's integrity? What obstacles do you think exist in measuring something like integrity?

REFERENCES

Anonymous. (1998, February 15). Officers had sex chats with teen. *The Atlanta Journal and Constitution*, 6A.

Brewer, G. A., & Selden, S. C. (1998). Whistle blowers in the federal civil service: new evidence of the public service ethic. *Journal of Public Administration Research and Theory, 8*, 413–439.

Cancino, J. M., & Enriquez, R. (2004). A qualitative analysis of officer peer retaliation. *Policing: An International Journal of Police Strategies and Management, 27*(3), 320–340.

Farrell, D. (1983). Exit, voice, loyalty, and neglect as responses to job dissatisfaction: a multidimensional-scaling study. *Academy of Management Journal, 26*(4), 596–607.

Hirschman, A. O. (1970). *Exit, Voice and Loyalty: Responses to Decline in Firms, Organizations and States*. Boston: Harvard University Press.

Human Rights Watch (1998). Shielded from Justice: Police Brutality and Accountability in the United States. New York: Human Rights Watch.

Kenney, D. J., & McNamara, R. P. (1999). *Police and Policing: Contemporary Issues*. Westport, CT: Praeger.

Klockars, C. B., Ivkovich, S. K., Harver, W. E., & Haberfeld, M. R. (2000, May). *The Measurement of Police Integrity*. Department of Justice. National Institute of Justice. Washington, D.C.

Klockars, C. B., Ivkovic, S. K., & Haberfeld, M. (2004). *The Contours of Police Integrity*. Thousand Oaks, CA: Sage Publications.

Klockars, C. B., Ivkovic, S. K., & Haberfeld, M. (2006). *Enhancing Police Integrity*. New York: Springer Publishing.

Kohlberg, L. (1984). *The Psychology of Moral Development: The Nature and Validity of Moral Stages*. San Francisco: Harper & Row.

Law Enforcement Management and Administrative Statistics. (2000). Department of Justice. Bureau of Justice Statistics.Washington, D.C.

Lipsky, M. (1980). *Street-Level Bureaucracy: Dilemmas of the Individual in Public Services*. New York: Russell Sage Foundation.

Lundman, R. J. (1980). *Police Behavior*. New York: Oxford University Press.

Maynard-Moody, S., & Musheno, M. (2000). State agent or citizen agent: two narratives of discretion. *Journal of Public Administration Research and Theory, 10*(3), 329–358.

Maynard-Moody, S., Musheno, M., & Palumbo, D. (1990). Street-wise social policy: resolving the dilemma of street-level influence and successful implementation. *The Western Political Quarterly, 43*(4), 833–848.

Oliver, W. (2006). The fourth era of policing: Homeland Security. *International Review of Law, Computers & Technology, 20*(1–2), 49–62.

Paoline III, E. A. (2001). *Rethinking Police Culture: Officers' Occupational Attitudes*. New York: LFB Scholarly Publishing LLC.

Raines, J. B. (2005). Law enforcement policy: use of force. *Law Enforcement Executive Forum, 5*(4), 97–104.

Rusbult, C. E., Farrell, D., Rogers, G., & Mainous, A. G. (1988). Impact of exchange variables on exit, voice, loyalty, and neglect: an integrative model of responses to declining job-satisfaction. *Academy of Management Journal, 31*(3), 599–627.

Rusbult, C. E., Zembrodt, I. M., & Gunn, L. K. (1982). Exit, voice, loyalty, and neglect: responses to dissatisfaction in romantic involvements. *Journal of Personality and Social Psychology, 43*(6), 1230–1242.

Skolnick, J., & Bayley, D. (1986). *The New Blue Line: Police Innovation in Six American Cities.*. New York: Free Press.

Skolnick, J., & Fyfe, J. (1993). *Above the Law: Police and the Excessive Use of Force*. New York: Maxwell MacMillan International.

Steinberg, S. S., & Austern, D. T. (1990). *Government, Ethics, and Managers: A Guide to Solving Ethical Dilemmas in the Public Sector*. Westport, CT: Praeger.

Trautman, N. E. (1997). *The National Law Enforcement Officer Disciplinary Research Project*. Long Beach, MS: The Ethics Institute.

Vila, B., & Morris, C. (1999). *The Role of Police in American Society: A Documentary History*. Westport, CT: Greenwood Press.

Walker, S. (2004, January). *Best Practices in Policing*. Oakland, CA: University of Nebraska at Omaha.

Wilson, J. Q. (1968). *Varieties of Police Behavior*. New York: Antheneum.

Withey, M. J., & Cooper, W. H. (1989). Predicting exit, voice, loyalty, and neglect. *Administrative Science Quarterly, 34*(4), 521–539.

CHAPTER 2

Police Attitudes, Behavior, and Culture

OBJECTIVES

- Expose students to Lipsky's causes of unethical behavior in street-level bureaucrats, specifically police officers
- Discuss causes of unethical behavior according to various scholars such as Maynard-Moody, Musheno, Paoline, Jiao, Klockars, Engel, Worden, Brown, and Benedict, exploring discretion in policing, rational choice, situational factors, individual characteristics, organizational forces, and officer attitudes
- Explore elements of Wilson's bureaucratic organizational culture theories
- Study the socialization process for police officers
- Introduce the concepts of ethical awareness, standards, and action in law enforcement

Standards and institutionalized norms contribute to socialization within an organization. In private business, codes of ethics are considered a part of corporate culture. It is treated similarly to a mission statement for a company—a means of communicating the ethical mandates prescribed by the corporation (Simon, 1995). The current Police Code of Conduct was originally a resolution passed in 1957 at the annual International Association of Chiefs of Police (IACP) conference. The code was not altered again until the 1989 IACP conference. Further changes were made, and the final result was the creation of the Law Enforcement Code of Ethics and the Police Code of Conduct, which were approved by the

IACP in 1991 at their annual conference. These codes are discussed at length in Chapter 4 of this book.

These are the formal ethical standards of police officers. There are a number of factors in the environment of public servants that affect their decision making. The following section reviews factors impacting the street-level bureaucrat's ethical decision-making process.

CAUSES OF UNETHICAL BEHAVIOR IN STREET-LEVEL BUREAUCRATS

According to Michael Lipsky (1980), street-level bureaucrats face many challenges that can potentially lead to unethical behavior in public agencies. Resources, clients, goals, performance measures, alienation, discretion, hiring, training, personality, supervisors, and coworkers each contribute to the street-level bureaucrat's ethical decision making. For the street-level bureaucrat, generally, resources are limited. Clients are nonvoluntary. Goals are ambiguous, and performance measures are inadequate. The street-level bureaucrat has a great deal of discretion in carrying out his or her mission. Ultimately, the organizational culture, and in particular the attitudes and behavior of supervisors and coworkers, will impact how the street-level bureaucrat handles all of these issues. The following subsections explore each of these issues in turn, with the exception of organizational culture, which is addressed in the subsequent section.

Street-Level Bureaucrat Dilemmas of Public Service

Street-level bureaucrats enormously influence the public's lives every day. Agencies provide public benefits and have the authority to sanction the public. In essence, bureaucrats "hold the keys to a dimension of citizenship" (Lipsky, 1980, p. 4). Unfortunately, the essential work bureaucrats perform is subject to conditions that hinder the effective and efficient delivery of services. Bureaucrats generally face inadequate resources; continually increasing demand for services; ambiguous, conflicting, or vague goals; inadequate performance measures; and nonvoluntary clients (Lipsky, 1980). Police officers certainly face all of these dilemmas in public service. A lack of resources, ambiguous and conflicting goals, community relations, performance measures, and the alienated nature of their work are common to police agencies. These problems, coupled with the constant threat of violence, make for an extremely stressful work environment.

Bureaucrats are faced with limited resources that are generally inadequate to fulfill the requirements of their jobs. Should additional resources be made available, the public immediately uses them up, constantly hungering for more services. In other words, demand will inevitably catch up with supply. This cycle eventually brings the agency back to its original position. Constantly facing inadequate resources is stressful and places a great amount of pressure on the bureaucrat's time. It also creates conflict as agencies must meet Constitutional requirements of equity. They must provide the same level of protection to each citizen, when providing services to the community (Lipsky, 1980, pp. 27–30).

Although officers today have increased technology as a resource, a lack of resources is commonplace for police officers. In particular, a lack of "time to collect information, time to act" is perhaps the most difficult problem officers face daily. Officers also work under the threat of violence constantly creating added stress to their work. These two factors alienate officers from the community and strengthen the internal bond. Furthermore, they are forced to make split second decisions that given hindsight often do not pass public scrutiny (Lipsky, 1980).

Working with this lack of resources, bureaucrats must face nonvoluntary clients with whom they may experience conflict. This friction between bureaucrat and client makes it difficult sometimes to carry out the bureaucrat's tasks. One factor affecting this relationship is the fact that clients are usually not included as a reference group for bureaucrats, which greatly impacts the way in which services are delivered. Ultimately, this allows the bureaucrat the ability to abuse the bureaucrat/client relationship given that the client cannot walk away from the transaction (Lipsky, 1980, p. 56). The end result within the police culture is the creation of an "us/them" mentality attributed to police officers (Paoline, 2001). A similar mentality exists between police supervisors and subordinates (Scarborough et al., 1999; Whetstone, 2001).

Lipsky (1980) argues that bureaucrats have ambiguous goals and inadequate performance measurement given that their tasks revolve around public service. Furthermore, goals can be diverse and contradictory. Officers still face overwhelming demand not only to catch criminals, but also to become involved in the community, and now to prevent terrorist attacks in all public places, including public transportation. The more ambiguous the goals and the more dissimilar, the more important the relationship between bureaucrats and their co-workers in order to sustain morale at work. A lack of supervisor monitoring contributes to the inadequacy of performance measurement. Agencies are forced to use surrogate measures for performance measurement. This can cause bureaucrats to channel their focus in unintended ways. Police officers goals are ambiguous and sometimes conflicting—whether to maintain order or to enforce the law (Lipsky, 1980). As discussed in Chapter 1, the role of the police officer has dramatically changed over time. Currently, the officer must handle conflicting roles within society (Adcox, 2000). The relationship between the officer and his or her supervisor influences how an officer will ultimately resolve this conflict (Engel & Worden, 2003).

Another obstacle that police organizations face is the collection of performance measures because supervisors cannot directly monitor officers. Surrogate measures are used, such as arrest rates, citizen complaints, and conviction rates. These measures give an incomplete picture as to whether the officer is making positive value choices (Lipsky, 1980). Early warning systems used to detect potentially problem officers can rely on any number of criteria, including "citizen complaints, firearm-discharge and use-of-force reports, civil litigation, resisting-arrest incidents, and high-speed pursuits and vehicular damage." A vast majority of departments, however, do not use any type of early warning system (Walker et al., 2001).

Lipsky (1980, p. 75) pointed out that street-level bureaucratic work is alienated work. "Jobs that require workers to deny the basic humanity of others" can be considered alienating work. This results in the bureaucrat becoming "less concerned with protecting clients' interests and their own connection with clients" (Lipsky, 1980, p. 79). Alienated workers can become dissatisfied with their jobs, which leads to absenteeism and less than adequate job performance.

As for the police officer's attitude toward citizens, the street-level bureaucrat can easily become alienated from the client. Police are suspicious of the public they serve as a coping mechanism for dealing with the dangers of their profession. As a result, the police become socially isolated, which contributes to the strong peer loyalty officers enjoy (Paoline, 2003); however, one study contradicts the existence of the "us/them" mentality normally attributed to police officers. This same study found that officers were not generally distrustful of the public, but have a positive view of citizen cooperation (Paoline et al., 2000).

This concept of alienation still holds true today (Barker, 1999). The officer's relationship with the community greatly impacts ethical decision making. Although this relationship is between the individual officer and the community, the results impact the community's relationship with that officer's agency. Ultimately, it is the agency's policy that dictates that relationship between the officer and individuals within the community. Jiao (1998) suggested that police departments can improve efficiency and effectiveness if the proper policing model is matched with the community it serves. Building such a policing model requires analyzing police activities, police orientations, and the role of the community before major policy changes are made within a police organization (Jiao, 1998). Organizational change within police departments occurs generally as a result of a scandal captured by the media, which leads to public inquiry resulting in personnel changes within management (Robinette, 1991). This cycle suggests that the ideal policing model may not be in place within each community.

A tenuous relationship with the community cannot help relationships with clients. Studies show that the public's attitude toward the police is as important as the police's attitude toward the public they serve. Suspects who act disrespectfully to police officers are more likely to be arrested, cited, and/or subject to use of physical force (Engel, 2003; Klockars et al., 2004). This does not mean that people in general have a negative view of police officers. Many studies show that the general public has a positive opinion of the police (Brown & Benedict, 2002; Cao et al., 1996; Chermak & McGarrell, 2001; Cheurprakobkit & Bartsch, 1999; Priest & Carter, 1999).

According to Maynard-Moody and Musheno (2000), discretion is inevitable for the street-level bureaucrat. The work is done without direct supervision, and officers encounter unexpected situations that do not clearly match guidelines. Citizens have difficulty reporting police misconduct, and peers can be corrupt leading to the corrupt socialization of officers on the job. Maynard-Moody and Musheno (2000) sought to analyze street-level work discretion from two different perspectives or views—the dominant view, or state-agent narrative, which says that self-interest is the guiding force behind decisions, and the counter narrative of the citizen agent from the street-level worker who is responsive to the needs of the client basing decisions on their experience.

The dominant view sees street-level workers as policymakers whose job is to execute the laws the government passes. This view says that the street-level worker relies on self-interest in decision making—that is, what will make my life easier and what will get this case out of my life faster? This view acknowledges that sometimes the street-level worker will go above and beyond the call of duty—picking a small number of cases that seem worthy to give special attention to, but that the worker doesn't have the time or the resources to do so with every case (Maynard-Moody & Musheno, 2000).

The citizen-agent view sees the street-level worker as responsive to clients, experienced, relying on normative values rather than rules, and distrustful of politicians and supervisors who only create obstacles to helping the client. This is a view that street-level workers themselves hold. The Maynard-Moody and Musheno (2000) article relies on observation, interviews, a questionnaire, and archival research from five sites including two police departments, two vocational rehabilitation agencies, and one middle school in the United States.

One story involves a woman who came to the police department to complain about the police roughing up her husband when mistakenly arresting him. The woman had to pray for several days before coming in because the original incident was so frightening to her. In the first instance of police discretion, the police used discretion to brutalize her husband. In the second instance, the police officer used his discretion to help the woman file a complaint (Maynard-Moody & Musheno, 2000).

Lieutenant Ken Adcox (2000) of the El Paso Police Department pointed out that both line officers and managers exercise discretion in their jobs. Adcox (2000, p. 17) focused on the unsupervised line officer making quick decisions with "immense autonomy and latitude." Although Adcox (2000) recognized the necessity of police discretion, relying on Lewis (1991), Adcox (2000) also recognized the subsequent potential for unethical behavior.

The poor working conditions of street-level bureaucrats alone do not account for unethical behavior. Several theories of deviant behavior are relevant to the hypotheses explored in this study. In particular, police officer attitudes, organizational deviance, and several sociological theories deserve mention here.

Factors That Influence Police Officer Attitudes and Behavior

What is the relationship between attitudes and behaviors in individuals? Is there a relationship between the two? Finding a causal link between attitudes and behavior is challenging considering the multitude of factors that can influence both. Measuring attitudes and behavior for police officers has primarily focused on factors that influence arrest behavior because it is the most convenient data available. Very little has been explored with respect to police officer attitudes and behavior related to ethical decision making.

Socialization begins for officers during their new recruit training and continues on the job throughout their careers. Measuring the impact of socialization is difficult given the nature of police work. One measure is officer attitude. There are a significant number of qualitative and quantitative studies that explore police officer attitudes (Engel & Worden, 2003). Most of these studies analyze what impact officer attitudes have on police service, arrest rates, detecting crime, use of coercion, and whether officers shirk their duties (Riksheim & Chermak, 1993). Social psychology research, in general, finds that the link between attitudes and behavior is mediated by situational factors such as social norms, peer norms, and peer behavior (Engel & Worden, 2003).

From about the mid 1960s through 1993, approximately 545 social science articles were published testing whether there is a relationship between attitudes and behavior in people generally. Of these studies, 40% have found no relationship, whereas the remaining studies have found either a positive or a negative relationship. Riksheim and Chermak (1993) analyzed these studies searching for those that pertain specifically to police officers according to service behavior, detection behavior, arrest behavior, and use of force behavior and found approximately 135 articles that examine these relationships within police agencies.

Approximately 25 studies have been conducted with respect to whether or not length of service has any impact on police behavior. Ten of those studies found either a positive or negative relationship, whereas 15 of those studies found no relationship. Meanwhile, 50 studies have been conducted that examine the relationship between attitudes of police officers and police behavior. Thirty six of those studies found no relationship while fourteen found either a positive or negative relationship. For example, there is a positive relationship between seriousness of the offense and an officer's willingness to arrest. The more serious the offense, the more willing the officer is to make an arrest. Meanwhile, there is a negative relationship between gender of the suspect and an officer's willingness to make an arrest. Officers are less willing to make an arrest where the suspect is female in domestic violence situations.

Fifty-five studies have explored the relationship between the seriousness of the crime committed and police behavior. Fifty one of those studies found either a positive or negative relationship, whereas four studies found no relationship. For example, where the seriousness of the crime committed is measured by weapon usage, the more serious the crime/weapon used, the more likely the officer will make an arrest as opposed to relying on mediation or referral to a third party for assistance. Departmental size has been studied five times, with four of those studies finding either a positive or negative relationship (Riksheim & Chermak, 1993). For example, some studies have shown that officers from smaller agencies conduct more traffic stops.

In other research, peer behavior and supervisory influence have been shown to impact officer behavior (Engel & Worden, 2003). Officers with high levels of trust, cooperation, group cohesion, and social support will be more successful with community policing (Robinson, 2003); however, officer assignment to community policing does not affect arrest rates (Novak et al., 2002). Also, studies exploring whether statutory language affects arrest rates have found mixed results (Finn et al., 2004). It is unclear whether departmental policies, such as having a pro-arrest policy in domestic disturbances, have an effect on officer behavior (Robinson & Chandek, 2000).

One study found a relationship between negative police officer attitudes and police use of force. Officers who viewed the general public, legal restrictions, and supervisors negatively while holding favorable opinions regarding aggressive police tactics and crime fighting were more apt to use coercion in carrying out their duties (Terrill et al., 2003). The officer's attitude toward the victim has a profound effect on an officer's decision to arrest (Robinson & Chandek, 2000); however, no relationship was found between police officers with authoritarian personality traits and police misconduct (Henkel & Sheehan, 1997).

As for socialization effects, there has been some research that suggests the possibility of socialization impacting police misconduct. Limited research has shown a relationship between years of service and cynicism. Officers enter the force with low levels of cynicism, which steadily increase during the first 10 years on the force. Eventually cynicism declines somewhat creating a relatively curvilinear relationship (Hickman et al., 2004). There is an intriguing similarity with the emergence of unethical behavior. Research shows that the average officer who commits an ethics violation is 32 years old, with approximately 5 to 10 years of law enforcement experience at the time of his or her transgression (Trautman, 1997). Sociological theories that include the effects of socialization offer possible explanations of officer misconduct and are explored in the following section.

Situational Factors Affecting Attitudes and Behavior

Situational variables that affect officer behavior in making arrests include the seriousness of the offenses, harm to the victim, and whether a weapon is involved in the crime (Robinson & Chandek, 2000). The decision to arrest is made expeditiously in response to a variety of situational factors, including seriousness of the offense, characteristics of the suspect and the victim, harm to the victim, and the presence of a weapon. The attitudes about misconduct and an officer's decision to report misconduct reflect a different kind of decision process. It is not unreflective behavior directed at disconnected clients. The decision to report officer misconduct is made after the fact and is directed at peers. Despite these differences, the seriousness of the offense is a factor to consider in evaluating an officer's willingness to report misconduct.

Terrill and Mastrofski (2002) conducted a study that took situational determinants into consideration when observing police officers during arrests. Officers did respond to factors such as whether the suspect resisted and safety concerns. Other studies have shown that the more serious the offense involved, the more likely the officer will use force (Friedrich, 1977; Garner et al., 1996; Kavanagh, 1994; Worden, 1995). These studies considered factors such as the seriousness of the offense and violent behavior of the suspect, as well as other factors such as race, intoxication of suspect, presence of bystanders, and whether the officer initiated contact.

Organizational Factors Affecting Attitudes and Behavior

Organizational factors such as size of agency, departmental bureaucratization, and police presence or the number of police officers patrolling within a community have also been found to affect officer behavior (Klinger, 2004). Organizational structure also can influence the ethical orientation of police officers. Van Wart (1998, p. 15) argued, "Organizational values are embedded in the organizational design." Some deviant behavior happens as a result of a concerted effort of many individuals within an organization, supported by organizational internal norms, peers, and supervisors.

The hierarchical structure of an organization can also impact behavior within the organization. For example, Kraska and Kappeler (1997) attribute the military model with the creation of an environment that fosters the use of force.

There are essentially three primary similarities between military and police organizations. First, both institutions are highly structured, hierarchical command organizations. Each uses the same basic chain of command hierarchical structure, which relies on rank for authority. Coupled with this similarity is the fact that both use similar jargon such as the names of rank and position. Finally, both institutions have similar communication structures. Each sees the flow of information within the organization as unidirectional—flowing from the top down through the hierarchy of authority (Hodgson, 2001). The reason the military and law enforcement are so similar is a result of the direct involvement the military has had in law enforcement historically. Even today, law enforcement is directly impacted by the military. Since their inception in the mid 1960s, there has been a sharp increase in the number of Special Weapons and Tactical teams that are military units (Weber, 1999).

Some scholars have examined the impact of department size, although the findings are not conclusive. Etzioni (1975) and Slovak (1986) indicated that larger police departments result in coercive measures toward the public they serve due to a lack of adequate supervision. Chatterton (1983) added that officers in large departments can become disconnected resulting in deviant behavior on the job. Other research demonstrates differences in behavior but does not attempt to show whether variations are inappropriate. The arrest rates for driving under the influence in very small agencies (five or fewer officers) were three times higher than arrest rates in large agencies (100 or more officers) (Mastrofski & Ritti, 1996). On the other hand, research conducting in the 1970s showed that officers in larger agencies tended to arrest and use force more often than their counterparts in smaller agencies (Klinger, 2004). According to these studies, it is not clear whether size of agency has a consistent impact on behavior.

Caiden and Caiden (1977) analyzed organizational corruption and the relationship between the individual and the agency. Organizational corruption focuses on an agency culture in which individuals within the organization accept unethical acts. Unethical bureaucrats are protected and whistleblowers are not only discouraged, but also punished for coming forward (Caiden & Caiden, 1977). Adams and Balfour (1998) argued that where organizational goals and proper authority exist within an agency, the administrator's discretion in making value judgments is removed. Administrative evil occurs when administrators forget what history has shown, repackage something evil, and define it as good. Administrators who forget their purpose and/or abandon their sense of accountability through neutral competence can cause great public harm (Adams & Balfour, 1998).

According to Lundman (1980), in order for organizational deviance to occur, there have to be several conditions present. The deviant acts "must be contrary to norms or rules maintained by others external to the police department," and these acts "must be supported by internal operating norms which conflict with the police organization's formal goals and rules" (Lundman, 1980, p. 140). Recruitment, socialization, peers, and supervisors must all support these internal operating norms of deviant behavior. These conditions combined support organizational deviance.

There is very limited research that explores Lundman's theory of organizational deviance. Cao et al. (2000) tested Lundman's theory using citizen complaints against police officers with respect to the use of physical force and found partial support. Their study found that field training, in-service training, length of service, arrest rate, and the population size served each had an impact on the number of citizen complaints. Departments that had field training and in-service training regarding use of force had lower citizen complaint rates. The longer an officer served, the lower the complaint rate. Also, departments serving larger populations and with higher arrest rates, experienced higher citizen complaint rates (Cao et al., 2000).

Alpert and MacDonald (2001) studied the impact that agency-level characteristics have on police use of force. Agency-level characteristics included whether an agency was accredited by the Commission on Accreditation for Law Enforcement Agencies, whether an agency was accredited by its state, whether the agency was unionized, whether an agency used data collected on use of force for management and administrative purposes, and whether use of force forms were completed by supervisors or individual officers. The study controlled for level of danger within the jurisdiction and the region within the United States.

Alpert and MacDonald (2001) found that some agency characteristics impact an officer's use of force. Agencies that required supervisors to fill out use of force forms experienced lower rates of force by officers.

Accreditation and unionization did not impact an officer's use of force, however, and those agencies that used data for management and administrative purposes experienced higher rates of force by officers. The agency characteristics used in the Alpert and MacDonald (2001) study are not available within the data set that is the subject of the present research; however, the results offer some partial support for the effect that organizational factors have on police behavior.

Individual Factors Affecting Attitudes and Behavior

Individual factors such as length of service, rank, and job assignment affect officer behavior (McElvain & Kposowa, 2004). Van Wart (1998) recognizes the impact that expertise has on the amount of discretion afforded to public administrators. Administrators with higher levels of expertise enjoy more discretion and decision making within an agency. For example, officers and detectives are different. While detectives are considered a promotion, this position generally does not have supervisory responsibilities. Still, in a few studies that have looked at differences in specialization of job assignment in police agencies, no appreciable difference between how police officers carry out their duties in specialized versus nonspecialized departments was found (Mastrofski et al., 1995; Novak et al., 1999).

What impact does expertise have on police officers? Controlling for race, gender, and age, officers with 5 to 9 years of experience were 12 times more likely to be investigated for misuse of force than their colleagues who had served for 20 years or more (McElvain & Kposowa, 2004). Race and gender were not found to be a significant factor in predicting misuse of force investigations; however, age and prior investigation were both significant (race, gender, and age are not available in the NIJ study). The younger the officer, the more likely to be investigated for misuse of force, and officers who had been investigated at least once were more likely to be investigated again during their careers (McElvain & Kposowa, 2004). Unfortunately, there is a lack of research regarding the impact that rank supervisory position and job assignment have on police behavior. Only a few studies have looked at differences in specialization of job assignment in police agencies and they found no appreciable difference between how police officers carry out their duties in specialized versus non-specialized departments (Mastrofski et al., 1995; Novak et al., 1999).

Paoline (2001) identified five types of police officers based on attitudes and background characteristics. These five types are Tough-Cops,

Clean-Beat Crime-Fighters, Avoiders, Problem-Solvers, and Professionals. These groups affect relationships with citizens and supervisors, attitudes toward legal restrictions and community policing, and attitudes toward their role in society (Paoline, 2001).

Tough-Cops hold negative attitudes toward citizens, supervisors, legal restrictions, order maintenance, and community policing. This type of officer believes in pursuing the law enforcement role, aggressive policing, and only handling serious violations. Clean-Beat Crime-Fighters are similar to Tough-Cops, but value legal restrictions, order maintenance, and pursuing all types of illegal behavior (Paoline, 2001).

Avoiders are also like Tough-Cops, but they are neutral in their attitudes toward supervisors. Avoiders, as the name implies, avoid work and aggressive behavior in order to keep from drawing attention to themselves. Problem Solvers and Professionals have positive relationships with citizens and supervisors. Both types value order maintenance and community policing. Problem-Solvers, however, see legal restrictions as an impediment to their work and are neutral in their attitude toward their role in enforcing the law. Problem-Solvers also believe in focusing their energies on serious problems (Paoline, 2001).

Paoline's research questioned the single moral order concept of police culture. He highlighted the differences in attitudes within police culture and identified an additional seven subcultures in his research. Van Maanen (1973) analyzed stages of cultural socialization for police officers instead of categorizing officers as Paoline and Wilson have done. According to Van Maanen (1973), there are four stages of police socialization into the organization, which include a pre-entry choice, introduction, encounter, and metamorphosis stages.

The first stage, pre-entry choice, acknowledges the individual's choice to become a police officer. This stage recognizes that most individuals who choose to become police officers hold similar values as those values held within the law enforcement profession. The second stage, introduction, involves the new recruit's training phase within formal instruction. The third stage, encounter, includes the new recruits on-the-job training with a senior police officer after initial new recruit training is completed. In the final stage, metamorphosis, the officer adapts to the nature of police work and is impacted by peer reinforcement of group norms.

Although these four stages were first created over 30 years ago, the stages still are accurate today (Adcox, 2000). The stages focus on the beginning of an officer's career where the primary socialization occurs. An officer's ethical decision making is most impacted within stage 3. Relying in part on Sykes (1994), Adcox (2000, p. 22) highlighted the importance of stage 3:

> These initial experiences can either set the stage for ethical behavior or teach the rationalization of inappropriate conduct. The actions of others speak far louder than any written policy, and the peer group becomes the most powerful conveyor of the unwritten code of conduct.

Stage 3, or the period when officers are receiving on-the-job training, is critical to the development of an officer's ethical decision making. Stage 3 is when peers inculcate norms, or as Adox characterizes it, the "unwritten code of conduct" (Adcox, 2000, p. 22). Individual and organizational factors impact individual attitudes and values shaped by the organization's structure and culture. These factors impact officers through hiring, socialization, and training. The following section explores the organizational culture of police agencies.

ORGANIZATIONAL CULTURE

Wilson (1989) explained that bureaucratic behavior depends on the bureaucratic culture, which includes "the situations they encounter, their prior experiences and personal beliefs, the expectations of their peers, and the array of interests in which their agency is embedded" (Wilson, 1989, p. 27). There are numerous definitions of culture. Most definitions highlight the importance of attitudes, as well as the situation-dependent nature of bureaucratic behavior. Paoline (2001, p. 7) uses a culmination of various definitions, including "attitudes and values that are shared and socially transmitted among groups of people, in an attempt to cope with common problems and/or situations." Van Wart (1998, p. 63) defined professional culture as one that is "expressed in norms, symbols, and a world-view." What, then, is the organizational culture of law enforcement?

Wilson (1968) introduced the concept of the "bureaucracy problem," which is getting street-level bureaucrats to do the right thing. Wilson's (1968) study involved observing patrolmen in eight communities and describing their daily routine behavior. The study identifies three styles of policing—the watchman, legalistic, and service styles. Each style guides the officer in the administration of daily duties (Wilson, 1968).

Wilson's theories regarding policing styles have been extremely influential on the study of police culture. His study, however, was conducted over 35 years ago and was limited to a highly selective sample of eight agencies in the Northeastern United States. As previously discussed, the role of the police officer in the United States has changed dramatically over time. Community policing is the latest change affecting the delivery of police services. Wilson's styles of policing are complimentary to the community-policing model; however, the service style of policing is most congruent with community policing. This study does not analyze the impact of community policing on Wilson's styles of policing, however, as the data are not sufficient to explore these possibilities.

Smith (1984) has shown some support for Wilson's theory that the level of professionalism and bureaucratization in a police agency affects its arrest rates. Smith (1984) examined 60 police agencies regarding professionalism and bureaucratization. Bureaucratization and professionalism did impact how officers perform their duties; however, most of Wilson's theories, in particular the influence of local political culture, were not supported in Smith's study.

Wilson (1968) defined political culture in four categories, which include high-professional council-manager, low-professional council-manager, nonpartisan mayor council, and partisan mayor-council. Wilson (1968) theorized that these forms of local government impacted the style of policing within the corresponding local police department. Wilson (1968) found support for his theory, however, several studies since then have been unable to support Wilson's theory (Hassell & Zhao, 2003; Langworthy, 1986; Smith, 1984).

There are other public administration theories regarding public sector culture that are not specific to police culture but that are useful here. One such theory identifies four types of organizational culture and the impact each has on its members. These four types include rational cultures, hierarchical cultures, group or team cultures, and adaptive cultures. These organizational culture types are derived from the competing values approach (CVA) developed by Quinn and Rohrbaugh (1981). CVA is a framework that argues that where values compete within an organization there is conflict. When an organization favors one value, it is to the detriment of the corresponding competing value (Quinn & Rohrbaugh, 1981).

Buenger et al. (1996) tested Quinn and Rohrbaugh's competing values framework within the Air Force. The study found support for CVA. Where an agency placed emphasis on one value, the corresponding competing value received less attention than its counterpart. Previous studies have found support for CVA in modeling organizational forms and studying leadership styles (Quinn, 1984; Quinn & Hall, 1983; Quinn & Rohrbaugh, 1983).

The data available for analysis in this study do not permit examining the organizational differences explored in this section. This study addresses differences in officer attitudes at different stages of their careers through length of service and rank. The section that follows directly explores the officer's socialization process further. Later sections discuss an officer's attitudes, values, and norms are investigated to determine how these characteristics exist and how they are shaped within the police culture.

The Individual Police Officer and the Socialization Process

There is conflicting research regarding the impact the socialization process has on an officer's ethical orientation. Recent research indicates that new recruits have a significantly different ethical perspective from that of seasoned officers. According to Catlin and Maupin (2004), new recruits tend to be idealistic in their ethical orientation, whereas officers who have been on the job for at least one year are more relativistic in their ethical orientation. This difference highlights the importance of how officers are hired, formally trained, and ultimately integrated into the police culture.

An officer's personality, the hiring process, and their formal training each play a role in shaping the ethical decision making of this street-level bureaucrat (Kraska & Kappeler, 1998; Lyman, 1999). The officer's personality can be measured through the Myers-Briggs Type Indicator (MBTI). Stages of moral development are commonly measured through the Defining Issues Test (DIT). These two tests are not commonly used in the hiring process for police officers (Hughes, 2003). Whether these tests should be used in hiring decisions is not the subject of this study; however, these tests do offer insight into the police officer psyche. This section explores the police officer's personality, including research regarding their stages of moral development and MBTI results, as well as current screening practices for hiring law enforcement and formal training.

Moral Development

Klockars et al. (2004) has shown that ethical awareness is a major factor affecting ethical behavior, and this research will examine this relationship in depth. For background, it is important to understand how ethical awareness is formed in the individual. Lawrence Kohlberg (1984) proposed a theory of moral development with six stages. During the first two preconventional stages, the individual makes ethical decisions based on whether they will be punished and the concept of reciprocity. Decisions rest on external concerns and not standards or norms. The next two conventional stages are marked by moral values, right and wrong, expectations of others, maintaining the social order, and a sense of duty to others. The final two postconventional stages are characterized by rules, legality, duty of contract, mutual trust and respect, and utilitarianism.

Kohlberg's stages of moral development have been validated across cultures, age, and gender using primarily a written instrument, sometimes combined with personal interviews. There has been some discussion in the literature regarding whether there is a gender bias in the instrument; however, testing has validated the instrument to be between 70% and 80% reliable (Kohlberg, 1984). The written instrument currently used was developed by Rest et al. (2000) and is known as the Defining Issues Test 2 (DIT 2).

The DIT 2 consists of three moral dilemma scenarios followed by a series of questions regarding what outcome the respondent will choose and ranking their reasoning for choosing that particular outcome. Questions are assigned scores based on how respondents rank their responses (Kohlberg, 1984). The DIT has been administered to individuals of various professions and ages. Generally, as people age, as their IQ increases, and/or as they advance through their education, they progress through the stages of development.

Nolan (2000) applied Kohlberg's stages of moral development to police officers in Boston. The study tested new recruits, as well as seasoned officers, some who had been subjected to specialized ethics training. The findings indicated that respondents fell in the conventional stage of Kohlberg's moral development scale. There was no difference in the study between officers who had received specialized training and those who had not (Nolan, 2000). Unfortunately, the study did not explore the implications of its results with respect to police misconduct.

The Nolan dissertation did find that the police officer participants had high stage 4 scores in Kohlberg's stages of moral development. Stage 4 is characterized by making moral decisions based on rules, laws, and regulations. Individuals who score high in stage 4 are interested in duty and social order, self-respect, and societal obligations. The Nolan dissertation also found that participant officers scored at the level of moral development equal to an American child between the ages of 11 and 13 (Nolan, 2000).

Stewart and Sprinthall (1994) adapted Kohlberg's instrument to the public administration environment. The Stewart-Sprinthall Management Survey was administered to 485 public managers with most administrators falling within stage 4 and the highest stage, the principled stage, which includes stages 5 and 6. The tendency was for administrators to rely on stage 4 reasoning (Stewart & Sprinthall, 1994).

What is the significance of stage 4 moral development for public administrators? Stewart and Sprinthall (1991, p. 253) observed that stage 4 development "may provide some protection against the ruthless exploitation for personal gain," or lower stage reasoning, but "it may also provide a built-in resistance to learning principled reasoning." Stewart and Sprinthall also noted that Rohr (1978) would characterize stage 4 reasoning as "low road" decision making within administrative ethics. The next question becomes what factors influence the stages of moral development?

Studies have shown that age, IQ, occupation, and education are the biggest factors impacting an individual's progression through the stages of moral development (Rest et al., 2000). The more education one has and the older one gets, the higher the level of moral development for the average adult (Wilson et al., 1992). Some occupations actually foster moral development through positive mentoring practices, such as the study of medicine, resulting in the advancement of doctors through the stages of moral development (Coleman & Wilkins, 2002).

The Nolan DIT results correspond with the personality characteristics found in police officers through the MBTI. Lynch and McMahon (1984) found that law enforcement officers generally are Introverted, Sensing, Thinking, and Judging (ISTJ). This combination includes individuals who are dependable, decisive, quiet, serious, thorough, detail oriented, and logical. Sensing and Judging (SJ) individuals are responsible, duty bound, and feel a sense of obligation within society. They are known as society's stabilizers. The SJ is talented at "establishing policies, rules, schedules, routines, regulations and hierarchy" (Lynch & McMahon, 1984, p. 14).

It is not surprising that police work would attract individuals who are rule oriented in their personalities and level of moral development. The selection of individuals who meet organizational expectations may influence the socialization process, as those with similar attitudes will be hired making socialization within the police culture easier (Bowen et al., 1991;

Kristof-Brown, 2000). It is surprising that the moral development of police officers in the Nolan study ranked fairly low in comparison to other professions such as enlisted men in the Navy. The Nolan study respondents ranked at the same level as prison inmates (Coleman & Wilkins, 2002).

One would hope that the hiring process would screen out questionable moral development in potential cadets. The hiring process for police officers varies greatly across the United States. Ideally, a department will take past behavior of the applicant into consideration, as well as age, IQ, and education. Unfortunately, not all departments make intelligent hiring decisions. For example, one police applicant scored highly in cognitive ability during the hiring process and was denied employment on this basis (Hughes, 2003). Normally, applicants who do well on hiring tests are accepted for employment on that basis, not denied for that very reason.

Authoritarian personality has been a major concern among scholars and observers of police behavior. There are several views of the origins of authoritarian attitudes in police behavior. One study found that the police do not necessarily attract persons with authoritarian personalities (Brown & Willis, 1985). Authoritarianism may be linked to the demands placed on officers by their agency, an officer's job assignment, amount of contact with the general public, rank, and length of service (Carlson & Sutton, 1975; Genz & Lester, 1976; Hageman, 1979; Lefkowitz, 1974; McNamara, 1967). Many scholars argue that police officers take on authoritarian personalities after less than 2 years on the job (McNamara, 1967). Authoritarian personalities are shaped by circumstances, as opposed to socialization, such as exposure to conflict, contact with the public, lower rank, and exposure to high crime areas. Henkel and Sheehan (1997) tested whether authoritarianism is the greatest factor influencing police misconduct. Henkel and Sheehan, however, found no support in their research for the hypothesis that authoritarianism is the greatest factor influencing police misconduct. If officers do harbor authoritarian attitudes, there is no support that these attitudes influence their behavior.

The NIJ Study, Ethical Awareness, Standards, and Action

The fundamental questions that this study seeks to analyze revolve around the ethical attitudes of police officers and the impact these attitudes have on the officer's willingness to take one form of action. These attitudes are grounded in the officer's awareness of ethical and unethical behavior within the context of the officer's work environment. An individual's ethical awareness is derived from the individual's values and moral character. Ethical awareness is the basis for an individual's attitudes toward rules, regulations, and policy. An individual's ethical awareness ultimately determines whether an individual will take ethical action. The police officer's ethical awareness reflects the officer's cognizance of ethical and unethical behavior, as well as the rules, regulations, and policy of the agency. The rules, regulations, and policy provide the backdrop, but the standards by which the officer serves are those that he or she will apply to instances of misconduct. Combined, awareness and standards impact whether the individual is willing to take action (Guy, 1991; Huddleston & Sands, 1995; Truelson, 1991).

Klockars et al. (2004) has shown that ethical awareness is related to ethical standards and action. In this study, the analysis starts with an examination of the nature of the ethical awareness itself. Although it is clear that officers favor discipline and are more likely to report an offense if they believe that it is very serious, how do the attitudes about seriousness of the police officers compare to objective measures?

According to Lipsky (1980), police officers face limited resources, nonvoluntary clients, ambiguous goals, inadequate performance measures, and alienation coupled with a great deal of discretion in carrying out duties. The officer's organizational culture, attitudes, and behavior of supervisors and coworkers impact how the street-level bureaucrat handles the ethical decision-making process. This study elucidates police officers' ethical decision making by analyzing their attitudes and behavior.

DISCUSSION QUESTIONS

1. Lipsky's concepts regarding the causes of unethical behavior have been around since 1980. Are these concepts outdated? Do they still ring true? How would you modify them today?
2. Compare Lipsky's framework against other scholars, discussing discretion, situational factors, individual characteristics, organizational forces, and officer attitudes. Do these scholars contradict or compliment one another?
3. Wilson's bureaucratic theorizing began in the late 1960s. Are Wilson's concepts outdated? How has Wilson modified these concepts over the years? How would you modify his approach?

4. Do you think that the socialization process for police officers should be highly formalized (training, mentoring, etc.), or do you think it should be informal? What are the benefits and drawbacks of each?
5. Research regarding authoritarian personalities in law enforcement yield mixed results. What impact do you think, based on your personal experiences, authoritarian personalities have in the workplace?

REFERENCES

Adams, G. B., & Balfour, D. L. (1998). *Unmasking Administrative Evil.* Thousand Oaks, CA: Sage Publications.

Adcox, K. L. (2000, January). Doing bad things for good reasons. *The Police Chief, 67*(1), 17–28.

Alpert, G. P., & MacDonald, J. M. (2001). Police use of force: an analysis of organizational characteristics. *Justice Quarterly, 18*(2), 393–409.

Barker, J. C. (1999). *Danger, Duty, and Disillusion: The Worldview of Los Angeles Police Officers.* Prospect Heights, IL: Waveland.

Bowen, D. E., Ledford Jr., G. E., & Nathan, B. R. (1991). Hiring for the organization, not the job. *Academy of Management Executive, 5*(4), 35–51.

Brown, B., & Benedict, W. R. (2002). Perceptions of the Police: Past findings, methodological issues, conceptual issues and policy implications. *Policing: An International Journal of Police Strategies and Management, 25*(3), 543–580.

Brown, L., & Willis, A. (1985). Authoritarianism in British police recruits—importation, socialization or myth. *Journal of Occupational Psychology, 58*(2), 97–108.

Buenger, V., Daft, R. L., Conlon, E. J., & Austin, J. (1996). Competing values in organizations: contextual influences and structural consequences. *Organization Science, 7*(5), 557–576.

Caiden, G. E., & Caiden, N. J. (1977). Developments in research: administrative corruption. *Public Administration Review, 37*(2), 301–309.

Cao, L., Deng, X., & Barton, S. (2000). A test of Lundman's organizational product thesis with data on citizen complaints. *Policing: An International Journal of Police Strategies and Management, 23*(3), 356–373.

Cao, L., Frank, J. and Cullen, F. T. (1996). Race, community context, and confidence in police. *American Journal of Police, 15,* 3–22.

Carlson, H. M., & Sutton, M. S. (1975). The effects of different police roles on attitudes and values. *The Journal of Psychology, 91,* 57–64.

Catlin, D. W., & Maupin, J. R. (2004). A two cohort study of the ethical orientations of state police officers. *Policing: An International Journal of Police Strategies and Management, 27*(3), 289–301.

Chatterton, M. (1983). *Police Work and Assault Charges in the Police Organization.* Cambridge, MA: MIT Press.

Chermak, S., & McGarrell, E. F. (2001). Citizens' perceptions of aggressive traffic enforcement strategies. *Justice Quarterly, 18,* 365–391.

Cheurprakobkit, S., & Bartsch, R. A. (1999). Police work and the police profession: assessing attitudes of city officials, Spanish-speaking Hispanics, and their English-speaking counterparts. *Journal of Criminal Justice, 27,* 87–100.

Coleman, R., & Wilkins, L. (2002). Searching for the ethical journalist: an exploratory study of the moral development of news workers. *Journal of Mass Media Ethics, 17*(3), 209–225.

Engel, R. S. (2003). Explaining suspects' resistance and disrespect toward police. *Journal of Criminal Justice, 31,* 475–492.

Engel, R. S., & Worden, R. E. (2003). Police officers' attitudes, behavior, and supervisory influences: an analysis of problem solving. *Criminology, 41*(1), 131–166.

Etzioni, A. (1975). *A Comparative Analysis of Complex Organizations.* New York: Free Press.

Finn, M. A., Blackwell, B. S., Stalans, L. J., Studdard, S., & Dugan, L. (2004). Dual arrest decisions in domestic violence cases: the influence of departmental policies. *Crime & Delinquency, 50*(4), 565–589.

Friedrich, R. J. (1977). *The Impact of Organizational, Individual, and Situational Factors on Police Behavior.* Ann Arbor, MI: University of Michigan.

Garner, J. H., Buchanan, J., Schade, T., & Hepburn, J. (1996). Understanding the continuum of force by and against the police. *National Institute of Justice.* 25–77.

Genz, J. L., & Lester, D. (1976). Authoritarianism in policemen as a function of experience. *Journal of Police Science and Administration, 4,* 9–13.

Guy, M. E. (1991). *Using High Reliability Management to Promote Ethical Decision Making.* San Francisco: Jossey-Bass.

Hageman, M. J. (1979). Who joins the force for what reasons: an argument for "the new breed." *Journal of Police Science and Administration, 7,* 206–210.

Hassell, K. D., & Zhao, J. S. (2003). Structural arrangements in large municipal police organizations. *Policing: An International Journal of Police Strategies and Management, 26*(2), 231–250.

Henkel, J., & Sheehan, E. P. (1997). Relation of police misconduct to authoritarianism. *Journal of Social Behavior & Personality, 12*(2), 551–556.

Hickman, M. J., Piquero, N. L., & Piquero, A. R. (2004). The validity of Niederhoffer's cynicism scale. *Journal of Criminal Justice, 32,* 1–13.

Hodgson, J. F. (2001). Police violence in Canada and the USA: analysis and management. *Policing: An International Journal of Police Strategies and Management, 24*(4), 520–549.

Huddleston, M. W., & Sands, J. C. (1995). Enforcing administrative ethics. *The Annals of the American Academy of Political and Social Science, 537,* 139–149.

Hughes, T. T. (2003). Jordan v. the City of New London, police hiring and IQ. *Policing: An International Journal of Police Strategies and Management, 26*(2), 298–312.

Jiao, A. Y. (1998). Matching police-community expectations: a method of determining policing models. *Journal of Criminal Justice, 26*(4), 291–306.

Kavanagh, J. (1994). Ph.D. dissertation. *The Occurrence of Force in Arrest Encounters.* Newark, NJ: Rutgers University.

Klinger, D. A. (2004). Environment and organization: reviving a perspective on the police. *The Annals of the American Academy of Political and Social Science, 593,* 119–136.

Klockars, C. B., Ivkovic, S. K., & Haberfeld, M. (2004). *The Contours of Police Integrity.* Thousand Oaks, CA: Sage Publications.

Kohlberg, L. (1984). *The Psychology of Moral Development: The Nature and Validity of Moral Stages.* San Francisco: Harper & Row.

Kraska, P. B., & Kappeler, V. E. (1997). Militarizing American police: the rise and normalization of paramilitary units. *Social Problems, 44,* 1–18.

Kraska, P. B., & Kappeler, V. E. (1998). A textual critique of community policing: police adaptation to high modernity. *Policing: An International Journal of Police Strategies and Management, 21*(2), 293–313.

Kristof-Brown, A. L. (2000). Perceived applicant fit: distinguishing between recruiters' perceptions of person-job and person-organization fit. *Personnel Psychology, 53*(3), 643–671.

Langworthy, R. H. (1986). *The Structure of Police Organizations.* Westport, CT: Praeger.

Lefkowitz, J. (1974). Job attitudes of police: overall description and demographic correlates. *Journal of Vocational Behavior, 5,* 221–230.

Lewis, C. (1991). *The Ethics Challenge in Public Service.* San Francisco: Jossey-Bass.

Lipsky, M. (1980). *Street-Level Bureaucracy: Dilemmas of the Individual in Public Services.* New York: Russell Sage Foundation.

Lundman, R. J. (1980). *Police Behavior.* New York: Oxford University Press.

Lyman, M. (1999). *The Police: An Introduction.* New York: Prentice Hall.

Lynch, R. G., & McMahon, R. R. (1984). *Getting to Know Policemen Personally.* Chapel Hill, NC: Institute of Government.

Mastrofski, S. D., & Ritti, R. R. (1996). Police training and the effects of organization on drunk driving enforcement. *Justice Quarterly, 13*(2), 291–320.

Mastrofski, S. D., Worden, R. E., & Snipes, J. B. (1995). Law enforcement in a time of community policing. *Criminology, 33*(4), 539–603.

Maynard-Moody, S., & Musheno, M. (2000). State agent or citizen agent: two narratives of discretion. *Journal of Public Administration Research and Theory, 10*(3), 329–358.

McElvain, J. P., & Kposowa, A. J. (2004). Police officer characteristics and internal affairs investigations for use of force allegations. *Journal of Criminal Justice, 32,* 265–279.

McNamara, J. (1967). The police: six sociological essays. In D. Bordua (ed.), *Uncertainties in Police Work: The Relevance of Police Recruits* (pp. 163–252). New York: John Wiley.

Nolan, T. W. (2000). *Toward Probity: The Moral Milieu of the Police Station House.* Boston: Boston University.

Novak, K., Hartman, J., Holsinger, A. J., & Turner, M. G. (1999). The effects of aggressive policing of disorder on serious crime. *Policing: An International Journal of Police Strategies and Management, 22*(2), 171–190.

Novak, K. J., Frank, J., Smith, B. W., & Engel, R. S. (2002). Revisiting the decision to arrest: comparing beat and community officers. *Crime & Delinquency, 48*(1), 70–98.

Paoline III, E. A. (2001). *Rethinking Police Culture: Officers' Occupational Attitudes.* New York: LFB Scholarly Publishing LLC.

Paoline III, E. A. (2003). Taking stock: toward a richer understanding of police culture. *Journal of Criminal Justice, 31,* 199–214.

Paoline III, E. A., Myers, S. M., & Worden, R. E. (2000). Police culture, individualism, and community policing: evidence from two police departments. *Justice Quarterly, 17*(3), 575–605.

Priest, T. B., & Carter, D. B. (1999). Evaluations of police performance in African-American sample. *Journal of Criminal Justice, 27,* 457–465.

Quinn, R. E. (1984). *Applying the Competing Values Approach to Leadership.* New York: Pergamon Press.

Quinn, R. E., & Rohrbaugh, J. (1981). A competing values approach to organizational effectiveness. *Public Productivity Review, 5,* 122–140.

Quinn, R. E., & Hall, R. H. (1983). *Environments, Organizations, and Policymakers: Toward an Integrative Framework.* Beverly Hills, CA: Sage Publications, Inc.

Rest, J. R., Narvaez, D., Thoma, S. J., & Bebeau, M. J. (2000). A neo-Kohlbergian approach to morality research. *Journal of Moral Education, 29*(4), 381–395.

Riksheim, E. C., & Chermak, S. M. (1993). Causes of police behavior revisited. *Journal of Criminal Justice, 21,* 353–382.

Robinette, H. M. (1991, January). Police ethics: leadership and ethics training for police administrators. *The Police Chief, 58*(1), 42–47.

Robinson, A. L. (2003). The impact of police social capital on officer performance of community policing. *Policing: An International Journal of Police Strategies and Management, 26*(4), 656–689.

Robinson, A. L., & Chandek, M. S. (2000). The domestic violence arrest decision: examining demographic, attitudinal, and situational variables. *Crime & Delinquency, 46*(1), 18–37.

Rohr, J. A. (1978). *Ethics for Bureaucrats: An Essay on Law and Values.* New York: Marcel Dekker.

Scarborough, K. E., Van Tubergen, G. N., Gaines, L. K., & Whitlow, S. S. (1999). An examination of police officers' motivation to participate in the promotional process. *Police Quarterly, 2*(3), 302–320.

Simon, R. (1995). Control in an age of empowerment. *Harvard Business Review, 73*(2), 80–88.

Slovak, J. S. (1986). *Styles of Urban Policing: Organization, Environment, and Police Styles in Selected American Cities.* New York: New York University Press.

Smith, D. A. (1984). The organizational context of legal control. *Criminology, 22*(1), 19–38.

Stewart, D. W., & Sprinthall, N. A. (1991). *Strengthening Ethical Judgment in Public Administration.* (Ethical Frontiers in Public Management ed.). San Francisco, CA: Jossey-Bass.

Stewart, D. W., & Sprinthall, N. A. (1994). Moral development in public administration. In T. Cooper, (ed.). *Handbook of Administrative Ethics* (pp. 325–348). New York: Marcel Dekker.

Sykes, G. W. (1994, Summer). That's the way we do things around here. *The Ethics Roll Call, 2,* 3.

Terrill, W., & Mastrofski, S. D. (2002). Situational and officer-based determinants of police coercion. *Justice Quarterly, 19*(2), 215–248.

Terrill, W., Paoline III, E. A., & Manning, P. K. (2003). Police culture and coercion. *Criminology, 41*(4), 1003–1034.

Trautman, N. E. (1997). *The National Law Enforcement Officer Disciplinary Research Project.* Long Beach, MS: The Ethics Institute.

Truelson, J. A. (1991). *New Strategies for Institutional Controls* (pp. 225–242). San Francisco: Jossey-Bass.

Van Maanen, J. (1973). Observations of the Making of a Policeman. *Human Organization, 32,* 407–418.

Van Wart, M. (1998). *Changing Public Sector Values.* New York: Garland Publishing, Inc.

Walker, S., Alpert, G. P., & Kenney, D. J. (2001, July). *Early Warning Systems: Responding to the Problem Police Officer.* Washington, D.C.: National Institute of Justice.

Weber, D. C. (1999, August 26). *Warrior Cops: The Ominous Growth of Paramilitarism in American Police Departments.* Washington, D.C.: CATO Institute.

Whetstone, T. S. (2001). Copping Out: Why Police Officers Decline to Participate in the Sergeant's Promotional Process. *American Journal of Criminal Justice, 25*(2), 147–159.

Wilson, J. Q. (1968). *Varieties of Police Behavior.* New York: Antheneum.

Wilson, J. Q. (1989). *Bureaucracy: What Government Agencies Do and Why They Do It.* New York: Basic Books.

Wilson, K. L., Rest, J. R., Boldizar, J. P., & Deemer, D. K. (1992). Moral judgment development: the effects of education and occupation. *Social Justice Research, 5*(1), 31–48.

Worden, R. E. (1995). *The Causes of Police Brutality: Theory and Evidence on Police Use of Force.* Washington, DC: Police Executive Research Forum.

CHAPTER 3

Deviant Behavior and Modeling Police Officer Misconduct

OBJECTIVES

- Review some of the basic theories of social deviance, including the Differential Association Theory and the Social Control Theory, and provide elements of the respective structural models
- Examine a National Institute of Justice study, including general characteristics of the respondents, the survey instrument, and some of the variables
- Apply the Differential Association Theory and the Social Control Theory to the National Institute of Justice study by assigning variables to the structural models
- Analyze the National Institute of Justice data using structural equation modeling to determine which theory, the Differential Association Theory or the Social Control Theory, best fits the data, thus possibly explaining some police misconduct behavior

Sociological theories regarding crime and delinquency provide a perspective relevant to police misconduct, but these theories are generally applied to adolescent delinquent behavior. These theories also may be applicable to police officer subcultures. Sociological theories of crime and deviant behavior are useful in pursuing later analysis of socialization factors related to police culture. Although deviant behavior theories are traditionally used to explain crime, deviant behavior by definition does not have to be criminal behavior. It can be any behavior considered deviant from social norms (Kornhauser, 1978). Some of the misconduct explored in this book does include criminal behavior, and all of the misconduct is a deviation from social norms. There are many sociological theories purporting to explain deviant behavior; however, two main theories are the basis for most other deviant behavior theories—the Differential Association Theory (DAT) and the Social Control Theory (SCT). The data analysis in this chapter is an attempt to apply these two competing sociological theories to police corruption.

According to Tabachnick and Fidell (2001), structural equation modeling (SEM) can be used to test competing theories. Existing theoretical models of these two theories from the literature will be compared using SEM. These models will be tested using data collected by the National Institute of Justice (NIJ) regarding police integrity. This chapter briefly examines these two competing sociological theories. Finally, structural equation models applying this data will be analyzed and compared quantitatively using the SPSS and AMOS computer statistical software programs.

GENERAL THEORIES OF DEVIANT BEHAVIOR

The DAT

Edwin Sutherland is considered the father of DAT. *Principles of Criminology*, Sutherland's seminal work on the subject, was first published in 1934 and is currently in its 11th edition despite Sutherland's death in 1950 (Sutherland et al., 1970). According to Sutherland, criminal behavior is learned in intimate relationships and personal groups. Individuals commit crime when they have learned "an excess of definitions favorable to law violation over definitions unfavorable to law violation" (Matsueda, quoting Sutherland, 1988). Essentially, through communication within groups, individuals learn techniques, motives, and rationalizations for committing deviant acts.

Definitions favorable to crime are weighted by the frequency, duration, priority, and intensity of the relationships within the personal groups. Cultural deviance theory is a result of culture and subculture supporting norms that are different from those of society. A culture or subculture exists, recruits new members, establishes norms that conflict with the norms of society at large, and supports criminalized behavior. This encouragement of criminal behavior causes delinquency and crime (Kornhauser, 1978).

Based on a review of Sutherland's theory, Matsueda identifies five relevant variables of causal relationships within a DAT model. These variables include background of the respondent, parental supervision, peer relationships, definitions favorable/unfavorable to crime, and delinquency. According to DAT, an individual's background, relationships with peers, and parental supervision shape whether the individual will develop definitions favorable or unfavorable to crime. An individual's background will also determine the way in which he or she is supervised and the types of peers with whom he or she associates. A copy of Matsueda's basic model can be found in Figure 3–1 (Matsueda, 1982).

These five variables are the latent variables, constructs, or unobserved variables. The observed variables used for each can vary depending on the researcher and the data set available for analysis. Typically, observed background variables include the respondent's age, socioeconomic status, family life, and perceptions of living conditions. Observed parental supervision variables include questions regarding whether a parent keeps track of where their child is and with whom. Relationships with peers can be measured by how much respect the respondent has for that peer. Definitions favorable and unfavorable to crime can be measured through attitudes toward law enforcement, other delinquents, and victims (Matsueda, 1982).

Several fundamental differences exist between DAT and SCT. First, DAT asserts that criminal behavior is learned, not innate, as this chapter explores in the next section. Second, DAT stresses the importance of subcultures through the overwhelming influence of peers on criminal behavior,

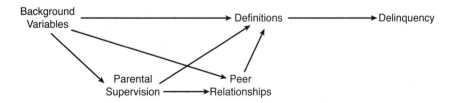

FIGURE 3–1 Model Derived from Differential Association Theory

which is the exact opposite of SCT. Finally, DAT focuses on the importance of culture overall as influential to the formation of definitions ultimately leading to delinquent behavior. Not all social theorists subscribe to DAT. Some social scientists argue that the potential for deviant behavior is within each of us.

The Social Control Theory

If Sutherland is the father of DAT, then Travis Hirschi may be the father of SCT. Hirschi, relying on Durkheim, Hobbes, Matza and others, brought attention to this theory of criminal behavior in his 1969 *Causes of Delinquency*. According to Hirschi, we are all born delinquent, but controls within society constrain our behavior. Constraints on behavior can be internal or external, direct or indirect (Kornhauser, 1978). Social bonds, particularly to parents, have the greatest impact on whether individuals will commit deviant acts (Hirschi, 2002).

Hirschi describes these social bonds as attachment, commitment, involvement, and belief. Attachment to parents, school, and peers "assumes that the bond of affection for conventional persons is a major deterrent to crime" (Hirschi, 2002). Attachment can be measured by the amount of supervision and communication between the adult and the adolescent respondent, the amount of contact with the peer, or the performance in school. Commitment refers to the stake the respondent has in conformity within society, which can be measured in adolescents by the frequency with which they engage in adult behaviors such as smoking, dating, and drinking alcohol. Involvement in conventional activities is measured through homework and hobbies, whereas belief in values and norms is measured in attitudes toward law enforcement, delinquents, and victims (Hirschi, 2002). Hirschi argues that variables measuring behavior are preferable when testing control theories (Hirschi & Gottfredson, 1990).

Attachments constrain behavior, according to Hirschi, keeping people from committing delinquent behavior out of fear. In Hirschi's model, there is a hypothesized attachment to peers and parents for delinquency. Hirschi asserts that attachment can cause delinquency by influencing belief in a single moral order, leading to delinquency through lack of supervision. According to SCT, peers are not important, but parents are very important. Delinquents are unable to become attached to anyone. Social controls are weak, and delinquents are then able to act out their innate desire to commit delinquent acts (Hirschi, 2002; Kornhauser, 1978).

Wiatrowski et al. (1981) have created a complex structural model of the social bonds discussed in Hirschi's SCT. The relevant variables include attachment to parents, socioeconomic status and ability, belief, and attachment/involvement/commitment to school. These variables each directly and indirectly impact delinquency. The model created by Wiatrowski et al. (1981) is in Figure 3–2.

Another sociological theory suggests that deviance amongst police officers is a result of an imbalance between three key variables, which include motivation, constraint, and opportunity (Tittle, 1995). Another study used the same scenarios from the NIJ study with additional control variables added to the survey instrument. The study administered the instrument to officers in Philadelphia. The results were analyzed to determine whether the amount of control that officers are subject to in relationship to the amount of control they have in their environment affects their decision to report peer misconduct (Hickman et al., 2001). The Hickman et al. (2001) study relies on Tittle's (1995) control balance theory. This control balance theory is based on the potential deviant becoming aware of an imbalance of control in a given situation and using deviant behavior in order to regain control over the situation (Tittle, 1995). The Hickman et al. (2001) study did show a relationship such that officers with less control over the situation were more likely to report peer misconduct.

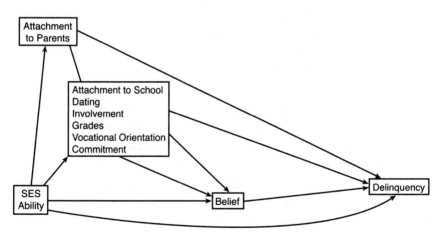

SES = socioeconomic status

FIGURE 3–2 Complex Model of the Social Bond

Therefore, officers may be impacted by poor working conditions, definitions favorable to crime, and unethical behavior through intimate work relationships, weak social bonds, and/or an imbalance of motivation, constraint, and opportunity (Tittle, 1995).

THE NIJ STUDY

The NIJ conducted a study measuring the integrity of police officers from 30 different agencies in the United States. The NIJ study focuses on corruption at the organizational level, as opposed to behavioral corruption. The authors use this approach in an effort to avoid willingness to report problems that often arise when asking officers directly whether they have been a party to corrupt behavior. The NIJ study asks officers for their perceptions regarding agency rules, corresponding punishment, and willingness to report a peer's unethical behavior (Klockars et al., 2000).

The Survey to Police Officers

The survey instrument used in the NIJ study included 11 case scenarios describing police misconduct. The case scenarios range from not very serious, to intermediately serious, to very serious in nature. Some of the activities included in the case scenarios are conflict of interest, bribery, theft, and excessive force. The 11 case scenarios and the corresponding abbreviations in the data set are in Table 3–1 (Klockars et al., 2000).

Each case scenario is followed by seven questions capturing the police officer's opinion regarding the misconduct scenario. Two questions asked officers to rate the seriousness of the case scenario from their own perspective and from that of their peers. Two additional questions addressed what disciplinary action the officer felt should be taken and what disciplinary action the officer felt would be taken in the case scenario. The officer's willingness to report the misconduct was another question, as well as a question regarding whether the officer felt that his or her peers would report the misconduct. A final question addressed whether the officer believed the misconduct was a violation of their agency's official policy. A copy of the seven questions and the corresponding abbreviations in the data set is in Table 3–2 (Klockars et al., 2000).

Finally, the study asked officers general questions regarding their background. Each officer responded to eight additional questions such as rank, assignment of duties, and size of agency. One open-ended question

Table 3-1 Case Scenarios from the Survey Instrument and Relevant International Association of Chiefs of Police Standards of Conduct

**Case 1
busin**
A police officer runs his own private business in which he sells and installs security devices, such as alarms, special locks, etc. He does this work during his off-duty hours.

Does not violate any standard

**Case 2
meals**
A police officer routinely accepts free meals, cigarettes, and other items of small value from merchants on his beat. He does not solicit these gifts and is careful not to abuse the generosity of those who give gifts to him.

IV. A. 8 (a) Officers shall report any unsolicited gifts, gratuities, or other items of value they receive and shall provide a full report of the circumstances of their receipt if directed.

**Case 3
speed**
A police officer stops a motorist for speeding. The officer agrees to accept a personal gift of half of the amount of the fine in exchange for not issuing a citation.

IV. A. 8 (b) Officers shall not use their authority or position for financial gain, for obtaining or granting privileges or favors not otherwise available to them or others except as a private citizen, to avoid the consequences of illegal acts for themselves or for others, to barter, solicit, or accept any goods or services whether for the officer or for another.

**Case 4
holi**
A police officer is widely liked in the community, and on holidays local merchants and restaurant and bar owners show their appreciation for his attention by giving him gifts of food and liquor.

IV. A. 8 (a) Officers shall report any unsolicited gifts, gratuities, or other items of value they receive and shall provide a full report of the circumstances of their receipt if directed.

**Case 5
burg**
A police officer discovers a burglary of a jewelry shop. The display cases are smashed and it is obvious that many items have been taken. While searching the shop, he takes a watch, worth about two days pay for that officer. He reports that the watch had been stolen during the burglary.

IV. A. 1 (a) Officers shall not violate any law or any agency policy, rule or procedure.

IV. A. 8 (c) Officers shall not purchase, convert to their own use, or have any claim to any found, impounded, abandoned, or recovered property, or any property held or released as evidence.

**Case 6
auto**
A police officer has a private arrangement with a local auto body shop to refer the owners of the cars damaged in the accidents to the shop. In exchange for each referral, he receives a payment of 5% of the repair bill from the shop owner.

IV. A. 8 (e) Officers are prohibited from using information gained through their position as a law enforcement officer to advance financial or other private interests of themselves or others.

**Case 7
super**
A police officer, who happens to be a very good auto mechanic, is scheduled to work during coming holidays. A supervisor offers to give him these days off, if he agrees to tune-up his supervisor's personal car. Evaluate the SUPERVISOR'S behavior.

(continues)

Table 3–1 Case Scenarios from the Survey Instrument and Relevant International Association of Chiefs of Police Standards of Conduct (continued)

IV. A. 8 (b) Officers shall not use their authority or position for financial gain, for obtaining or granting privileges or favors not otherwise available to them or others except as a private citizen, to avoid the consequences of illegal acts for themselves or for others, to barter, solicit, or accept any goods or services whether for the officer or for another.

Case 8
alch

At 2 A.M. a police officer, who is on duty, is driving his patrol car on a deserted road. He sees a vehicle that has been driven off the road and is stuck in a ditch. He approaches the vehicle and observes that the driver is not hurt but is obviously intoxicated. He also finds that the driver is a police officer. Instead of reporting this accident and offense he transports the driver to his home.

IV. A. 8 (b) Officers shall not use their authority or position for financial gain, for obtaining or granting privileges or favors not otherwise available to them or others except as a private citizen, to avoid the consequences of illegal acts for themselves or for others, to barter, solicit, or accept any goods or services whether for the officer or for another.

Case 9
bar

A police officer finds a bar on his beat that is still serving drinks a half hour past its legal closing time. Instead of reporting this violation, the police officer agrees to accept a couple of free drinks from the owner.

IV. A. 8 (b) Officers shall not use their authority or position for financial gain, for obtaining or granting privileges or favors not otherwise available to them or others except as a private citizen, to avoid the consequences of illegal acts for themselves or for others, to barter, solicit, or accept any goods or services whether for the officer or for another.

It is not clear whether the free drinks are consumed while on duty. If so, these standards would also apply:

IV. A. 6 (a) Officers shall not consume any intoxicating beverage while on duty unless authorized by a supervisor.

IV. A. 6 (c) An officer shall not be under the influence of alcohol in a public place, whether on or off duty.

Case 10
force

Two police officers on foot patrol surprise a man who is attempting to break into an automobile. The man flees. They chase him for about two blocks before apprehending him by tackling him and wrestling him to the ground. After he is under control both officers punch him a couple of times in the stomach as punishment for fleeing and resisting.

IV. A. 5 (c) While recognizing the need to demonstrate authority and control over criminal suspects and prisoners, officers shall adhere to this agency's use-of-force policy and shall observe the civil rights and protect the well-being of those in their charge.

Case 11
wallet

A police officer finds a wallet in a parking lot. It contains the amount of money equivalent to a full-day's pay for that officer. He reports the wallet as lost property, but keeps the money for himself.

IV. A. 8 (c) Officers shall not purchase, convert to their own use, or have any claim to any found, impounded, abandoned, or recovered property, or any property held or released as evidence.

Table 3-2 Questions, Possible Responses, and Coding from the Survey Instrument

Abbreviations	Questions and Possible Responses
OS	How serious do YOU consider this behavior to be?
	1 not at all serious – 5 very serious
MS	How serious do MOST POLICE OFFICERS IN YOUR AGENCY consider this behavior to be?
	1 not at all serious – 5 very serious
VI	Would this behavior be regarded as a violation of official policy in your agency?
	1 definitely not – 5 definitely yes
OR	Do you think YOU would report a fellow police officer who engaged in this behavior?
	1 definitely not – 5 definitely yes
MR	Do you think MOST POLICE OFFICERS IN YOUR AGENCY would report a fellow police officer who engaged in this behavior?
	1 definitely not – 5 definitely yes
OD	If an officer in your agency engaged in this behavior and was discovered doing so, what if any discipline do YOU think SHOULD follow?
	1 none, 2 verbal reprimand, 3 written reprimand, 4 period of suspension without pay, 5 demotion in rank, 6 dismissal
MD	If an officer in your agency engaged in this behavior and was discovered doing so, what if any discipline do YOU think WOULD follow?
	1 none, 2 verbal reprimand, 3 written reprimand, 4 period of suspension without pay, 5 demotion in rank, 6 dismissal

---

was also included, allowing officers to add comments; however, the responses to this question are not included in the SPSS data set, as they require qualitative analysis. A copy of the general questions that are a part of the SPSS data set and the corresponding abbreviations is in Table 3–3 (Klockars et al., 2000).

Characteristics of the Police Agencies Involved in the Survey

The survey instrument was completed by 3,237 officers from 30 police agencies in the United States. Most of these agencies are located in the Northeast, and were not chosen randomly. The authors chose these agencies because of an existing relationship allowing access to these agencies.

Table 3–3 Background Questions, Possible Responses, Corresponding Abbreviations

Abbreviation	Questions and Possible Responses
lengthg	How many years have you been a police officer?
	Less than 1;1-2; 3-5; 5-10; 11-15; 16-20; over 20
lengthpp	How many years have you been employed at your current police agency?
	Less than 1; 1-2; 3-5; 5-10; 11-15; 16-20; over 20
rank	What is your rank?
	Recruit, Corporal, Lieutenant, Colonel, Officer, Deputy, Detective IO, Sergeant, Captain, Major, Chief/Sheriff, Other
assign	Which of the following best describes your current assignment?
	Patrol, Detective/Investigative, Special Operations (vice, juvenile, etc.), Communications, Administrative, Other
supervis	Are you a supervisor or non-supervisor?
	Non-Supervisor, Supervisor (unit supervisor, group supervisor, chief/sheriff)
agency	Which of the following best describes your police agency?
	Very Large Municipal Police (more than 500 sworn officers), Large Municipal Police (201-500 sworn officers), Medium-Sized Municipal Police (76-200 sworn officers), Small Municipal Police (25-75 sworn officers), Very Small Municipal Police (less than 25 sworn officers), State Police, Sheriff, County Police

The authors do not indicate how many agencies were invited to participate; however, the authors do admit that some agencies declined to participate despite assurances of anonymity and confidentiality (Klockars et al., 2000).

Approximately 60% of respondents work in very large agencies with over 500 officers on duty. Almost 20% of respondents work in large agencies with a range from 201 to 500 sworn officers. Meanwhile, 9% of respondents work in medium-size agencies with 76 to 200 officers; 8.5% work in small agencies with 25 to 75 officers, and the remaining less than 3% work in small agencies with fewer than 25 sworn officers. The average respondent has been an officer for approximately 10.3 years; 63.1% of respondents work in patrol or traffic, and only 1 in 5 respondents is a supervisor (Klockars et al., 2000).

NIJ's Survey Techniques

The NIJ compares mean scores of respondents at the agency level. Three case scenarios offer the greatest differences in mean scores between agencies. These three case scenarios involved officers accepting kickbacks, officers accepting alcohol in exchange for ignoring a bar closing late, and officers using excessive force. Based on these mean comparisons, the authors give each agency an integrity score and then rank the agencies according to the integrity score (Klockars et al., 2000).

The integrity score is based on an agency's mean score as compared with the mean scores of the other 29 agencies. An agency that ranked in the top third of all mean scores received 3 points, and an agency in the middle third received 2 points, whereas agencies in the bottom third only received 1 point. These points were totaled for each question and aggregated. The range of possible integrity scores then began at 11 for those agencies who remained in the lowest third for all questions up to a possible 33 points for agencies that remained in the top third of mean scores in all case scenario responses (Klockars et al., 2000).

Given the potential bias in the sample, it is hard to say whether the results reported in the NIJ study accurately measure an agency's integrity. A more effective study would have randomly sampled the population of police agencies across the United States to alleviate this potential bias. It also would be interesting to compare integrity means of police officers with the general public to see whether police officers are significantly different.

DATA ANALYSIS

The NIJ study provides data at the individual level of analysis, making it accessible to multiple forms of data analysis. One advantage of using this data set is that it is very large, allowing for easy deletion of outliers and missing values, as well as the use of cross validation, if necessary. A second advantage is that it contains responses creating approximately 88 variables, including a broad range of misconduct and background information. Finally, the data are very recent, collected in 2000, making it timely and relatively open to evaluation.

Screening the Data

The first step in screening the data set included deleting missing values for the relevant variables. A second step in screening the data that was unique to this data set involved honesty of the respondents in completing the survey data. One question added to the end of the survey instrument asked officers who did respond to the survey whether they were truthful in responding to the survey questions. According to the authors, approximately 2.2% of the officers responded "no" to this question, with approximately 1.8% not responding. These 4% of respondents were deleted from the analysis. The NIJ study chose only to delete the "no" responses to this question.

The third step involved checking for multicollinearity or singularity. SEM assumes absence of multicollinearity or singularity among variables. The variable length of service in general was dropped from the DAT model, and length of service for the agency was dropped for the SCT model. These two variables were redundant. The variables were selected for each model based on path coefficients in order to give each model the advantage of the highest path coefficient. One other variable had a high estimate in the SCT model relating to the reporting of a superior's misconduct. The variable "superior" was dropped from the SCT model, as it was adequately represented by three other supervisor measures.

SEM also assumes absence of outliers. After removal of missing cases, potentially untruthful officers, and outliers, the data set contained 2,689 cases.

SEM assumes linearity. Finally, residual matrices need to be analyzed in order to detect systematic error. As both models are somewhat similar in error, no further adjustments were made. These residuals will help explain the relative fit of these models discussed in the following sections. Analyzing the LaGrange Multiplier test was not helpful in solving this problem. Experimenting with adding parameters to the model based on the highest modification index scores for unobserved variables did not add to the model fit for either model.

The Differential Association Model

Choosing the DAT Observed Variables

The DAT model relies on variables that reflect the theory. As DAT measures delinquent behavior, the three scenarios chosen for this model were ranked by police officers as very serious. In the NIJ study, the scenarios were ranked according to six of the seven questions in the survey instrument. The one question not included asked respondents whether their department had a policy regarding the behavior in question. The three most seriously ranked scenarios were included as observed variables in the model as they most resemble deviant behavior.

The unobserved variable for delinquency is represented by the survey responses to whether the respondent's agency had a policy regarding the behavior in question. Departments that have a policy regarding the behavior in question have defined the behavior in question as delinquent. The scenarios used for this unobserved variable included case number 5 (burgvi) and case number 11 (walletvi). A comparison of means for responses to all case scenarios reveals that most agencies have a policy against the three scenarios chosen for this model, with case 11 (walletvi) receiving the highest score and cases 3 (speedvi) and 5 (burgvi) tied for second place. Running the model in AMOS with case 5 (burgvi) yielded a higher regression weight, however. Running the program with all three scenarios yield mixed results in the goodness-of-fit measurements. The regression weight for case 11 (walletvi) was .31, whereas the regression weight for case 5 (burgvi) was .24, indicating that both observed variables are strong indicators for the latent variable representing delinquent behavior.

Peer relationships were measured using the difference between the officer's perceptions and what they believe to be the perceptions of their peers. The responses to what officers believed were the perceptions of their peers regarding misconduct was subtracted from the responses to the question regarding their own perceptions of what officers believe to be misconduct (i.e., speedos – speedms). This created a new variable labeled "peer" with the corresponding case number (i.e., speedos – speedms = peer3; burgos – burgms = peer5). These two new variables were then recoded as follows in Table 3–4.

The recalculation of these two questions most directly reflects the officer's perception of their relationship with their peers. The two most seriously ranked scenarios for this question were case 5 (burgos/burgms) and case 3 (speedos/speedms). The results yielded significant regression weights of .51 for case 3 (speedos/speedms) and .74 for case 5 (burgos/burgms), indicating that these observed variables strongly predict the relationship between an officer and his or her peers.

Definitions favorable or unfavorable to crime were measured by responses to the question regarding the perception of the respondent. This question reflects the opinion of the officer directly regarding what they believe to be delinquent behavior. The two most seriously ranked scenarios according to officers were case 3 (speedos) and case 5 (burgos). The regression weights

Table 3–4 Peer Variable

Significance	Old Value	New Value
Officers have a close relationship with their peers because there is no difference between the officer's perception of misconduct and the officer's perception regarding that of their peers	0	5
Officers have a good relationship with their peers because there is only a slight difference between the officer's perception of misconduct and the officer's perception regarding that of their peers	1	4
Officers have an uncertain relationship with their peers because there is a significant difference between the officer's perception of misconduct and the officer's perception regarding that of their peers	2	3
Officers do not have a good relationship with their peers because there is a big difference between the officer's perception of misconduct and the officer's perception regarding that of their peers	3	2
Officers have a bad relationship with their peers because there is an extremely large difference between the officer's perception of misconduct and the officer's perception regarding that of their peers	4	1

were significant yielding .46 for case 3 (speedos) and .66 for case 5 (burgos), indicating that these observed variables strongly predict whether officers have definitions favorable or unfavorable to crime.

Background was measured using several observed variables, including rank, length of service in the agency, the size of the agency, and whether the officer is a supervisor. The length of service in general was left out because of multicollinearity as previously mentioned. The length of service in the agency adequately covered this area of the officer's background. Regression weights were significant.

Supervision of the officer was measured with question number 7 asking respondents about the type of punishment the officer misconduct would receive under the case scenario. Interestingly, the two most seriously ranked case scenarios for this question were case 5 (burgmd) and case 11 (walletmd). The regression weights for these two observed variables are .69 and .72, respectively. These observed variables strongly predict supervision of officers.

Effect of Latent Variables on Delinquent Behavior for the DAT Model

According to the model, Supervision has the strongest direct effect on Definitions with a path coefficient or beta weight of .29, and a total causal effect of .317, while Background, with a beta weight of .04 and a total causal effect of .098, has the least direct effect on Definitions. Peer Relationships have a .08 direct effect on Definitions. These results are in contrast to DAT, which would hypothesize the strongest effect on Definitions would be Peer Relationships.

The total causal effects for each of the latent variables with respect to Delinquency yield similar results. The total causal effect of Peer Relationships on Delinquency is .080, the lowest effect contradicting DAT. Background, with a total causal effect of .094, is the next highest causal effect on Delinquency. The highest causal effect on Delinquency was Supervision with a .302 total causal effect. Accordingly, these results indicate that Supervision is the best predictor of delinquency with police officers. The direct effect of Definitions on Delinquency was extremely strong in the DAT model with a .95 path coefficient. A copy of the model with unstandardized and standardized regressions, as well as the accompanying AMOS output, can be found in Figure 3–3.

Evaluating the DAT Model

As a preliminary matter, the critical ratios and P values reported in the regression weight table of the data suggests deleting some parameters. Background to Definitions, Definitions to Delinquency, Delinquency to walletvi and burgvi each have critical ratios below 2 and P values greater than .05. Deleting any of these parameters, with the exception of Background to Definitions, is problematic for the model and contrary to theory. Also, deleting these parameters one at a time did not yield significant chi-square difference test results.

Assessing the goodness of fit for this model requires looking beyond chi-square scores of significance as the sample size is so large. As expected, the chi-square was found to be significant, which is undesirable in a good fitting model.

Considering the goodness-of-fit measures for DAT, the model passes 8 of 11 goodness-of-fit tests. DAT passed GFI, AGFI, RMR, CFI, NFI, RMSEA, IFI, and RFI. The fit tests that DAT failed included TLI, PNFI,

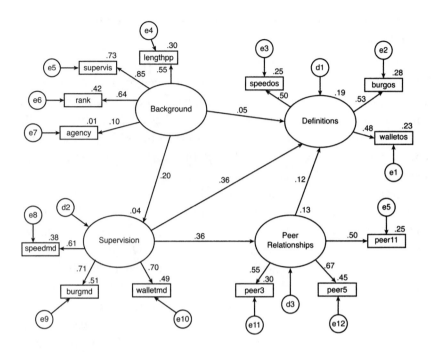

FIGURE 3–3 AMOS: Differential Association Theory

and PCFI. According to these tests, although not perfect, the model can be considered a good fit. Table 3–5 shows the goodness-of-fit scores for the DAT model compared to threshold values.

The Social Control Model

Choosing the SCT Observed Variables

The SCT model also relies on variables that reflect the theory. Again, the most serious scenarios were used in this model. As SCT relies heavily on behavioral observed variables, the variables for belief were exclusively behavioral. The five most serious cases were used for the question regarding whether an officer would report the relevant misconduct.

The observed variables for delinquency were similar to that of the DAT model; however, all three of the most serious cases were used without detracting from the overall model. Attachment to supervisor was measured similarly relying on officer's opinions regarding supervisor misconduct described in case 7. The SCT model differs in that socioeconomic status and ability are separated from achievement and commitment that

Table 3–5 Goodness of Fit for DAT Model

GFI	values > .90 or .95, depending on textbook	.981
AGFI	values > .90	.969
RMR	close to zero	.040
CFI	values > .90 or .95, depending on textbook	.930
NFI	values > .90	.919
TLI	values > .95	.904
RFI	close to 1	.889
IFI	values > .90	.931
RMSEA	values < .06	.046
PNFI	should not drop in value from NFI	.669
PCFI	should not drop in value from CFI	.677

DAT characterizes as background. A copy of the model with unstandardized and standardized regressions, as well as the accompanying AMOS output, can be found in Figure 3–4.

The model suggests deleting the parameters from Achievement/Commitment to Belief, from Attachment to Supervisor to Delinquency, from Achievement/Commitment to Delinquency, and from SES/Ability to Delinquency; however, these relationships are critical to SCT, and removal did not make a significant impact on the goodness-of-fit measures for this model. Overall, the regression weights between unobserved and observed variables were strong, whereas the weights between unobserved variables were significantly weaker. The strongest regression weights between unobserved variables were those from SES/Ability to Belief and from Attachment to Supervisor to Belief, indicating the strongest relationships. SCT suggests that the relationship between Belief and Delinquency should be the strongest; however, this model does not reflect such findings.

The regression weights were significant for relationships between observed variables and unobserved variables. For example, the regression weights for observed variables and Belief ranged from .66 to .86, with four of the five observed variables weighted over .82, suggesting a strong relationship. Other particularly strong regression weights can be found in the relationship between the observed variables of superos, superod, and supermr and Attachment to Supervisor, which were .66, .80, and .90, respectively.

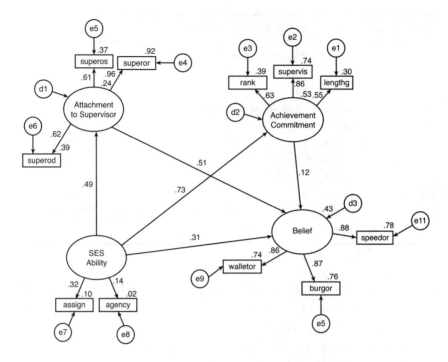

FIGURE 3–4 AMOS: Social Control Theory

Effect of Latent Variables on Delinquent Behavior for the SCT Model

According to the model, Attachment to Supervisor has the strongest direct effect on Belief with a path coefficient or beta weight of .73, and a total causal effect of .384. SES/Ability, with a beta weight of .42 and a total causal effect of .500, has the next highest direct effect on Belief and the highest total causal effect on Belief. Achievement/Commitment has a −.10 direct effect on Belief. These results are partially in contrast to SCT with respect to Achievement/Commitment. SCT would hypothesize that Achievement/Commitment would have a stronger effect and a positive effect on Belief.

The total causal effects for each of the latent variables with respect to Delinquency yield similar results. The total causal effect of SES/Ability, Achievement/Commitment, and Belief on Delinquency is .225, −.214, .216, respectively. SCT would hypothesize Belief having the strongest effect on Delinquency and Achievement/Commitment having a positive effect on Delinquency. Attachment to Supervisor, with a total causal effect of .087, is the lowest causal effect on Delinquency. Accordingly, these results indicate that SES/Ability may be the best predictor of delinquency with police officers. The direct effect of Belief on Delinquency was significant, but not as strong as SES/Ability, with a .22 path coefficient for Belief and a .26 path coefficient for SES/Ability.

Evaluating the SCT Model

Goodness-of-fit measures for the SCT model show that it is generally a good fitting model, passing 7 of the 11 goodness-of-fit tests. The 7 tests passed by the model include GFI, AGFI, RMR, CFI, NFI, RFI, and IFI. The four tests failed by the model include TLI, RMSEA, PNFI, and PCFI. The only difference between SCT and DAT is that DAT passed the RMSEA test. Table 3–6 shows the goodness-of-fit scores for SCT compared with the threshold values.

Comparing the AIC, BCC, and BIC for both models, however, shows that DAT is a better fitting model than SCT. All three scores are significantly lower for DAT than for SCT. One advantage to the SCT model, however, is that it was possible to include four more variables in the analysis than in the DAT model without affecting any of the goodness of fit measures significantly; however, this may be attributed to the unique qualities of this data set and not the models themselves. Table 3–7 compares all of the goodness of fit measures for both models.

Table 3–6 Goodness of Fit for SCT

GFI	values > .90 or .95, depending on textbook	.951
AGFI	values > .90	.929
RMR	close to zero	.077
CFI	values > .90 or .95, depending on textbook	.937
NFI	values > .90	.931
TLI	values > .95	.920
RFI	close to 1	.913
IFI	values > .90	.937
RMSEA	values < .06	.062
PNFI	should not drop in value from NFI	.737
PCFI	should not drop in value from CFI	.742

Table 3-7 Goodness of Fit for SCT and DAT

Goodness of Fit Test	SCT	DAT
GFI	.951	.981
AGFI	.929	.969
RMR	.077	.040
CFI	.937	.930
NFI	.931	.919
TLI	.920	.904
RFI	.913	.889
IFI	.937	.931
RMSEA	.062	.046
PNFI	.737	.669
PCFI	.742	.677
AIC	1147.623	375.970
BCC	1148.14	376.262
BIC	1503.073	627.425

CONCLUSION

There are some limits to this data analysis. First, the data were collected in order to measure police integrity, not to test sociological theories. Choosing observed variables that explain these models was an imperfect process. With 88 variables to choose from within the NIJ study, it was a daunting task, requiring qualitative analysis of the variables to determine which best described the latent constructs provided in each theory.

Another limitation of applying this data set to the models chosen addresses the issue of using cross sectional data instead of longitudinal. Sociological literature favors the use of longitudinal data for studying deviant behavior, particularly in the SCT literature. Longitudinal data, however, are not always available, as is the case here, and are often substituted in similar research studies.

Deviant behavior affects everyone in society, especially deviant behavior by those in positions of power. Understanding the police officer's perspective as a subordinate within the criminal justice system is an important step toward understanding misconduct within their ranks.

The NIJ study did not test any theories. There is no discussion within the NIJ study as to whether any of these variables are important in explaining theories of deviant behavior among police officers. This book suggests that these variables are important to theory and should be explored in future research. The data analysis in this chapter suggests that police officers learn deviant behavior in intimate social groups, specifically from their peers at work. How officers view their supervisors also plays a role. Further research is needed to validate the reliability of DAT within the context of police organizations.

DISCUSSION QUESTIONS

1. Do you believe that people are born with tendencies toward deviant behavior, or do you think these behaviors are learned in social groups?
2. What factors do you think most impact socially deviant behavior? Relationships with parents? Relationships with friends? School? Heredity?
3. If you were a law enforcement officer, would you be willing to report a fellow officer for any of the misconduct in the scenarios from the NIJ survey?
4. Have you ever witnessed anyone cheat, steal, or lie? Did you report that person or turn that person in to an authority figure? Why or why not?
5. The structural model suggests that DAT is a slightly better fit than the SCT model. What does this mean? Can both theories be true or are they mutually exclusive?

REFERENCES

Hickman, M. J., Piquero, A. R., Lawton, B. A., & Greene, J. R. (2001). Applying Tittle's Control Balance Theory to police deviance. *Policing: An International Journal of Police Strategies and Management, 24*(4), 497–519.

Hirschi, T. (2002). *Causes of Delinquency.* Berkeley, CA: University of California Press.

Hirschi, T., & Gottfredson, M. R. (1990). *A General Theory of Crime.* Stanford, CA: Stanford University Press.

Klockars, C. B., Ivkovich, S. K., Harver, W. E., & Haberfeld, M. R. (2000, May). *The Measurement of Police Integrity.* Washington, D.C.: National Institute of Justice.

Kornhauser, R. R. (1978). *Social Sources of Delinquency*. Chicago: University of Chicago Press.

Matsueda, Ross L. 1988. The Current State of Differential Association Theory." *Crime and Delinquency, 34*, 277–306.

Matsueda, R. L. (1982). Testing control theory and differential association: a causal modeling approach. *American Sociological Review, 47*(4), 489–504.

Sutherland, E. H., Cressey, D. R., & Luckenbill, D. F. (1970). *Principles of Criminology*. Philadelphia: Lippincott.

Tabachnick, B. G., & Fidell, L. S. (2001). *Using Multivariate Statistics*. Needham Heights, MA: Allyn & Bacon.

Tittle, C. R. (1995). *Control Balance: Toward a General Theory of Deviance (Crime and Society)*. New York: Westview Press.

Wiatrowski, M. D., & Griswold, D. B., & Roberts, M. K. (1981). Social Control Theory and delinquency. *American Sociological Review, 46*(5), 525–541.

CHAPTER 4

Police Officer Ethics Training

OBJECTIVES

- Consider the various ethics training opportunities available for law enforcement in the United States
- Give a brief history and description of both the Code of Conduct and Code of Ethics for law enforcement
- Present qualitative research including interviews, questionnaires, archival data, and observations of police ethics training
- Scrutinize the implications that this research has with respect to police officer ethics training in the United States

Even without screening out individuals in the hiring process who are not functioning at a high level of moral development, an agency could use training in order to promote an ethical work environment. The purpose of this chapter is to analyze police officer ethics training. A 1997 survey of ethics training for law enforcement discovered that over 70% of respondents offered 4 hours or less of ethics training (IACP [International Association of Chiefs of Police], 1998). Over 83% of respondents indicated that they offered ethics training to new officers, and approximately 72% of agencies offer ethics training beyond new recruit training (IACP, 1998). The focus of this chapter is the use in ethics training of the Code of Conduct, one component of a code of ethics for law enforcement. The data attempt to capture the perspective of police officers in management training, as well as the perspective of their instructors. This research relies on qualitative methodology, including observation, open-ended questionnaires, archival data gathering, and interviewing.

Understanding how police officers are trained in ethical decision making is an important step in understanding how police officers make ethical and moral decisions in their police work. Police officers who are undergoing management training provide a good starting point, as these officers have been on the force for many years. There is an increased likelihood that officers in management training have had ethical training in the past.

INTRODUCTION TO ETHICS

Ethics Training

At the beginning of this research project, I was surprised to discover that ethics training is rarely, if ever, conducted internally within police departments (Trautman, 2000). Sherman (1982), Hodgson (2001), and Harrison (1999) each reveal that learning ethical decision making for police officers most often occurs on the job, with no time for the officer to reflect during the heat of the battle. Each author argues, however, that ethics education during Basic Law Enforcement Training (BLET) is preferable to give the officers an opportunity to work through ethical dilemmas before facing similar situations at work.

Training that occurs after BLET is commonly referred to as In-Service Training (IST) and consists of a variety of topics, sometimes related to ethics. Unfortunately, some police administrators view IST ethics training as problematic. These administrators fear that requiring ethics training may make the administrator look incompetent (Trautman, 2000). In other words, administrators who need to place their officers in ethics training must have unethical officers and/or must be bad leaders. What I discovered from an informal interview of a colleague of mine in law enforcement is that although some departments may offer ethics training as IST, attendance is often not required by officers.

In the 1992 national training package created by the Central Planning and Training Unit for police officers, no "explicit reference to the significance of ethics" was made with respect to investigative interviewing techniques used by police officers (Newton, 1998). Trautman (2000) argued that a lack of ethical training, in general, is a recipe for corruption. Training and education in ethics for law enforcement are paramount to avoiding corruption (Harrison, 1999). Donahue and Felts

(1993) supported this view and asserted that police ethics are in a state of crisis and ethical training is needed.

There seems to be a consensus that working through real-life problems is the best ethics training for law enforcement. Relying on Sherman (1982), Delattre (1991) supported ethics training that focuses on the value choices that law enforcement officers make and general ethical dilemmas that officers face in their day-to-day work. Kleinig (1999) suggested that simply relying on codes of ethics in training is not enough. Bristow (1975) and Kleinig (1999) advocated linking the police code of ethics with actual real-life problems and cases to help officers work through ethical dilemmas and issues in the classroom. Trautman (2000) and Donahue and Felts (1993) also supported open discussion and ethical-dilemma simulation training. My initial observations have uncovered that there is very little discussion and/or simulation training available to officers.

Although there is some consensus regarding ethics training for law enforcement, there is also some diversity of opinion with respect to emphasis of material and training techniques advocated by different scholars. Not all scholars agree that codes of ethics should be the focus of law enforcement ethics training (IACP In-Service Training Manual). Meanwhile, Crawshaw (1998) advocated that law enforcement rely on codes of ethics for guidance in ethical decision making. Donahue and Felts (1993) would agree with this analysis as they focus on codes as ethical guidance for officers. Crawshaw (1998) suggested using video-tape recording, not only as evidence in interviewing suspects, but also as a training tool for officers to review interviewing techniques with their supervisors. No other literature mentions the use of video-tape recording in their training. Trautman (2000) advocates implementing mandatory internal ethics training in every police department; however, this view is not mentioned by others.

This diversity of opinion suggests a disparity in techniques and curriculum from region to region. This lack of continuity in ethics training for law enforcement could be the source of problems with respect to police corruption in the United States. My observations have shown that curriculum among the programs studied herein varies significantly. Hence, part of the focus of this study is to look at exactly what is being taught and how it is being taught to police officers across the country in management training programs. For comparison purposes, this research also looks at what is being taught and how it is being taught to new recruits in North Carolina. From this body of data, I hope to determine whether and in what way the Police Code of Conduct is incorporated into these training programs for law enforcement.

The Police Code of Conduct

The Law Enforcement Code of Ethics was originally contemplated as an oath of office rather than as a traditional code of ethics. The creation of a separate code of ethics and code of conduct was initially in response to the desire to have an oath of office for use at graduation ceremonies. This required shortening the original code created in 1957, which was undesirable as most agreed with the basic value statements contained in the original 1957 code. The solution was the creation of two separate documents, the Code of Ethics and the Police Code of Conduct. The Law Enforcement Code of Ethics is found in Figure 4–1, and the Police Code of Conduct is found in Figure 4–2.

The Police Code of Conduct contains nine main headings, which are referred to as ethical mandates that officers should turn to for guidance in performing their jobs. Each mandate contains a brief description of how a police officer should conduct himself or herself on the job. The entire document fits onto one page. According to the 1992 Police Chief article introducing it, the Police Code of Conduct reprinted in their magazine is at least "suitable for framing." A content analysis of the Police Code of Conduct reveals 24 distinct, nonclassified precepts within the nine mandates. This content analysis will be used as a coding scheme to analyze the instructor materials for law enforcement ethics courses. This coding scheme will be used to determine whether elements of the Police Code of Conduct are included indirectly in police officer ethics training. The content analysis can be found in Table 4–1.

The literature does not indicate whether the Police Code of Conduct is included in any training for officers. Some of the literature even advocates avoiding too much of a focus on codes as opposed to philosophical issues (IACP training materials are available online at http://www.theiacp.org). After analyzing five police officer training programs in the United States who were promised anonymity, only one of the programs included a copy of the Police Code of Conduct in its entirety, along with an in-depth discussion of its mandates. One other program included the Police Code of Ethics along with the American Society for Public Administration Code of Ethics. Essentially, these two documents combined cover all of the elements found in the Police Code of Conduct, especially the Police Code of Ethics. One of the sets of training materials did not include either, but the instructor always ends his or her lecture with a recitation of the Police Code of Ethics.

Law Enforcement Code of Ethics

As a law enforcement officer, my fundamental duty is to serve the community; to safeguard lives and property; to protect the innocent against deception, the weak against oppression or intimidation and the peaceful against violence or disorder; and to respect the constitutional rights of all to liberty, equality and justice.

I will keep my private life unsullied as an example to all and will behave in a manner that does not bring discredit to me or to my agency. I will maintain courageous calm in the face of danger, scorn or ridicule; develop self-restraint; and be constantly mindful of the welfare of others. Honest in thought and deed both in my personal and official life, I will be exemplary in obeying the law and regulations of my department. Whatever I see or hear of a confidential nature or that is confided to me in my official capacity will be kept ever secret unless revelation is necessary in the performance of my duty.

I will never act officiously or permit personal feelings, prejudices, political beliefs, aspirations, animosities or friendships to influence my decisions. With no compromise for crime and with relentless prosecution of criminals, I will enforce the law courteously and appropriately without fear of favor, malice or ill will, never employing unnecessary force or violence and never accepting gratuities.

I recognize the badge of my office as a symbol of public faith, and I accept it as a public trust to be held so long as I am true to the ethics of police service. I will never engage in acts of corruption or bribery, nor will I condone such acts by other police officers. I will cooperate with all legally authorized agencies and their representatives in the pursuit of justice.

I know that I alone am responsible for my own standard of professional performance and will take every reasonable opportunity to enhance and improve my level of knowledge and competence.

I will constantly strive to achieve these objectives and ideals, dedicating myself before God to my chosen profession . . . law enforcement.

FIGURE 4–1 Law Enforcement Code of Ethics

Police Code of Conduct

All law enforcement officers must be fully aware of the ethical responsibilities of their position and must strive constantly to live up to the highest possible standards of professional policing. The International Association of Chiefs of Police believes it important that police officers have clear advice and counsel available to assist them in performing their duties consistent with these standards, and has adopted the following ethical mandates as guidelines to meet these ends.

Primary Responsibilities of a Police Officer

A police officer acts as an official representative of government who is required and trusted to work within the law. The officer's powers and duties are conferred by statute. The fundamental duties of a police officer include serving the community, safeguarding lives and property, protecting the innocent, keeping the peace and ensuring the rights of all to liberty, equality and justice.

Performance of the Duties of a Police Officer

A police officer shall perform all duties impartially, without favor or affection or ill will and without regard to status, sex, race, religion, political belief or aspiration. All citizens will be treated equally with courtesy, consideration and dignity.

Officers will never allow personal feelings, animosities or friendships to influence official conduct. Laws will be enforced appropriately and courteously and, in carrying out their responsibilities, officers will strive to obtain maximum cooperation from the public. They will conduct themselves in appearance and department in such a manner as to inspire confidence and respect for the position of the public trust they hold.

Discretion

A police officer will use responsibly the discretion vested in his position and exercise it within the law. The principle of reasonableness will guide the officer's determinations, and the officer will consider all surrounding circumstances in determining whether any legal action shall be taken.

Consistent and wise use of discretion, based on professional policing competence, will do much to preserve good relationships and retain the confidence of the public. There can be difficulty in choosing between conflicting courses of action. It is important to remember that a timely word of advice rather than arrest - which may be correct in appropriate circumstances-, can be a more effective means of achieving a desired end.

Use of Force

A police officer will never employ unnecessary force or violence and will use only such force in the discharge of duty as is reasonable in all circumstances.

The use of force should be used only with the greatest restraint and only after discussion, negotiation and persuasion have been found to be inappropriate or ineffective. While the use of force is occasionally unavoidable, every police officer will refrain from unnecessary infliction of pain or suffering and will never engage in cruel, degrading or inhumane treatment of any person.

Confidentiality

Whatever a police officer sees, hears or learns of that is of a confidential nature will be kept secret unless the performance of duty or legal provision requires otherwise.

Members of the public have a right to security and privacy and information obtained about them must not be improperly divulged.

Integrity

A police officer will not engage in acts of corruption or bribery, nor will an officer condone such acts by other police officers.

The public demands that the integrity of police officers be above reproach. Police officers must, therefore, avoid any conduct that might compromise integrity and thus undercut the public confidence in a law enforcement agency. Officers will refuse to accept any gifts, presents, subscriptions, favors, gratuities or promises that could be interpreted as seeking to cause the officer to refrain from performing official responsibilities honestly and within the law. Police officers must not receive private or special advantage from their official status. Respect from the public cannot be bought; it can only be earned and cultivated.

Cooperation with Other Police Officers and Agencies

Police officers will cooperate with all legally authorized agencies and their representatives in the pursuit of justice.

An officer or agency may be one among many organizations that may provide law enforcement services to a jurisdiction. It is imperative that a police officer assists colleagues fully and completely with respect and consideration at all times.

Personal-Professional Capabilities

Police officers will be responsible for their own standard of professional performance and will take every reasonable opportunity to enhance and improve their level of knowledge and competence.

Through study and experience, a police officer can acquire the high level of knowledge and competence that is essential for the efficient and effective performance of duty. The acquisition of knowledge is a never-ending process of personal and professional development that should be pursued constantly.

Private Life

Police officers will behave in a manner that does not bring discredit to their agencies or themselves. A police officer's character and conduct while off duty must always be exemplary, thus maintaining a position of respect in the community in which he or she lives and serves. The officer's personal behavior must be beyond reproach.

FIGURE 4–2 Police Code of Conduct

Table 4-1 Content Analysis of the Law Enforcement Code of Conduct

1 Primary Responsibilities of a Police Officer

   a. the fundamental duties of a police officer include serving the community

   b. the fundamental duties of a police officer include safeguarding lives and property

   c. the fundamental duties of a police officer include protecting the innocent

   d. the fundamental duties of a police officer include keeping the peace

   e. the fundamental duties of a police officer include ensuring the rights of all to liberty, equality and justice

2 Performance of the Duties of a Police Officer

   a. a police officer shall perform all duties impartially, without favor

   b. a police officer shall perform all duties impartially, without ill will

   c. a police officer shall perform all duties impartially, without regard to status, sex, race, religion, political belief or aspiration

   d. police officers will conduct themselves in appearance and deportment in such a manner as to inspire confidence and respect

3 Discretion

   a. consistent use of discretion

   b. wise use of discretion

   c. discretion based on professional policing competence

4 Use of Force

   a. a police officer will never employ unnecessary force or violence

   b. every police officer will refrain from unnecessary infliction of pain and suffering and will never engage in cruel, degrading or inhuman treatment of any person

5 Confidentiality

   a. whatever a police officer sees, hears or learns of that is of a confidential nature will be kept secret

6 Integrity

   a. a police officer will not engage in acts of corruption

   b. a police officer will not engage in acts of bribery

   c. a police officer will not condone such acts of corruption or bribery by other officers

   d. police officers must avoid any conduct that might compromise integrity

   e. officers will refuse to accept any gifts, presents, subscriptions, favors, gratuities or promises that could be interpreted as seeking to cause the officer to refrain from performing official responsibilities

   f. police officers must not receive private or special advantage from their official status

(continues)

Table 4–1 Content Analysis of the Law Enforcement Code of Conduct (continued)

---

7 Cooperation with Other Police Officers and Agencies

    a. police officers will cooperate with all legally authorized agencies and their representatives in the pursuit of justice

8 Personal-Professional Capabilities

    a. police officers will be responsible for their own standard of professional performance and will take every reasonable opportunity to enhance and improve their level of knowledge and competence

9 Private Life

    a. a police officer's character and conduct while off duty must always be exemplary

---

In private business, codes of ethics are considered a part of corporate culture. It is treated like a mission statement for a company—a means of communicating the ethical mandates prescribed by the corporation (Simon, 1995). Whether the Police Code of Conduct can be viewed as a mission statement is not clear. It is only minimally beneficial as a communication tool, expressing what those in power expect of their subordinates. The mandates and accompanying explanations within the Police Code of Conduct are fairly obvious. Officers are required to safeguard property and lives fairly, avoid unnecessary use of excessive force, avoid corruption, use consistent and wise discretion, keep confidences when appropriate, cooperate with other law enforcement agencies, and exhibit exemplary behavior off duty. Arguably, even if not communicated within a code, most officers would recognize corruption.

The purpose of the Law Enforcement Code of Ethics is to swear officers into office during graduation ceremonies. What then is the purpose of the Police Code of Conduct? According to the 1992 Police Chief article introducing it, the Police Code of Conduct reprinted in their magazine is at least "suitable for framing." Is the Police Code of Conduct suitable for more than framing? If so, how do officers incorporate their Code of Conduct into their everyday policing? This chapter attempts to determine whether the Police Code of Conduct is either directly or indirectly included in ethics training for law enforcement. A variety of data-collecting methods are used to accomplish this goal.

ETHICS TRAINING PROGRAMS FOR POLICE OFFICERS

This study relied on three forms of data gathering methods and is supplemented with archival research. The first data-gathering method included interviews of four instructors from management training programs and one in-person interview of a new recruit training instructor. The second data-gathering method included open-ended written questionnaires to police officers in two ethics training courses. The final method included observation of two ethics training classes. This study gathered archival data from police officer management training programs in the United States. Currently, there are six programs in existence providing this type of training. They include the following:

1. Administrative Officers Management Program (AOMP), North Carolina State University, Raleigh, North Carolina
2. The Institute for Law Enforcement Administration (ILEA), Richardson, Texas
3. Police Executive Leadership Program (PELP), Johns Hopkins University, Columbia, Maryland
4. The Southern Police Institute (SPI), University of Louisville, Louisville, Kentucky
5. Center for Public Safety Management Training (NUCPS), Northwestern University, Evanston, Illinois
6. Senior Management Institute for Police, Police Executive Research Forum (PERF), Washington, D.C. (with classes held at Boston University)

There is one other program operated by the FBI Academy in Quantico, Virginia; however, officers who attend this program have usually gone through one of the previously listed programs as it is highly competitive; therefore, inclusion of this program would be duplicative.

Interviewing Ethics Training Coordinators

First, an attempt was made to gather instructor data from all six programs. Instructors teaching ethics in the management programs were contacted for an interview over the phone. Individuals from AOMP, ILEA, PELP, and SPI were reached; however, the instructor from PELP was unable to complete a phone interview due to a recent stroke. The remaining instructors were asked what information, generally speaking, is covered in their ethics training. Instructors were also asked whether they think the Code of Conduct should be included in ethics training. These questions give a basic understanding of what instructors cover in ethics training.

Many instructors went much further to include information about other programs outside of their own, scholars within the field, and even grant opportunities. Originally, I had decided to use a formalized interviewing guide; however, after I began conducting interviews, I could see clearly that different instructors with different backgrounds were not each going to be able to answer the same questions. I tried to ask very few questions, allowing the instructors to open up and share their wealth of knowledge.

I also discovered that some noninstructors of ethics courses in these programs could provide valuable information. For example, I reached an instructor who does not teach for SPI, but who does teach ethics at the University of Louisville. He sent me a syllabus and talked at length on the phone about his course. I also talked to the director of the ILEA program, who provided a wealth of information on outside resources in addition to a full description of the various programs offered by ILEA. The ILEA program offers such a wide variety of ethics programs that talking to an individual instructor of any one of these was not as useful as talking to the director who could describe all of the various ILEA ethics programs.

Open-Ended Questionnaires to Police Officers in Ethics Training

Police officer data were collected from the AOMP program, a Wake Technical Community College management training program, and the State Highway Patrol BLET program. All officers who were enrolled in these programs and present in class on the day that the questionnaires were administered were given the opportunity to complete the questionnaires. There were 85 officers enrolled in three classes. A total of 15 officers chose not to complete questionnaires, and 3 were absent from class. Sixty-seven officers completed questionnaires.

Officers had approximately 15 to 30 minutes to respond to the questionnaires, depending on the flexibility of the instructor. The questions asked officers to describe any police officer ethics training they have had before their management training, what they expect this ethics training to include, whether they believe this ethical training is necessary and why they feel this way, what they believe should be included in ethics training for police officers, and what they believe should be in a code of ethics for police officers.

The open-ended written question gave me data that officers may not have been comfortable sharing with each other publicly in focus groups. It also encouraged those officers who may not be very vocal to participate at least on paper. The written question also elicited responses that reflected everything that instinctually comes to the officer's mind without allowing time for prolonged reflection. This data provided depth of knowledge for this study. For each form of data collected, participant identity was kept anonymous. A statement regarding anonymity and confidentiality was included with the open-ended written questionnaire.

Attending Police Ethics Training

The final component of my research involved observation of two nonethics training courses for comparison and two ethics training classes in North Carolina. Observation and field notes of officers were recorded during the ethics portion of their training in the Wake Technical Community College (Wake Tech) management training program and the State Highway Patrol (SHP) program. Nonethics training courses conducted by the same instructor were observed in the AOMP program on 2 separate days. Teaching materials from AOMP, ILEA, PELP, SPI, and SMIP were also collected.

Observations lasted anywhere from 1 to 6 hours, depending on the course. The 1-hour component observed was a nonethics practical skills course on Microsoft Excel. The other nonethics course was a traditional theory-based discussion of budgetary issues for law enforcement that lasted approximately 2 hours. Both of these courses were a part of a larger management training program that lasts approximately 16 weeks. The AOMP program uses three instructors to teach a variety of different topics.

The Wake Tech ethics course lasted approximately 3.5 hours. This course was not a part of a structured program such as the AOMP program. Students in this course register for one or more management courses through Wake Tech. The instructor of the ethics portion of this course was not the regular instructor for the course. The SHP ethics course was 6 hours in length; however, normally it runs 16 hours. This ethics course is just one part of a 29-week BLET course for the SHP. Like the Wake Tech program, the instructor of the ethics portion of this course was not the regular instructor for the course.

RESULTS OF COLLECTING INFORMATION FROM THE TRAINING PROGRAMS

Observations of Police Ethics Courses: Talk the Talk and Walk the Walk

I observed two ethics training courses for law enforcement occurring in classrooms in both Garner and Cary. These courses included the Wake Tech program for management training and the BLET program for the SHP. These training courses service police officers from North Carolina to Florida. Officers were exposed, sometimes for the first time, to ethics training. Officers had anywhere from 0 to 25 years on the force. New recruits, senior, and middle managers were taught by fellow officers and nonofficers.

Some officers took notes, whereas others just listened intently. No one slept, and no one read or tried to accomplish other work; only one student was out of both classes. Officers and instructors are serious about their training, but they are also humorous with one another, incorporating laughter into their interactions. The classes ranged from 9 students to 48. Classes ranged from very interactive to virtually no interaction between students and very little between students and the instructor. I observed four classes, two about ethics and two AOMP classes about general management issues for comparison.

The materials used in the two ethics courses were not uniform, did not draw from the same data, and did not incorporate the same concepts. Each focused on different research and used different teaching styles to convey how to handle ethical issues for law enforcement. There appears to be no general framework to draw from for instructors.

There is obviously a culture, a sense of camaraderie among officers. Jargon is used frequently in the lecture and by officers. For example, one instructor kept relying on the phrase "if you talk the talk, you have to walk the walk," as a reference to leadership by managers as a way of instilling ethical behavior in police officers. Another instructor said several times "every dog has his day"—meaning that those officers who violate ethics will eventually be caught.

Officers in management training are eager to share their experiences. New recruits do not have much to share as they lack the experience. Several tell personal stories in the management training courses. One officer mentioned a time when he pulled over a car for speeding and the driver "flashed his badge" without rolling down the window as a means of escaping a ticket. This phenomenon was referred to as "professional courtesy" by the officer. Another officer admitted that he had accepted free admission into a local movie theater, something that is not allowed under the Police Code of Conduct. One officer responded to a question regarding absolute honesty by offering that "one person who walked this earth was absolutely honest all the time—Jesus Christ."

Everyone is comfortable with one another. There does not appear to be a fear of speaking up, even against other cops, especially in jurisdictions outside North Carolina that are not well respected by the existing community. Honesty is encouraged by the instructor and the students, who offer surprising personal experiences that are self-deprecating or sometimes graphic. One instructor admits that her son "flashed my business card" after being pulled over for speeding. The instructor admitted her anger at her son's arrogance.

Occasionally, some mild profanity can work its way into the discussion, depending on the instructor's use of similar language. In one class, the instructor praised a leader who called her in as a young officer and called her a "jackass" for aggressive police behavior. The officers followed with stories of "assholes" who had "flashed their badge" in order to get out of speeding tickets or free admission to the movies. The SHP class was much more formal and did not use profanity.

Instructor Interviews: Part Teacher, Part Preacher

Of the six management training programs, I interviewed only one actual instructor of ethics for law enforcement within these programs. I did discuss ethics for law enforcement with three other instructors who teach either ethics, in general, or within one of the management training programs. From these informal phone interviews, I was able to gather some useful information.

Each phone interview led me to further research in the area of ethics training for law enforcement. Dr. Sykes from the ILEA program suggested that I contact Dr. Klockars at the University of Delaware regarding an integrity study Dr. Klockars concluded recently. I have since received a copy of this unpublished work. Dr. Van Dyke from NUCPS directed me to the National Institute for Justice and suggested that I contact six other scholars in this area of research.

I learned a lot about the average law enforcement officer who is a student in the courses taught within management training programs. The average law enforcement officer is a white male with more than 5 years of experience on the force and a supervisor or manager in their respective program. There are more differences than similarities among officers in these programs. The years of experience, age, level of command, area of law enforcement, region, and general background vary dramatically among programs.

I was able to interview personally during breaks the instructor, First Sergeant Ken Castelloe, had for the SHP training program. This course is in addition to the state mandate of 4 hours that is taught at the beginning of the 29-week term for these students. He sees his role as "part preacher, part teacher." The instructor suggested many great resources for future research. He referenced Barbara Walters documentary work that was created a decade ago. He also mentioned that Trautman heads up the Ethics Institute in Florida. The instructor recommended a great program in California that has online materials.

Dr. Van Dyke indicated that it was his experience that when ethics training is brought to a law enforcement agency it is "usually brought to a department because of a screw up." As a result, ethics training is "a rough sell for many officers." This could explain the lack of sufficient ethics training for law officers discussed in the literature. Dr. Van Dyke also praised highly the ILEA program as "academically sound."

Ethics Instructor Materials: We Are Accountable to Each Other

I received instructor materials from two of the six management training programs discussed—previously here—AOMP and PELP. I also received some SPI materials that originated from a professor, J. Price Foster, who teaches a graduate level justice administration course through the University of Louisville. This course is not actually taught through the SPI program, but the SPI directed me to Professor Foster, who indicated that a small number of law enforcement regularly register for his course. I also located instructor materials from the IACP online, from (Wake Tech), and from the SHP. Of the three programs that I did not receive materials from, one program, ILEA, sent materials 2 weeks prior to Thanksgiving, and I have not received them to date. I have not been able to ascertain who teaches ethics at the other missing programs—NUCPS and PERF.

Of those five programs that I have materials for, each has similarities and differences. Three of the program materials were put together by academics who have little or no actual police experience—AOMP, SPI, and PELP. These instructors teach either at a university and/or possess an advanced degree within the field they teach. Two sets of program materials were put together by a nonacademic—Wake Tech and SHP. The IACP materials do not indicate who prepared the materials for this program.

Only one of the programs, PELP, included a copy of the Police Code of Conduct in its entirety along with an in-depth discussion of its mandates. One other program, AOMP, included the Police Code of Ethics along with the American Society of Public Administrators Code of Ethics. Essentially, these two documents combined cover all of the elements found in the Police Code of Conduct, especially the Police Code of Ethics. The SHP training materials do not include either, but the instructor always ends his lecture with a recitation of the police code of ethics.

The IACP materials, SHP materials, and SPI materials do not include a copy of the Police Code of Conduct. Each, however, discusses the elements of the code indirectly in depth. The only concepts that are not well covered in these materials that are a part of the code are the concepts of keeping confidences and cooperating with other law enforcement agencies. These two essentially missing concepts are implied in some areas. For example, the IACP materials mention "We are accountable to each other" and "We believe that cooperation and team work will enable us to combine our diverse backgrounds, skills and styles to achieve common goals." Cooperating with other agencies is not explicit in these two statements, but it is implied.

The Wake Tech materials focused on three mandates found in the Police Code of Conduct. These elements include police use of discretion, use of force, and integrity. The other elements of the Police Code of Conduct were missing from these materials, as well as the accompanying lecture. Fortunately, I also attended the course where these materials were distributed.

Another difference between the Wake Tech materials and the other materials is that the Wake Tech materials had no discussion of philosophical issues relating to ethics and morals. The IACP materials had a limited discussion of philosophical materials. For example, the IACP materials focused on the general moral decline of society as an explanation for increased police corruption and scandal. The IACP materials point to "a significant and continuing decline in moral and ethical standards in many areas of life" and "the increasing number of individuals who reject responsibility for their own actions." The IACP argues

> The combination of these two factors—the lowering of moral standards and the failure of individuals to accept responsibility for the consequences of their own acts—produce a 'what's wrong with that?' mentality across a broad spectrum of U.S. society. The abnormal has become normal; the immoral has become commonplace. Obviously, the police are not to blame for this state of affairs, it is a phenomenon of modern society as a whole. However, it would be naive to believe that the police are not directly and drastically affected by it.

This argument is a large portion of the teaching materials, pointing the finger of blame on society for police officer corruption. There is no discussion of philosophical theories and only a few scholars are cited.

The remaining materials, including the SHP materials, quote Aristotle, Kant, and modern-day scholars regarding philosophical tenants of morality. The PELP materials are authored by the instructor and include multiple examples of moral reasoning based on a review of philosophical literature. My favorite teaching exercise described in these materials is used to illustrate the shortcomings of a theory known as individual moral subjectivism where judging moral behavior is based on whether one thinks or believes the act is morally sound.

> I often find an undergraduate or young police officer who claims to be an individual moral subjectivist and I ask whether I might borrow his or her watch. Because it is very early in their experiences with me, they generally consent to give me the watch in question, whereupon I promptly put the watch in my trouser pocket and proclaim that I agree wholeheartedly with individual subjectivism. In fact, I think that it would be morally good if I keep the watch, and thus, using that first theory, I would be morally right. Now the wisest of the real watch owners usually respond by saying that he or she thinks or feels or believes that it would be morally good if I gave the watch back to its rightful owner, and I, of course, point out that, using individual moral subjectivism, he or she is right too; however, I still have the watch.

This is an excellent example of how these materials apply the philosophical concepts discussed in the materials.

The SPI materials are scholarly works from two different books that focus on the application of philosophical issues in law enforcement ethical decision making. These materials are full of real-life examples of law enforcement ethical situations. One chapter uses *Serpico* and *Prince of the City* as examples of popular movies that explore ethical issues for law enforcement. The AOMP materials are the shortest in length, relying more on lecture than written materials; however, the AOMP lecture discusses scholarly journal articles relating to ethical issues for public administrators in general. The SHP materials are PowerPoint slides relaying information in an outline format.

The most surprising discovery, which makes it the most interesting, was the overall tone of the IACP materials. All of the other materials were overall very positive in tone, promoting the concept of police officers making ethical choices. The IACP materials, however, had an interesting perspective with respect to its discussion of the decline of morals in society and the part that the media plays in this ethical decline.

For example, the IACP materials boldly state without backup documentation that most observers agree that "moral standards of contemporary society have fallen far below the norms of the past." As for the media's role, without citing any sources, the IACP materials argue that "some observers feel that the problem of police ethics is no worse now than it has ever been, but is simply more widely publicized today than in years past." The materials go on to report that "lowered social standards are becoming accepted as normal by our society." The entire document is peppered with references to the public's lack of values and acceptance of responsibility. These overgeneralizations about the public make the tone of these materials quite different from the tone of all of the other materials collected.

Open-Ended Questionnaires of Police Officers: Mismatched Expectations

Over 90% of officers in management training who responded to the questionnaire reported that they had prior ethics training. Two thirds of the officers have received more than one ethics training course through BLET, IST, or elsewhere. When the new recruits are added to the analysis of data, there are still only 37% of officers who have not had some prior ethics training, law enforcement or otherwise. This was an interesting finding as the literature review and my phone interview with Dr. Van Dyke each suggest that most officers have not had ethics training. When I interviewed the director of the ILEA program, he indicated that over 6,000 officers have been through their Train the Trainer program for ethics, suggesting that the literature may not be current on this issue.

Approximately 87% of all officers responding to the questionnaire believe that the current ethics training is necessary. Over half, 58%, believe that ethics training is necessary for police officers either because there is not enough training currently or to reinforce police officer ethics. One officer in management training remarked that training was necessary.

> It is easy to loose [sic] focus when you spend much of your time around criminals, lawyers (no offense) and government people who use their positions for personal gains. People need to be regularly reminded of their commitment. The flexible way some members of the justice system view 'truth' tends to cause people to wander in their commitment to right. Also, the deals that occur in the back rooms and hallway of the courthouse.

The remaining respondents believe that the current training was necessary for reasons such as "public trust," "public perception," or some combination of these responses.

Of those who responded that the ethics training was not necessary, their reasoning was unanimous that ethics cannot be taught—officers are either ethical or not. One management training officer explained

> Ethics is inside the person, and no matter how much ethics training is received a person will not suddenly have ethics. Obtaining ethics begins a [sic] childhood from parents, peers, early education, etc. if you have them in adulthood, you have them, no short 1 or 2 day class is going to instill ethics in a person.

Aristotle would agree with this reasoning (Delattre, 2002, quoting Aristotle at 5).

> It is a matter of real importance whether our early education confirms in us one set of habits or another. It would be nearer the truth to say that it makes a very great difference indeed, in fact all the difference in the world.

On the other hand, Aristotle also argued that working through ethical decision making through argument was another way of instilling ethics in students. This concept of ethics not being teachable was also discussed in the literature as a misconception regarding ethics training. Trautman (2000) and Martinelli and Pollock (2000) saw this as an excuse by law enforcement management to avoid implementing ethics training.

When asked what they expected ethics training to include, 39% of the officers expected an emphasis on codes of ethics, norms, "court cases," and/or "rules." When asked what officers believe should be in ethics training, one third of officers responded that "decision making" should be covered. Overall, two thirds of officers expected something different would be taught in police officer ethics training from what they believed should be taught in the ethics program. This statistic did not change regardless of whether the officers were in management training or new recruit training.

To me, these results suggest somewhat mismatched expectations in students. It may suggest that officers do not fully understand why they are being submitted to ethics training, the purpose of ethics training, or what they should be getting out of an ethics course. Further research would have to explore this phenomenon more in depth. This finding is one of the interesting discoveries that I did not expect. I especially did not expect that the results would be the same whether the officer was new to the force or in management.

When asked what should be in a code of ethics for police officers, 16.4% responded with the IACP Code of Conduct. It is unclear whether officers did not think of the code or whether they are not familiar with the code. Officer responses included many elements found in the IACP Code of Conduct. For example, responses included "integrity," "honesty," "professionalism," and "personal behavior beyond reproach." A new recruit officer suggested a few guidelines that combined concepts of professionalism and philosophical perspectives.

> Not to do anything that he/she would not do in front of a TV camera or in front of his/her parents. If one is ashamed of an act he/she has performed, then chances are what that person did was not the best choice that person could have made. The goal is not just to stop unethical behavior, but to hopefully change there [sic] perspective so that they (people) know in their hearts that the unethical conduct is wrong. Though different reasonings, we as an agency have accomplished the same learned behaviors by doing these things. We have taken away escape routes so that officers will not make the wrong choices, when it comes to ethical dilemmas. Hopefully these teaching [sic] will change hearts and will become more genuine. Psychological tests to get into agencies will also help eliminate people that think unethically.

There were approximately 18% of officers who advocated some combination of elements in a code of ethics, rather than focusing on just one concept.

Another concept found in the IACP Code of Conduct (1992) is the concept of equal treatment. One new recruit officer responded that what he/she believes should be in a code of ethics revolves around this issue of fairness and equality.

> Just to focus on the fact that just because they are the law they are not above it. The LEO [law enforcement officer] should understand that everyone should be treated fairly—equally no matter what the circumstance is.

These remarks mirroring the IACP Code of Ethics were another interesting discovery for me because I am curious about how police officers view their code. Further research on this issue is needed to clarify how familiar officers are with the various codes within law enforcement and their perceptions of those codes.

SIGNIFICANCE AND CONCLUSION OF THIS RESEARCH

The Ethics of Studying Ethics

I had several ethical issues arise while gathering data for this research. First, there are not many training facilities for law enforcement in the city where I conducted this research so maintaining anonymity when reporting the findings is challenging. If I identify where I attended new recruit officer training, then essentially there are only three possible places for officers to receive this type of training. I have determined that leaving the name of the city out of any published findings will ensure anonymity.

There seemed to be a problem with respect to officers feeling uncomfortable being completely honest while I was observing their classes. Admitting unethical behavior in front of a stranger is difficult, especially a stranger who is recording every word. My presence alone may have encouraged officers to omit information and/or change facts in their class discussions. It may also have had an effect on the instructors' behavior, as well. They may have prepared differently for teaching ethics knowing that I was observing their class. I know when I teach that I change my behavior if I know a colleague is going to be critiquing my teaching.

I have visited several class settings and administered questionnaires to subjects during my research this semester. The questionnaire contains an informed consent that each subject must sign, detailing the scope of the project and who to contact if they have questions. The first class that I visited had about 26 students. Each student signed the informed consent and filled out the questionnaire. Fifteen students from two different classes were unwilling to sign the informed consent, although some were willing to fill out the questionnaire without signing the informed consent. This presented me with two separate ethical dilemmas.

First, do I allow all of the students to fill out the questionnaire and use their responses despite not having informed consents from all of the students? I explained how I had no control over the informed consent, that it was necessary, required by the school, and basically how it would be kept separate from the questionnaires so that names could not be matched up with responses. Still, the 15 students who dissented would not bend on this issue, and I could not accept questionnaires from them.

Second, the difference between the classes boiled down to an issue of trust. I had established trust with the AOMP class, but not the SHP or the Wake Tech classes where I was a complete stranger before administering the questionnaire. I spoke with the instructor from the AOMP course and two people on my dissertation committee. We all agreed that I had established trust with the first class by visiting their class prior to the questionnaire, being affiliated with NCSU, which sponsored the courses they were currently taking, and having a rapport with their instructor who they all knew fairly well.

This ethical issue is more insidious than most and is one that all ethnographers face. How close do we become with our subjects so that we can gather the research we need? How do we instill trust in our subjects without crossing the line of familiarity? I have determined that it is safe to establish an ongoing communication with ethics instructors and to visit their classrooms in person in order to establish rapport. If my goal was to expose police officers and their unethical behavior, then I might feel more uncomfortable with establishing trust in order to gather my data; however, I plan on looking at what is taught in ethics courses to police officers. An unethical approach to an ethics study is probably not the best choice.

Police Officer Ethical Decision Making: Where the Rubber Hits the Road

Unethical behavior affects everyone in society, especially unethical behavior by those in positions of power. Understanding the police officer's perspective is an important step toward understanding ethical and unethical behavior within their ranks. Having ethics training and a code of ethics are ineffective tools if they are developed without police officer perspectives in mind. This research is a step toward understanding police officers, their ethics training, and their relationship with their code of ethics.

What I have discovered is that the ethical training analyzed and observed in this study may not be a good preparation for ethical decision-making. Whether it is effective depends on the instructor and the materials used by that instructor. Some materials were more comprehensive than others, combining philosophical issues, examples, decision-making scenarios, and discussion of the Police Code of Conduct. Other materials were not as comprehensive.

Ethical instruction was also inconsistent in its delivery of ethical concepts, one program being more comprehensive than the other; however, neither program that I observed walked students through decision-making exercises. Future research observing ethics programs across the United States is needed to determine whether this is the norm or the exception. My dissertation will attempt to study further the issues raised here.

According to the IACP, "Personal integrity and a conscious decision to do the right thing even in the face of sometimes overwhelming pressure to do otherwise are where the rubber hits the road in the ethical decision-making environment." The concepts studied in this project hopefully shed some light on the police officer's training for facing his or her ethical decision-making environment. In other words, this study has attempted to analyze how police officers prepare for when the rubber hits the road in their careers.

DISCUSSION QUESTIONS

1. How important is ethics training for law enforcement? How much time should be allotted for this type of training? When do you think it is most important—during new officer training, ongoing, mid-career?
2. How should the Code of Conduct be used in day-to-day policing? What about the Code of Ethics? How important is it for officers to learn these documents?
3. Was there anything about the results from the interviews, questionnaires, archival data, or observations that surprised you? What do you think was most notable from this data? Explain why this is important based on what has been discussed thus far in the text.
4. What implications do you think this data has on police officer ethics training? What are some of the limitations of this data?

REFERENCES

Bristow, A. P. (1975). *You and the Law Enforcement Code of Ethics.* Santa Cruz, CA: Davis Publishing Co.

Crawshaw, R. (1998). *Human Rights and Policing.* Boston: Kluwer Law International.

Delattre, E. J. (2002). *Character and Cops: Ethics in Policing, Fourth ed.* Lanham, MD: American Enterprise Institute Press, p. 6.

Delattre, E.J. (1991). *Against Brutality and Corruption: Integrity, Wisdom, and Professionalism.* Rockville: National Institute of Justice/NCJRS paper reproduction.

Donahue, M. E., & Felts, A. A. (1993). Police ethics—a critical perspective. *Journal of Criminal Justice, 21*(4), 339–352.

Harrison, B. (1999). Noble cause corruption and the police ethic. *FBI Law Enforcement Bulletin,* August, 1–7.

Hodgson, J. F. (2001). Police violence in Canada and the USA: analysis and management. *Policing: An International Journal of Police Strategies and Management, 24*(4), 520–549.

International Association of Chiefs of Police. (1998, January). Ethics training in law enforcement. *The Police Chief, LXV,* 14–24.

International Association of Chiefs of Police National Law Enforcement Policy Center. Standards of Conduct, 1992, *The Police Chief.*

Kleinig, J. (1999). *The Ethics of Policing.* New York: Cambridge University Press.

Martinelli, T. J., & Pollock, J. M. (2000, October). Law enforcement ethics, lawsuits, and liability: defusing deliberate indifference. *The Police Chief,* 52–67.

Newton, T. (1998). The Place of Ethics in Investigative Interviewing by Police Officers. *The Howard Journal of Criminal Justice, 37*(1), 52–69.

Sherman, L. (1982). Learning police ethics. *Criminal Justice Ethics, 1*(1), 10–19.

Simon, R. (1995). Control in an age of empowerment. *Harvard Business Review, 73*(2), 80–88.

Trautman, N. (2000). The corruption continuum: how law enforcement organizations become corrupt. *Public Management, 82*(6), 16–20.

CHAPTER 5

Measuring Attitudes Toward Police Misconduct

OBJECTIVES

- Further describe the National Institute of Justice study of 1977
- Characterize unethical behavior of police officers through the use of case scenarios
- Identify variables in the National Institute of Justice study that depict ethical awareness, standards, and action in police officers
- Further explore the concepts of ethical awareness, standards, and action in law enforcement
- Suggest some hypotheses for ethical awareness, standards, and action in law enforcement as they are impacted by individual, organizational, and social factors

This chapter explores a National Institute of Justice (NIJ) study conducted in 1997. The NIJ study did not use random sampling in its data collection, but collected data from agencies based on prior relationships and convenience. The authors do not indicate how many agencies were invited to participate; however, included in the NIJ study are agencies from 11 different states that are not identified in order to honor promises of anonymity made during administration of the instrument (Klockars et al., 2000). This lack of random sampling creates both an internal validity selection bias issue and an external validity issue. Thus, statistical significance cannot be established from data analysis, and results may not be generalized to police officers in the United States.

This data set is unique, however. The survey instrument for the NIJ study was completed by 3,237 officers from 30 police agencies in the United States (Klockars et al., 2000). The study received a 55.5% overall response rate. The size of the data set, the number of variables, and the subject matter are extremely valuable. The sampling unit for this study is the individual level and the agency level. The NIJ study also collected data at both the individual and agency levels. As the sample is a convenience sample and not random, this sample is treated as a population.

In police agencies where officers rank misconduct as very serious, the officers are more willing to report peers for misconduct. There was very little difference between the officer's individual attitude toward the misconduct and what they believed their peer's attitudes would be toward the misconduct (Klockars et al., 2004). Unfortunately, the Klockars study did not analyze the strength of the relationships, only a comparison of means.[1]

THE INSTRUMENT

The instrument used by the NIJ captured police officer attitudes toward police misconduct. As mentioned in Chapter 1, this study has been administered to over 10,000 officers worldwide, thus bolstering content validity (Klockars et al., 2004).

Asking officers directly whether they have engaged in unethical behavior yields mixed results, as most people are reluctant to admit to unethical behavior. Officer attitudes toward misconduct, on the other hand, yield more reliable results. Two additional questions asking officers whether they have been truthful and whether they believe their peers have been truthful increased reliability of the instrument. The independent variables available in this study are the agency size, job assignment, supervisory status, rank, length of service, knowledge of existing policy, and perception regarding peer attitudes and behavior. The dependent variables are an officer's ethical awareness, ethical standards, and ethical action. A copy of the scenarios found in the instrument can be found in Chapter 3.

The authors selected police agencies and collected data from individual respondents. The NIJ report examines corruption by asking hypothetical

---

[1] Dr. Carl Klockars passed away on July 24, 2003, precluding additional analysis and publication on this topic.

questions regarding misconduct. Officers are more likely to respond to questions that do not ask officers directly whether they have been a party to corrupt behavior. The NIJ study asks officers for their perceptions regarding agency rules, corresponding punishment, and willingness to report a peer's unethical behavior (Klockars et al., 2000).

This research study will analyze the NIJ data using advanced statistical tools. To date, the NIJ data have been used to prepare descriptive studies that present the mean scores for questionnaire responses. One study exploring traditional sociological theories of crime and deviant behavior has used advanced statistical tools in analyzing the NIJ data (Hickman et al., 2001). This study expands the analysis to examine the NIJ data in the context of public administration literature as it relates to street level bureaucrats and policing.

The survey instrument used in the NIJ study included 11 case scenarios describing police misconduct. The case scenarios involve behaviors that range from not very serious to intermediately serious to very serious in nature. Some of the activities included in the case scenarios are conflict of interest, bribery, theft, and excessive force (Klockars et al., 2000). The first scenario, depicting a conflict of interest regarding off-duty employment, will not be used in this research, because it is not necessarily depicting misconduct. Many departments have policies regarding off-duty employment; however, most do not have a policy that such employment is a conflict of interest (Brunet, 2005).

Content validity is supported by the methods used to create the scenarios. The scenarios were created to be culturally neutral by avoiding the mention of specific holidays and currency amounts. Respondents were asked to assume that the police officers depicted in each scenario had 5 years of service and no previous disciplinary problems. Some of the case scenarios relied on previously published studies using the case scenario approach (Klockars et al., 2000). Chapter 3 includes the case scenarios and the corresponding International Association of Chiefs of Police (IACP) National Law Enforcement Standards of Conduct violation.

Several general standards of conduct apply to the scenarios, including a provision that prohibits officers from violating the law. Officers are also not allowed to engage in conduct that would discredit the officer and/or the agency. It could be argued that one provision in particular applies to case 8 that prohibits officers from interfering with or thwarting an internal or criminal investigation.

Each case scenario is followed by seven questions capturing the police officer's opinion regarding the misconduct scenario. Two questions asked officers to rate the seriousness of the case scenario from their own perspective and from that of their peers. Two additional questions addressed what disciplinary action the officer felt should be taken and what disciplinary action the officer felt would be taken in the case scenario. The officer's willingness to report the misconduct was another question, as well as a question regarding whether the officer felt their peers would report the misconduct. A final question addressed whether the officer believed the misconduct was a violation of their agency's official policy (Klockars et al., 2000). Chapter 3 includes the questions, possible responses, and corresponding coding.

The question asking respondents to consider how serious the behavior is will measure the officer's ethical awareness. The question regarding what discipline should follow from an officer engaging in the behavior will measure the officer's ethical standards. The question addressing the respondent's willingness to report the behavior will measure the officer's action. Although these questions alone do not adequately measure awareness, standards, and action completely, they do provide partial measures. Relying on partial measures reduces construct validity; however, the NIJ researchers did not collect multiple measures, nor did they use multiple methods in gathering their data.

The questions regarding what the respondent believes would be the responses of their peers to seriousness, punishment, and reporting allows a discrepancy measure. Whether there is a policy in a given agency is not as important as the respondent's knowledge of the existence of such policies and the certainty of that knowledge given the respondent's length of service and rank.

Finally, the survey asked officers general questions regarding their background and context, including rank, assignment of duties, and size of agency. Chapter 3 includes the general background questions, possible responses, and corresponding abbreviations.

STATISTICAL ANALYSIS

This research study seeks to identify the relationship between a police officer's attitude toward misconduct and whether that officer is willing to report peer misconduct. The appropriate statistical analysis tools include cross-tabs, gamma, and regression. Although gamma establishes the relationship between variables, multiple regression assesses the relative strength of this relationship. Multiple regression can also be used to determine the predictive nature of the independent variables with respect to the dependent variable in this study (Tabachnick & Fidell, 2001).

Variables

The hypotheses explored in this study address the fundamental question of whether there is a relationship between officer characteristics, attitudes regarding misconduct, and an officer reporting the unethical behavior of peers. The variables that are available for analysis within this data include officer attitudes regarding misconduct, officer attitudes regarding agency misconduct policies, officer attitudes regarding reporting peer misconduct, rank, supervisory position, length of service within an agency, length of service within law enforcement, job assignment, and agency size. Background questions about officers are limited in order to protect confidentiality; therefore, questions indicating gender and race were left off of the NIJ survey instrument (Klockars et al., 2004).

Figure 5–1 explores the characteristics of respondents within the NIJ study. These characteristics are defined by the NIJ study. Over 70% of respondents work in very large agencies (over 500 sworn officers), whereas approximately 7% of respondents work in large agencies (between 201 and 500 sworn officers). Approximately 11% of respondents work in medium-size agencies (76 to 200 sworn officers); 6.8% work in small agencies (25 to 75 sworn officers), and the remaining less than 3% work in very small agencies (less than 25 sworn officers). The typical respondent has been an officer for approximately 10 years. Officers who work in patrol or traffic comprise 66.7% of respondents. One in five respondents is a supervisor. There was only one sheriff agency respondent and only one county police respondent in this study, and thus, these agencies were added to the corresponding agency size.

Several of the hypotheses explore whether an officer who is not promoted will view misconduct more or less favorably than an officer who is promoted. An officer may achieve various levels of rank during their career. Not all agencies use each of the ranks explored in this study. Each agency can use rank in a different hierarchical order, and some ranks can be combined (i.e., lieutenant colonel). Rank within police agencies is similar to military organizations.

The ranks included in this study include officers, deputies, and corporals who are not supervisors. Detectives include detectives and investigators only. First-line managers include sergeants and corporals who are supervisors. Midlevel managers include captains and lieutenants. Senior managers include colonels, chiefs, and majors. These same labels are used throughout this study for analysis of ethical awareness, standards, and action.

This study also hypothesizes that length of service will have a curvilinear relationship to an officer's ethical awareness, standards, and action controlling for rank and supervisory status. It is important to examine an officer's experience or length of service with rank in mind as officers achieve higher rank and supervisory status as they gain more experience. This study, therefore, controls for supervisory status by examining length of service for nonsupervisors only.

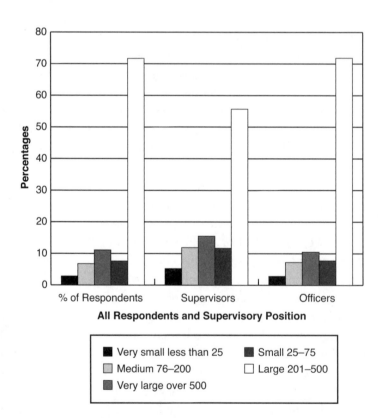

FIGURE 5-1 Percentages of Respondents and Supervisors by Agency Size

Not surprisingly, managers have been in service longer than officers. The majority of midlevel and senior managers have been in service for more than 20 years. Over 90% of midlevel managers have been in service for over sixteen years. Almost 79% of senior managers have been in service for over 16 years. First-line managers consist of almost equal one-third portions of officers who have been in service for 11 to 15 years, 16 to 20 years, and over 20 years. Approximately one third of all officers and one third of all detectives have been in service for 6 to 10 years. These results indicate that officers are likely to obtain promotion during years 6 through 15 of their careers. Figure 5–2 shows the characteristics of respondents by rank and length of service.

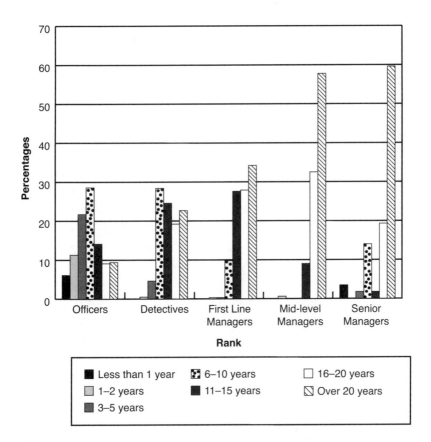

FIGURE 5–2 Percentages of Respondents According to Length of Service and Rank

The characteristics of rank and job assignment are somewhat redundant. The job assignment variable offers five possible categories, which include patrol, detective/investigative, special operations, communications, administrative, and other. There were only eight communications officers within the sample and these officers were merged with patrol.

Approximately 85% of patrol officers categorized their rank as officer, whereas 79.3% of detective/investigative officers characterized their rank as officer or detective/investigator. Although detective rank is a promotion, it does not necessarily involve a supervisory responsibility. As the results show later here, about 20% of detectives are managers, mostly first-line managers. Administrative officers tend by 66.5% to categorize their rank as management. As a result of this overlap, job assignment is not explored as a variable in the chapters that follow, although it is important to recognize that the assignments of patrol and investigation are embedded in the measure of rank for officers and detectives, respectively. Figure 5–3 explores the characteristics of respondents by rank and job assignment.

The independent variables that will be used for analysis in this study include the agency size, supervisory status (in cross-tabs only), rank (in regression analysis), length of service controlling for supervisory status, knowledge of existing policy, and perception regarding peer attitudes and behavior. Respondents were asked questions regarding the agency size, supervisory status, rank, and length of service as described earlier in this chapter. Respondents were also asked whether each scenario violated policy within their agency on a five point Likert-type scale with 1 equaling definitely not a violation and 5 equaling definitely a violation. For each scenario, respondents were asked how peers would respond to the same scenario with respect to awareness, standards, and action.

There are three dependent variables. Two of these become independent variables during the analysis. These dependent variables are ethical awareness, ethical standards, and ethical action. Ethical awareness is the officer's attitude regarding the seriousness of the misconduct in each scenario. Ethical standards include the officer's attitude toward punishment that should follow the police misconduct. Ethical action is the officer's willingness to report misconduct. Both ethical awareness and ethical standards become independent variables during the analysis.

To provide an overview of hypotheses that will be presented later, there are certain assumptions about the relationship among variables that will be tested. For ethical awareness, the variation in responses may be

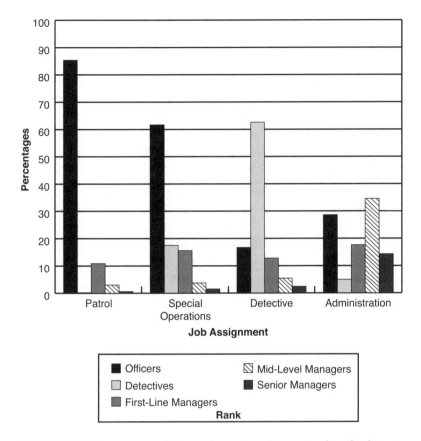

FIGURE 5–3 Percentages of Respondents According to Rank and Job Assignment

explained by the independent variables such as size of agency, length of service, rank, supervisory position, the perception of peer attitudes, and the perception of official policy regarding discipline.

For ethical standards, the variation in responses may be explained by ethical awareness, although "slippage" is expected. The attitude that a behavior is serious can be undercut by preferring "weak" discipline. Thus, attitude about discipline is considered to be a better indicator of the real judgment about the behavior than the attitude about seriousness.

For ethical action, the variation in responses can be explained by ethical awareness and ethical standards, as well as discrepancies in attitude between the individual officer and the attitudes of their peers, as well as official policy. With regard to reporting, attitudes of peers and official policy are considered to have a reinforcing or deterrent effect. An officer is more likely to break the code of silence if expected by his or her peers to do so and if it will be sustained by appropriate official disciplinary action. On the other hand, an officer is less likely to risk alienating peers who disapprove of his or her behavior and also less likely to deviate from informal norms if it appears that the agency will not provide discipline the officer feels is appropriate.

The survey instrument used in the NIJ study included 11 case scenarios describing police misconduct. Each scenario is followed by a series of questions, including one question asking the officer, "Do you think you would report a fellow police officer who engaged in this behavior?" This question is a direct measure of whether an officer is willing to report a peer for misconduct. This question asks officers directly what they would do under the circumstances, unlike the other questions in this instrument. These questions are designed to "probe the implications of the normative inclination to resist temptations to abuse the rights and privileges of one's office" (Klockars et al., 2004).

The officer's attitude toward misconduct is measured with this question: "How serious do you consider this behavior to be?" This question is asked following each scenario. This question is a direct measure of the officer's attitude regarding misconduct. Because there is a broad range of misconduct in the case scenarios, the respondents are more likely to answer honestly. Their responses would seem unreliable if they simply answered accepting a free meal is as serious as accepting a money bribe (Klockars et al., 2004). We will not presume, however, that the officer's attitudes about seriousness match standards for police conduct that can be derived from external sources. This is one of the issues to explore in the research.

The officer's attitude regarding the discipline that should follow misconduct is also measured within the instrument. This is an operational measure of ethical standards. Regardless of the attitude about the seriousness of the behavior, the preferred action indicates how the seriousness would be translated into discipline. The options given for response are limited to actual forms of punishment, which is problematic. The forms of punishment offered do not include formal sanctions such as transfer, fines, counseling, and delay in promotion or informal measures such as peer intervention or ostracism (Klockars et al., 2004).

Peer norms can be measured with this question: "How serious do most police officers in your agency consider this behavior to be?" Norms are those attitudes shared by a group. This question is also asked of each peer and those responses could be used as the measure; however, what is important is the respondent's belief and not the actual response of peers. Similarly, peer behavior is measured with this question: "Do you think most police officers in your agency would report a fellow police officer who engaged in this behavior?"

Categorizing Unethical Behavior

Measuring the impact that the nature of misconduct has on officer attitudes and behavior can be accomplished by categorizing the case scenarios. As noted previously here, the designers of the survey instrument intentionally presented cases that presented a broad range of misconduct, although the authors provided no guide indicating their ordering of the cases with respect to seriousness of misconduct. Two methods may be used: perception of respondents and external standards.

According to respondents, the case scenarios range from not very serious to intermediately serious to very serious in nature. Specifically, respondents ranked the least serious of the scenarios as conflict of interest, accepting free meals, accepting holiday gifts, and professional courtesy. According to respondents, the intermediately serious scenarios included excessive force, supervisor misconduct, alcohol bribes, and kickbacks. The scenarios that were considered very serious to respondents include stealing a wallet, stealing a watch, and accepting a money bribe.

One method for classifying the seriousness of officer misconduct by objective standards would involve assessing uniform codes of punishment for such misconduct. The limitation of this approach is that the punishment for misconduct varies from jurisdiction to jurisdiction and can differ within a state from county to county and among various agencies. There is a movement to make punishment more standardized by individual states in the same way federal sentencing guidelines are used, but there would still be differences between states in how they punish various forms of misconduct (Walker, 2004).

There is another way of classifying the data that reflects a principle-based approach to ethics. This approach uses external standards to judge the seriousness of actions rather than relying on the perceptions of officers, such as the respondents within the NIJ study. According to this approach, one can make independent judgments about officers' ethical sensitivity based on the extent to which their attitudes are consistent with ethical principles (Svara, 1997).

There are numerous definitions from scholars and commissioned government reports for three types of unethical behavior: misconduct, brutality, and corruption. The consensus among these materials is that misconduct includes behavior that violates police policy and usually involves some type of personal gain for the officer engaging in the misconduct. Acts of misconduct include favoritism, graft, prejudice, perjury, and brutality. Although considered misconduct, brutality or misuse of force is considered nearly as serious as corruption and is treated separately in the literature. Corruption is considered to be even more serious misbehavior. It can include behavior for personal gain and most often includes some type of illegal behavior. Acts of corruption include burglary, theft, bribery, kickbacks, payoffs, and other fixes (Hale, 1989).

Kolthoff et al. (2007) identified a typology of integrity violations for public officials. Their research is based on research conducted in the Netherlands. The typology is useful within the context of this study. The typology includes definitions of various types of corruption, as well as definitions of concepts such as bribing, theft, conflict of interest, improper use of authority, and private time misconduct.

Bribery falls under corruption and is defined to include the misuse of power for private gain and asking, offering, accepting bribes (Kolthoff et al., 2007). Bribery within the United States is similarly defined as the "offering, giving, receiving, or soliciting of something of value for the purpose of influencing the action of an official in the discharge of his or her public or legal duties" (Garner, 1999, p. 191). Kolthoff et al. (2007) define fraud and theft as an organizational private gain. Fraud and theft are treated separately under the law. The U.S. Black's Law Dictionary (1991) defines fraud as a deception with intent to cause injury to another, usually by convincing the victim to consensually part with something of value. Theft does not have the element of deception, but the two can be combined under the law.

The improper use of authority according to Kolthoff et al. (2007) only considers abuse that occurs as a result of noble intent. Improper use of authority with bad intentions is called nepotism, cronyism, and patronage. This typology, however, does not consider abuse of authority with bad intentions that does not fall within the three narrowly defined categories provided. Kolthoff et al. (2007) does recognize conflict of interest as the acceptance of something of value that might interfere with the public interest.

This study creates a typology that is specific to the scenarios listed within the NIJ study relying on the typologies identified by Kolthoff et al. (2007) and Hale (1989). Analysis of the NIJ data will be done according to four categories of seriousness: conflict of interest, exploiting authority, abuse of authority, and malfeasance. These classifications of misconduct and corruption are supported by the literature, and neither contradicts the discipline that would be received within the departments surveyed in the NIJ study (Hale, 1989).

In addition to categorizing the scenarios within this study based on current literature and existing legal definitions of crime and punishment, principal component factor analysis and bivariate correlation were used to confirm at least moderate correlation among the scenarios. Categorization according to the literature and correlation enhance construct validity, including convergent and discriminant validity. Principal component factor analysis confirms strong correlations among scenarios within each of the four categories, but not overly high correlations.

Categorizing the scenarios requires consideration of harm to third parties, benefits to the officer individually or collectively, and whether the misconduct is illegal behavior. The scenarios that involve minor instances of misconduct that do not involve harm to third parties or illegal behavior are categorized as conflict of interest. These scenarios include officers accepting gifts or food from local merchants. Scenarios where the officer uses their power as a police officer to take advantage of others for economic gain are characterized as exploiting authority. These two scenarios include the receipt of kickbacks and a violation of office policy.

The third group of misbehavior—abuse of authority—involves behavior not providing any direct economic benefit to the officer, but a psychic benefit instead. Abuse of authority is the wrongful exercise of lawful authority. The scenarios depict a violation of departmental policy, a human rights violation, and a violation of criminal law. Two of the three scenarios encourage what is considered professional courtesy where officers protect or shield one another from harm. Although not professional courtesy, the third scenario depicts conspiratorial behavior. Conspiracy is treated more seriously in criminal law, as it is potentially more dangerous than crimes committed by individuals (Samaha, 2005). One scenario depicts physical harm to a suspect, which is considered more serious in criminal law than economic harm (Samaha, 2005).

The final group of misbehavior includes criminal behavior that is considered malfeasance. A common law term, malfeasance includes illegal behavior that is attributed to public officials (Hale, 1989). Each of the three scenarios depicted within malfeasance involve illegal officer behavior including bribery and theft. Table 5–1 shows how the scenarios are categorized.

One scenario has been omitted from this analysis—the scenario that involves off-duty work, which potentially creates a conflict of interest. Not all departments in the United States have an off-duty conflict of interest policy for officers to follow. For most departments, having outside work is not a violation of policy at all; even work that is closely related to the job of a police officer (Brunet, 2005). Those that do have policies enforce different rules with respect to whether and how an officer will pursue outside employment. The survey responses clearly indicated that there is no relationship between this scenario and any of the others offered in this study.

The scenarios are represented in the law enforcement code of ethics. Conflict-of-interest scenarios and unnecessary force are explicitly forbidden by the code mandating that officers should never accept gratuities and should never employ unnecessary force. The code also generally directs officers to "develop self restraint," which contradicts both exploiting authority and abuse of authority scenarios. The code also requires that officers "enforce the law courteously and appropriately without fear or favor," which would prohibit behavior depicted with both exploiting authority and abuse of authority. Malfeasance is generally not allowed in that the code states officers should be "honest in thought and deed."

The scenarios are also covered by the IACP National Law Enforcement Standards of Conduct. The standards generally prohibit officers from violating the law, accepting gratuities without filing a report, or using their position for gain or advantage. The standards provide specific language prohibiting drinking alcohol on duty and, in particular, from drinking in public whether on or off duty. There is also a specific provision prohibiting misuse of force. The law prohibits misuse of force in the sense that misuse of force is technically an assault.

The scenarios that fall within each of the four categories are highly correlated according bivariate correlations. The categories are listed in order of seriousness according to the factors used to create the categories. For example, exploiting authority should be considered more serious than conflict of interest because there is greater harm to third parties. In order to condense the variables into these categories, means were used for the

Table 5–1 Case Scenarios by Nature of the Misconduct

Conflict of Interest

A police officer routinely accepts free meals, cigarettes, and other items of small value from merchants on his beat. He does not solicit these gifts and is careful not to abuse the generosity of those who give gifts to him.

A police officer is widely liked in the community, and on holidays local merchants and restaurant and bar owners show their appreciation for his attention by giving him gifts of food and liquor.

Exploiting Authority

A police officer has a private arrangement with a local auto body shop to refer the owners of the cars damaged in the accidents to the shop. In exchange for each referral, he receives a payment of 5% of the repair bill from the shop owner.

A police officer, who happens to be a very good auto mechanic, is scheduled to work during coming holidays. A supervisor offers to give him these days off, if he agrees to tune-up his supervisor's personal car. Evaluate the SUPERVISOR'S behavior.

Abuse of Authority

A police officer finds a bar on his beat that is still serving drinks a half hour past its legal closing time. Instead of reporting this violation, the police officer agrees to accept a couple of free drinks from the owner.

At 2 A.M. a police officer, who is on duty, is driving his patrol car on a deserted road. He sees a vehicle that has been driven off the road and is stuck in a ditch. He approaches the vehicle and observes that the driver is not hurt but is obviously intoxicated. He also finds that the driver is a police officer. Instead of reporting this accident and offense he transports the driver to his home.

Two police officers on foot patrol surprise a man who is attempting to break into an automobile. The man flees. They chase him for about two blocks before apprehending him by tackling him and wrestling him to the ground. After he is under control both officers punch him a couple of times in the stomach as punishment for fleeing and resisting.

Malfeasance

A police officer stops a motorist for speeding. The officer agrees to accept a personal gift of half of the amount of the fine in exchange for not issuing a citation.

A police officer discovers a burglary of a jewelry shop. The display cases are smashed and it is obvious that many items have been taken. While searching the shop, he takes a watch, worth about two days pay for that officer. He reports that the watch had been stolen during the burglary.

A police officer finds a wallet in a parking lot. It contains the amount of money equivalent to a full-day's pay for that officer. He reports the wallet as lost property, but keeps the money for himself.

scenarios falling into each category. For example, conflict of interest is the mean of the two scenarios depicting an officer accepting gratuities and accepting gifts on holidays. The following section explores the nature of this relationship and the hypotheses to be tested in this study.

Hypotheses—Ethical Awareness, Ethical Standards, and Ethical Action

The hypotheses analyze what factors impact officer attitudes toward misconduct and standards, as well as whether an officer will report peer misconduct. This study analyzes organizational and situational variables that impact officer attitudes and behavior. Organizational variables are measured by the size of an agency, an officer's job assignment and rank, and whether an officer is a supervisor. Situational factors are measured by the nature of the misconduct. Attitudes of peers, expected behavior of other officers, and departmental policy are measures of organizational culture. An officer's ethical awareness is measured according to their attitudes toward misconduct. Ethical standards are measured according to what an officer believes should be the punishment for misconduct. Ethical action is measured by whether an officer is willing to report peer misconduct.

H1: The more serious the misconduct, the higher an officer's ethical awareness.

H2: Officers who are supervisors will have higher ethical awareness.

H3: An officer's length of service controlling for rank and supervisory status will have a curvilinear relationship to an officer's ethical awareness.

H4: The size of the police agency will have no relationship to an officer's ethical awareness.

H5: An officer's awareness of existing policies regarding misconduct will positively impact that officer's ethical awareness.

H6: An officer's perceptions regarding peer ethical awareness will positively impact that officer's ethical awareness.

H7: The more serious the misconduct, the higher that officer's ethical standards.

H8: Officers who are supervisor will have higher ethical standards.

H9: An officer's length of service controlling for rank and supervisory status will have a curvilinear relationship to an officer's ethical standards.

H10: The size of the police agency will have no relationship to an officer's ethical standards.

H11: An officer's awareness of existing policies regarding misconduct will positively impact that officer's ethical standards.

H12: An officer's perceptions regarding peer ethical awareness and standards will positively impact that officer's ethical standards.

H13: The higher an officer's ethical awareness, the higher that officer's ethical standards.

H14: The more serious the misconduct, the greater the likelihood of an officer's ethical action.

H15: Officers who are supervisors are more likely to take ethical action.

H16: An officer's length of service controlling for rank and supervisory status will have a curvilinear relationship to the officer's ethical action.

H17: The size of the police agency will have no relationship to an officer's ethical action.

H18: An officer's awareness of existing policies regarding misconduct will positively impact that officer's willingness to take ethical action.

H19: An officer's ethical and perceptions regarding peer ethical awareness, standards, and action will positively impact that officer's willingness to take ethical action.

H20: The higher the officer's ethical awareness and standards, the greater the likelihood of an officer's ethical action.

The first six hypotheses examine the variation in awareness levels of officers. These hypotheses involve situational, individual, and organizational variables. Situational measures include seriousness of the misconduct for each misconduct scenario. The measures for individual factors include supervisory position, rank, and length of service in general. The organizational factors included in this study are agency size and policy.

H5, H11, and H18 explore an officer's awareness of existing policies regarding misconduct. This variable may be an indicator of how much an officer has been exposed to ethics training during his career. This variable also may indicate to some degree how committed supervisors are to communicating agency policy to subordinates. The results explored in this study regarding whether officers are aware of agency policies will suggest whether further training is necessary within an agency or system wide. Given that not much ethics training exists for officers, the expectation is that officers will be uncertain about whether policies exist regarding less serious misconduct depicted in the scenarios. Educators and police supervisors agree that ethics training is important for law enforcement, suggesting that this variable with have a substantial impact on an officer's ethical awareness, standards, and action.

H6, H12, and H19 explore an officer's awareness of perceptions regarding peer ethical awareness. This variable measures the importance an officer places on peer opinions, particularly when considering its impact on whether an officer will report misconduct. This variable essentially gives insight into the weight indirect peer pressure may have on an officer's ethical awareness, standards, and action. The solidarity depicted within law enforcement among peers suggests that this variable will have a big impact on an officer's awareness, standards, and action.

H2, H8, and H15 explore supervisory status, whereas H4, H10, and H17 explore the size of the agency. Individual and organizational variables have had mixed results with respect to impact on officer attitudes and behavior (Riksheim & Chermak, 1993). These hypotheses follow the police culture literature, which suggests that socialization and police culture shape attitudes (Paoline, 2001). If these hypotheses are correct, then supervisors and higher ranking officers believe that officer misconduct is more serious than nonsupervisors and lower ranking officers. Supervisors and higher ranking officers will also believe that more discipline is necessary and will be more likely to report misconduct than non-supervisors and lower ranking officers.

Hypotheses that explore length of service—H3, H9, and H16—are supported by Catlin and Maupin's (2004) findings that socialization on the job impacts an officer's ethical orientations. Analyzing the data to determine whether support exists for this hypothesis requires a comparison of means between officers at varying years of service. Actual years of service are not available in the NIJ data, only the categories indicated earlier in this chapter. In view of the expected impact of rank and supervisory status, length of service will be analyzed with a control for supervisory status.

There is very little research exploring the issue of agency size—H4, H10, and H17—and its impact on officer attitudes. Recent research suggests that local political culture has no impact on the organizational structure of law enforcement agencies (Hassell & Zhao, 2003). Most studies that do consider the organizational structure of a law enforcement agency do so within the context of the size of the city serviced by the officers and not the size of the agency itself (Riksheim & Chermak, 1993). Research that does exist related to size of agency is conflicting, suggesting that there is no relationship between size of agency and an officer's attitudes.

As for the impact of policy on officer attitudes—H5, H11, and H18— some studies have found a relationship between agency policy and officer behavior (Robinson & Chandek, 2000). Their study relies on hierarchical structure to influence the officer's attitude toward misconduct. One can argue, however, that community policing is changing the long-established relationship between size and hierarchy. Larger organizations are more likely to have eliminated formal hierarchical bureaucratic structures in community-based approaches (Kenney & McNamara, 1999).

In addition, larger agencies will have more resources for training and that can narrow the amount of discrepancy in attitudes between officers and their peers. This study hypothesizes that community policing and more extensive resources in larger agencies will have a positive effect on an officer's ethical awareness, standards, and action. On the other hand, bureaucratization and the stress-producing conditions of large cities where one finds larger agencies have a negative effect. Given the contradictory expectations regarding size, the hypothesis predicts no relationship.

From two perspectives, the nature of the misconduct itself—H1, H7, and H14—has an impact on an officer's attitude toward that misconduct, the discipline that should follow, and whether an officer is willing to report that misconduct. First, virtue-based approaches to ethics would suggest that the more an action violates norms of integrity, the more likely it is to be considered wrong, as should the disparity between principle and action (DeLattre, 2002). Second, some studies have shown a relationship between situational variables and officer behavior (Engel & Worden, 2003). This suggests that the nature of the misconduct itself has an impact on an officer's attitude toward that misconduct, the discipline that should follow, and whether an officer is willing to report that misconduct. The more serious the nature of the misconduct consistent with objective standards, the more serious the officer is likely to view that misconduct, the more discipline the officer will believe should follow, and the more likely the officer will report that misconduct.

Supervisors—H2, H8, and H15—will have been in police work long enough for the socialization process to shape their attitudes toward misconduct such that it will be in line with the attitudes of their peers. Furthermore, they have been selected to be supervisors because they meet agency standards and expectations and have incentives to uphold ethical norms. Similarly, as officers progress through their careers, they hold more prestigious job assignments and attain higher status through rank. Persons selected for promotion meet agency standards and expectations (Scarborough et al., 1999; Whetstone, 2001). Each of these variables— supervisory position, rank, length of service—contribute to the officer's attitude toward misconduct. The analysis will examine the separate and combined effects.

New officers—H3, H9, and H16—should have higher values than officers who have been in service for 3 to 10 years for two primary reasons. In part, this view is inferred from the finding that officers who are disciplined for misconduct are generally in their seventh year of service, as Trautman (1997) has shown. In addition, officers become more cynical during this phase of their careers (Hickman et al., 2004). As officers progress through their careers, their commitment to ethical values rise as they either receive promotion or come to terms with their careers (Barker, 1999). The exception to the standard expectation regarding length of service is officers who have been passed over for promotion or selection as supervisors. Negative socialization and/or the cumulative effects of longer service in stressful conditions together with possible resentment for not being promoted can lead to a decline in ethical values. Toward the end of a long period of service, however, self-selection may leave highly experienced officers with higher values than their colleagues who have intermediate periods of service.

All of these situational, individual, and organizational variables combined contribute to an officer's ethical awareness, ethical standards, and ethical action. An officer's socialization shapes the officer's attitude regarding how serious misconduct is in any given situation, whether discipline is warranted, and whether the officer will report the peer misconduct. Ethical awareness and standards ultimately affect an officer's ethical action.

Hypotheses 14 through 20 address the issue of what impacts an officer's decision to report misconduct. Klockars (2002) pointed out that police departments that have successfully broken the police code of silence have consistently upheld fair ethical standards for all officers. Ethical awareness and standards each contribute ultimately to whether an officer is willing to report peer misconduct. One possible explanation for mixed results in the literature when tying socialization, situational, individual, and organizational factors to behavior could be that these factors may only play an indirect role in shaping behavior. Attitudes may more directly impact behavior, whereas these socialization, situational, individual and organizational factors may more directly impact attitudes.

NIJ Data

The NIJ study provides data at the individual level of analysis, making it accessible to multiple forms of data analysis. One advantage of using this data set is that it is very large and missing values did not impact the overall number of respondents. A second advantage is that it contains responses creating approximately 88 variables, including a broad range of misconduct and background information. The majority of variables, 77 questions in the survey, explore the respondent's attitudes toward 11 different specific scenarios depicting officer behavior. The remaining 11 variables inquire into the respondent's background.

The statistical analysis tools that are appropriate to this study include gamma and regression. Each offers a different perspective for interpreting the data. Gamma is a measure of association that measures the strength of relationships between variables (Garson, 2006). Gamma ranges from +1 to –1 and measures the independent variables ability to predict the dependent variable's rank (Garson, 2006). Regression can establish the predictive power independent variables have with respect to a dependent variable (Tabachnick & Fidell, 2001). Combined, these tools offer a deeper understanding of the NIJ data than has been provided in earlier published reports.

The hypotheses explored in this study ask two basic questions. First, what is the strength of the relationship between the variables including organizational, situational, attitudinal, and behavioral variables? This question is best explored through gamma results. The second question revolves around the combined relative impact these variables have on the dependent variables. This question is best analyzed with the help of regression analysis.

Regression assumes linearity, interval level data, normal error terms, homoscedasticity, minimal measurement error, normal distributions, nonrecursivity, absence of multicollinearity, and additivity (Tabachnick & Fidell, 2001). Gamma assumes ordinal-level data and is used in place of Yule's Q when using dichotomous variables. Gamma also does not assume a random sample, as is the case with this study (Garson, 2006).

Screening the Data

The first step in screening the data that was unique to this data set involved honesty of the respondents in completing the survey data. One question added to the end of the survey instrument asked officers who did respond to the survey whether they were truthful in responding to the survey questions. According to the authors, approximately 2.2% of the officers responded "no" to this question, with approximately 1.8% not responding. These 4% of respondents were deleted from the analysis in this paper. The NIJ study chose only to delete the "no" responses to this question.

The next step involved meeting assumptions for regression. The assumptions discussed later here include interval level data, linearity, homoscedasticity, normal distributions, normal error terms, multicollinearity, and no overfitting of data. Most of the data are discrete in the form of a five-point Likert-type scale, which may be treated as if continuous (Tabachnick & Fidell, 2001). It is necessary to check the data for normality by running skew and kurtosis tests and requesting outliers. The test results show no significant skewness or kurtosis problems.

Scatterplots are used to determine whether observed variables have linear relationships, as this is not possible with unobserved variables. Although not perfect, linearity was not problematic with these variables. Residual plots and the analyses of outliers are tools used to determine violation of this assumption. Lack of homoscedasticity would be indicated on the residual plots by a funnel-shaped pattern. The homoscedasticity assumption was met with the NIJ data.

Regression assumes absence of multicollinearity or singularity among variables. Squared multiple correlations were analyzed from the data. The variable length of service in general was virtually identical to length of service for the agency, making the two variables redundant. As this study does not analyze data at the agency level, the variable length of service for the agency was dropped in order to avoid multicollinearity issues.

Analysis of a histogram for standardized residuals is the proper tool for determining whether this assumption has been met. If the histogram shows a normal curve, then the residual error terms can be assumed normally distributed.

Chapters 6, 7, and 8 reveal the results of the analysis discussed in this chapter.

DISCUSSION QUESTIONS

1. Discuss each of the case scenarios from the NIJ study. How serious is the behavior depicted in each scenario? What punishment do you think should follow? Would you be willing to report this type of behavior?
2. There are no standardized punishments (analogy: federal sentencing guidelines) for unethical/illegal behavior committed by police officers. Each jurisdiction varies, even within a state. Do you think there should be standardized punishments? What are the benefits to this approach? What are the drawbacks to such an approach?
3. Analyze each hypothesis presented within this chapter one at a time. Do you find support for each hypothesis in the research presented in this book? Do you find conflicting evidence?
4. Which hypotheses do you believe will be supported, and which do you think may not be supported by analyzing the data in the NIJ survey?
5. What impact does this data/survey have on policing, if any? What impact should it have?

REFERENCES

Barker, J. C. (1999). *Danger, Duty, and Disillusion: The Worldview of Los Angeles Police Officers*. Prospect Heights, IL: Waveland Press.

Brunet, J. R. (2008) Blurring the Line Between Public and Private Sectors: The Case of Police Off-Duty Employment *Public Personnel Management, 37*(2), 161–174.

Catlin, D. W., & Maupin, J. R. (2004). A two cohort study of the ethical orientations of state police officers. *Policing: An International Journal of Police Strategies and Management, 27*(3), 289–301.

Delattre, E. J. (2002). *Character and Cops: Ethics in Policing*. Lanham, MD: American Enterprise Institute Press.

Engel, R. S., & Worden, R. E. (2003). Police officers' attitudes, behavior, and supervisory influences: an analysis of problem solving. *Criminology, 41*(1), 131–166.

Garner, B.A. (ed.) (1999). *Black's Law Dictionary*, Seventh ed. St. Paul, MN: West Group, p. 191.

Garson, D. G. (2006). *Statnotes: Topics in Multivariate Analysis*. Retrieved August 31, 2006, from http://www2.chass.ncsu.edu/garson/pa765/statnote.htm.

Hale, D. C. (1989). Ideology of police misbehavior: analysis and recommendations. *Quarterly Journal of Ideology, 12*, 59–85.

Hassell, K. D., & Zhao, J. S. (2003). Structural arrangements in large municipal police organizations. *Policing: An International Journal of Police Strategies and Management, 26*(2), 231–250.

Hickman, M. J., Piquero, A. R., Lawton, B. A., & Greene, J. R. (2001). Applying Tittle's control balance theory to police deviance. *Policing: An International Journal of Police Strategies and Management, 24*(4), 497–519.

Hickman, M. J., Piquero, N. L., & Piquero, A. R. (2004). The validity of Niederhoffer's cynicism scale. *Journal of Criminal Justice, 32,* 1–13.

Kenney, D. J., & McNamara, R. P. (1999). *Police and Policing: Contemporary Issues.* Westport, CT: Praeger.

Kolthoff, E., Huberts, L., & Van Den Heuvel, H. (2007). The ethics of new public management: is integrity at stake? *Public Administration Quarterly, 30*(4), 399–439.

Klockars, C. B., Ivkovic, S. K., & Haberfeld, M. (2004). *The Contours of Police Integrity.* Thousand Oaks, CA: Sage Publications.

Klockars, C. B., Ivkovich, S. K., Harver, W. E., & Haberfeld, M. R. (2000, May). *The Measurement of Police Integrity.* Washington, D.C.: National Institute of Justice.

Paoline III, E. A. (2001). *Rethinking Police Culture: Officers' Occupational Attitudes.* New York: LFB Scholarly Publishing LLC.

Riksheim, E. C., & Chermak, S. M. (1993). Causes of police behavior revisited. *Journal of Criminal Justice, 21,* 353–382.

Robinson, A. L., & Chandek, M. S. (2000). The domestic violence arrest decision: examining demographic, attitudinal, and situational variables. *Crime & Delinquency, 46*(1), 18–37.

Samaha, J. (2005). *Criminal Law.* Belmont, CA: Thomson Wadsworth.

Scarborough, K. E., Van Tubergen, G. N., Gaines, L. K., & Whitlow, S. S. (1999). An examination of police officers' motivation to participate in the promotional process. *Police Quarterly, 2*(3), 302–320.

Svara, J. (1997). The ethical triangle: synthesizing the bases of administrative ethics. *Public Integrity Annual, 1,* 33–41.

Tabachnick, B. G., & Fidell, L. S. (2001). *Using Multivariate Statistics.* Needham Heights, MA: Allyn & Bacon.

Trautman, N. E. (1997). *The National Law Enforcement Officer Disciplinary Research Project.* Hanover, NH: The Ethics Institute.

Walker, S. (2004, January). *Best Practices in Policing.* Oakland, CA: University of Nebraska at Omaha.

Whetstone, T. S. (2001). Copping out: why police officers decline to participate in the sergeant's promotional process. *American Journal of Criminal Justice, 25*(2), 147–159.

CHAPTER 6

Ethical Awareness

OBJECTIVES

- Distinguish ethical awareness from ethical standards and action
- Identify the situational, individual, and organizational factors that impact ethical awareness of police officers
- Analyze the National Institute of Justice data, and apply it to the ethical awareness hypotheses
- Recognize the findings that were most surprising from the data analysis, including supervisory impact and conflicting views on misuse of force

This chapter analyzes the characteristics of the National Institute of Justice (NIJ) study with an emphasis on officer ethical awareness. This chapter looks at the individual characteristics of the officers who responded to the NIJ study followed by an analysis of ethical awareness cross-tabs, gamma, and regression analysis. The variables explored provide some insights into the individual characteristics of the officers responding to the study. Individual characteristics included the length of time an officer has served within law enforcement, the length of time an officer has served within the agency being surveyed, and the rank an officer holds. Because the length of time an officer has served within the agency being surveyed was highly correlated to the length of time the officer has served within law enforcement, only one of these two variables is used. Because the length of time the officer has been in law enforcement is more relevant to the results, it is used.

WHAT IS ETHICAL AWARENESS FOR POLICE OFFICERS?

Ethical awareness is a measure of the officer's attitude regarding the seriousness of the misconduct in each scenario. The ethical awareness measure later here was created averaging all of the scenario responses regarding seriousness of the misconduct. The scenarios were condensed for three reasons. First, condensing the scenarios from 11 to 4 greatly simplifies the quantitative analysis. Second, condensing the scenarios highlights the similarities in the scenarios and explores the categories of police misconduct. Finally, condensing the scenarios makes analysis of the nature of the misconduct simpler.

The scenarios fall into four categories, which include conflict of interest, exploiting authority, abuse of authority, and malfeasance. For each hypothesis explored in this study, the issue is whether there is a relationship between an officer's ethical awareness with the nature of the misconduct, individual, organizational, and behavioral variables. The first six hypotheses posit a relationship between these variables:

H1: The more serious the misconduct, the higher an officer's ethical awareness.

H2: Officers who are supervisors will have higher ethical awareness.

H3: An officer's length of service controlling for rank and supervisory status will have a curvilinear relationship to an officer's ethical awareness.

H4: The size of the police agency will have no relationship to an officer's ethical awareness.

H5: An officer's awareness of existing policies regarding misconduct will positively impact that officer's ethical awareness.

H6: An officer's perceptions regarding peer ethical awareness will positively impact that officer's ethical awareness.

Analyzing the nature of the misconduct requires including variables that distinguish the degree of seriousness of the misconduct. The seriousness of the misconduct is separated into four categories: conflict of interest, exploiting authority, abuse of authority, and malfeasance. The ethical awareness measure is the mean of all misconduct scenarios used in this study measured through the question "how serious do you consider this behavior to be?" The section that follows explores these hypotheses and analyzes the data using descriptive statistics.

SITUATIONAL, INDIVIDUAL, AND ORGANIZATIONAL FACTORS THAT AFFECT ETHICAL AWARENESS

This chapter focuses on an officer's ethical awareness by analyzing the nature of the misconduct, supervisory position, rank, years of service, agency size, policy, and the officer's perception of peer attitudes toward misconduct. The first hypothesis asserts that the more serious the misconduct, the higher an officer's ethical awareness; however, the strength of this relationship does not increase strictly in correspondence to the seriousness of the misconduct. Officers rate exploiting authority as more serious than abuse of authority, which contradicts objective standards based on harm to third parties, benefits to the officer, and legality. Objective measures would indicate that minor misconduct on the same 5-point Likert-type scale in this study should receive a three score as moderately serious. Exploiting authority should receive a four score as serious, whereas abuse of authority and corruption should each receive scores of five indicating very serious misconduct. The 5-point Likert-type scale used in the study offers five levels of seriousness for respondents.

The dependent variables explored in this study include the four types of police misconduct—conflict of interest, exploiting authority, abuse of authority, and malfeasance. Respondents rated each type of misconduct according to the level of seriousness of the misconduct. The four types of misconduct are presented in the order of seriousness expected within the results, not in the order of seriousness according to respondents. Percentages, number of respondents, and means are indicated in Table 6–1 according to the dependent variables.

Three important points emerge from these descriptive statistics. First, respondents generally view exploitation of authority as more serious than abuse of authority. Most (89%) respondents rate exploiting authority as serious to very serious with a majority rating this category of misconduct as very serious. In contrast, over half view abuse of authority as only moderately or less serious to serious. It is striking that using unnecessary force and overlooking the misconduct of an officer would be tolerated as relatively minor infractions by a majority of officers.

Second, respondents view exploiting authority almost as seriously as malfeasance. Certainly, malfeasance is in a class by itself with virtual unanimity that these actions are very serious violations of ethical norms.

Table 6-1 Ethical Awareness Dependent Variable Summary

	(1) Not Serious–(5) Very Serious			
	Conflict of Interest	Exploiting Authority	Abuse of Authority	Malfeasance
Not at all serious 1.5	24.3% (756)	0.5% (16)	7.6% (234)	.2% (6)
Slightly serious 1.6–2.5	29.3% (909)*	2.4% (74)	15.1% (468)	.3% (9)
Moderately serious 2.6–3.5	23.9% (741)	8.1% (250)	30.2% (936)	.6% (17)
Serious 3.6–4.5	14.3% (444)	32.0% (992)	30.3% (940)*	4.8% (149)
Very serious 4.6–5	8.2% (253)	57.0% (1771)*	16.8% (523)	94.1% (2923)*
Means	2.72	4.40	3.54	4.91

*largest percentage/(n)

A majority of respondents view exploiting authority as very serious (whereas only one-sixth view abusing authority in this way). It appears that officers are sensitive to the ethical inappropriateness of taking action to secure personal gain.

Finally, the manifestations of conflict of interest—accepting but not soliciting gratuities and holiday gifts—are not viewed to be as serious as objective standards would indicate that they should be. Despite the extensive attention focused on the free donut problem, a majority of officers view these behaviors as only slightly serious at worst. One in four respondents rated conflict of interest as not serious at all. Taking steps to secure personal benefits is generally perceived to be wrong, whereas accepting the gifts that come the officer's way is not.

Thus, the overall tendency of the respondents is to treat the cases as either very serious or serious for three of the four types of behavior. Abuse of authority, however, is considered less serious than exploiting authority, and conflict of interest is generally viewed as less than moderately serious. Respondents considered abuse of authority almost as serious as malfeasance. Except for the response to malfeasance, there are also significant majorities in the case of conflict of interest and abuse of authority whose level of awareness is well below what law enforcement professionals would consider to be acceptable, whereas only 1 in 10 consider exploiting authority to be no more than moderately serious. Even if ethical awareness is strongly related to ethical standards and ethical action in subsequent analysis, it is important to recognize that the level of awareness itself does not fully accord with objective standards of the seriousness of behavior and is uneven across law enforcement officers. Thus, these results show mixed support for hypothesis 1, which asserts that the more serious the misconduct, the higher the ethical awareness.

It is hypothesized that supervisory position will impact an officer's ethical awareness. Approximately 20% of respondents in this survey were supervisors, ranging from sergeants to captains. The typical officer (including detectives who are not supervisors) has been in service for 3 to 5 years, whereas the typical supervisor has been in office for over 16 years. Table 6–2 provides percentages, number of respondents, and means for ethical awareness attitudes according to supervisory position.

There are important differences in attitudes between supervisors and nonsupervisors, as indicated in Table 6-2. Among supervisors, 60% view

Table 6–2 Ethical Awareness and Supervisory Position

	(1) Not Serious–(5) Very Serious			
	Conflict of Interest	Exploiting Authority	Abuse of Authority	Malfeasance
Supervisor				
Not at all serious 1.5	9.8% (60)	0.0% (0)	3.1% (19)	0.2% (1)
Slightly serious 1.6–2.5	22.1% (136)	0.6% (4)	11.9% (73)	0.5% (3)
Moderately serious 2.6–3.5	29.0% (178)*	3.0% (18)	25.0% (153)	0.3% (2)
Serious 3.6–4.5	23.6% (145)	20.2% (124)	37.4% (230)*	2.8% (17)
Very serious 4.6–5	15.5% (95)	76.2% (468)*	22.6% (139)	96.2% (591)*
Means	3.34*	4.69*	3.84*	4.94*
Nonsupervisor				
Not at all serious 1.5	28.0% (693)	0.6% (16)	8.7% (215)	0.2% (5)
Slightly serious 1.6–2.5	31.1% (770)*	2.8% (70)	15.9% (393)	0.2% (6)
Moderately serious 2.6–3.5	22.6% (557)	9.4% (231)	31.4% (776)*	0.6% (15)
Serious 3.6–4.5	11.9% (295)	34.8% (860)	28.7% (707)	5.4% (132)
Very serious 4.6–5	6.4% (157)	52.4% (1295)*	15.3% (379)	93.6% (2315)*
Means	2.57	4.33	3.46	4.90
Gamma	.402**	.401**	.229**	.366**

*largest percentage/(n)/mean

**p < .05

abuse of authority as serious or very serious compared with 44% of non-supervisors. There is greater awareness of the seriousness of these actions, although a significant minority does not see the behaviors as serious. Among nonsupervisors, however, a clear majority has lax attitudes about these forms of abuse of authority. Similarly, one-third of supervisors view conflict of interest as no more than slightly serious compared with three out of five nonsupervisors.

Despite the clear difference, one must question what kind of example or leadership supervisors provide when two in five consider abuse to be no more than moderately serious and one in three do not consider conflict of interest to be more than slightly serious. The differences are not always as great at the other end of the awareness scales. For example, 76% of supervisors versus 52% of nonsupervisors consider exploiting authority to be very serious. A high consensus about ethical norms is reflected in shared agreement that malfeasance is a very serious offense. There is also, however, a shared avoidance of classifying abuse of authority as very serious, a view held by only 23% of supervisors and 15% of nonsupervisors.

Means for seriousness of misconduct are higher with supervisors than with nonsupervisors. The differences between means are larger for conflict of interest than the other types of misconduct with the least difference in means with respect to serious misconduct. Both supervisors and nonsupervisors find exploiting authority more serious than abuse of authority. Neither group, however, lends support to higher levels of ethical awareness according to type of misconduct, as abuse of authority is rated lower than exploiting authority. The only support for hypothesis 1 is that malfeasance has higher means than conflict of interest and both exploiting authority and abuse of authority have higher means than conflict of interest.

Gamma scores are moderately strong across all types of misconduct indicating a positive relationship between whether or not an officer is a supervisor and that officer's attitude toward misconduct. These results lend further support to hypothesis 2 that supervisors have higher ethical awareness than nonsupervisors. The lowest gamma weight occurs within abuse of authority indicating a weaker relationship with respect to this type of misconduct.

Rank is used as a control variable in this study. Officer rank is strongly tied to supervisory position and length of service. Officers may or may not achieve higher rank as they progress through their careers. Rank is explored in this chapter in Table 6–3 and is used as a control in the regression model later in this chapter.

Table 6–3 Ethical Awareness and Rank

| | (1) Not Serious–(5) Very Serious | | | |
	Conflict of Interest	Exploiting Authority	Abuse of Authority	Malfeasance
Officers				
Not at all serious 1.5	29.0% (609)	0.7% (14)	9.2% (192)	0.2% (4)
Slightly serious 1.6–2.5	31.3% (656)*	2.9% (61)	15.3% (321)	0.2% (5)
Moderately serious 2.6–3.5	22.2% (466)	9.6% (201)	31.6% (663)*	0.6% (12)
Serious 3.6–4.5	10.9% (229)	35.6% (748)	28.3% (593)	5.8% (121)
Very serious 4.6–5	6.6% (139)	51.2% (1075)*	15.6% (328)	93.2% (1958)*
Means	2.54	4.32	3.46	4.90
Detectives/Investigators				
Not at all serious 1.5	21.3% (79)	0.6% (2)	6.2% (23)	0.3% (1)
Slightly serious 1.6–2.5	29.9% (111)*	2.4% (9)	18.9% (70)	0.0% (0)
Moderately serious 2.6–3.5	25.1% (93)	7.8% (29)	30.7% (114)*	0.8% (3)
Serious 3.6–4.5	18.3% (68)	31.0% (115)	29.1% (108)	3.5% (13)
Very serious 4.6–5	5.4% (20)	58.2% (216)*	15.1% (56)	95.4% (354)*
Means	2.77	4.41	3.49	4.93
First-Line Managers				
Not at all serious 1.5	12.4% (47)	0.0% (0)	2.6% (10)	0.0% (0)
Slightly serious 1.6–2.5	24.0% (91)	0.5% (2)	13.2% (50)	0.6% (2)
Moderately serious 2.6–3.5	29.0% (110)*	2.7% (10)	25.9% (98)	0.0% (0)
Serious 3.6–4.5	22.2% (84)	22.4% (85)	35.1% (133)*	2.6% (10)
Very serious 4.6–5	12.4% (47)	74.4% (282)*	23.2% (88)	96.8% (367)*
Means	3.18	4.68	3.81	4.96*
Mid-Level Managers				
Not at all serious 1.5	6.5% (11)	0.0% (0)	3.6% (6)	0.0% (0)
Slightly serious 1.6–2.5	20.8% (35)	0.6% (1)	11.9% (20)	0.6% (1)
Moderately serious 2.6–3.5	29.8% (50)*	4.1% (7)	23.2% (39)	0.6% (1)
Serious 3.6–4.5	25.6% (43)	16.1% (27)	42.3% (71)*	3.0% (5)
Very serious 4.6–5	17.3% (29)	79.2% (133)*	19.0% (32)	95.8% (161)*
Means	3.49*	4.69	3.85	4.94
Senior Managers				
Not at all serious 1.5	14.0% (8)	0.0% (0)	3.5% (2)	1.8% (1)
Slightly serious 1.6–2.5	15.8% (9)	1.8% (1)	7.0% (4)	1.8% (1)
Moderately serious 2.6–3.5	26.3% (15)*	1.8% (1)	22.8% (13)	1.8% (1)
Serious 3.6–4.5	19.3% (11)	17.5% (10)	42.1% (24)*	0.0% (0)
Very serious 4.6–5	24.6% (14)	78.9% (45)*	24.6% (14)	94.6% (54)*
Means	3.46	4.72*	3.91*	4.84
Gamma	.289**	.279**	.143**	.320**

*largest percentage/(n)/mean

**p < .05

Regardless of rank, respondents rate exploiting authority as more serious than abuse of authority. Regardless of rank, respondents rate exploiting authority almost as seriously as malfeasance. A majority of officers (51%) and detectives/investigators (58%) view exploitation of authority as very serious, whereas an overwhelming majority of first-line managers (74%), mid-level managers (79%), and senior managers (79%) take this view. A majority of officers and detectives (56%) view abuse of authority as no more than moderately serious, whereas only 43% of first line managers, 39% of mid-level managers, and 33% of senior managers rate abuse of authority at the same relatively low level of seriousness. It would be expected that the managers would rate abuse of authority as more serious than nonmanagers, but at least managers are more likely to consider abuse of authority to be at least serious.

In support of hypothesis 2, conflict of interest percentages show that supervisors (managers) have higher ethical awareness than nonsupervisors (officers and detectives/investigators). A majority of officers (60%) rate conflict of interest as either not serious at all or only slightly serious. In contrast, 36% of first-line managers, 26% of mid-level managers, and 30% of senior managers take this view. As noted with regard to supervisors, however, even though the proportions who take a lax attitude are lower, there is a substantial minority of leaders sending an accommodating message about conflict of interest.

Mid-level managers have the highest overall means, whereas officers have the lowest overall means. There is a large range between supervisors (first-line managers, mid-level managers, and senior managers) and nonsupervisors (officers). Managers (first-line, mid, and senior) rate misconduct as more serious than other types of officers. Officers consistently rate misconduct as much less serious than other types of officers. All officers, regardless of rank, place exploiting authority as more serious than abuse of authority. Also, the range of means for conflict of interest is much larger than the other three types of misconduct.

Within rank, two interesting gaps in means emerge. The first notable mean gap is between first-line managers and officers. First-line managers include sergeants and corporals who are supervisors. First-line managers are first promotions for most officers, and thus, there is most likely the smallest gap in time between the transitions from officer to first-line manager. The second notable gap occurs between detectives and mid-level managers.

Detectives are usually somewhere in between first-line and mid-level managers within the hierarchical structure of the police organization. Their ethical awareness, however, is closer to officers than to first-line supervisors and substantially lower than the awareness level of mid-level managers.

As with supervisory status, gamma scores are moderately strong, although somewhat weaker, within rank than supervisory status. These results indicate that the higher the rank, the higher the officer's ethical awareness. The lowest gamma score, again, is within abuse of authority.

The findings for analysis of supervisory status and rank show very similar patterns. To simplify the presentation of data in future chapters, only supervisory status will be presented. Rank will be used, however, in regression analysis.

An officer's rank is also closely related to that officer's length of service within law enforcement, as those officers who are promoted have been in service longer than nonsupervisors. For this reason, it is important to control for these additional responsibilities when analyzing length of service. It is expected that an officer's length of service, controlling for rank and supervisory status, will have a curvilinear relationship to an officer's ethical awareness. In order to analyze the complex issue of length of service, it is necessary to control for supervisory status. The association of tenure and ethical awareness for nonsupervisors is presented in Table 6–4.

Regardless of the number of years an officer has served, respondents rate exploitation of authority as more serious than abuse of authority. A majority of officers with less than 1 year of service (55%) and officers with more than 6 years of service ranging from 50% to 61% rate exploitation of authority as very serious. In contrast, less than a majority of officers with 1 to 5 years of experience rate it as very serious, ranging from 45% to 47%. The percentages of officers who believe exploitation of authority is very serious increases as years of service increase over 6 years of service. Officers with less than 1 year of service have a higher percentage of respondents (55%) that believe exploiting authority is very serious than officers with 6 to 10 years of service (50%). These results highlight the curvilinear relationship hypothesized with years of service where officers have higher ethical awareness with less than 1 year of service, ethical awareness declines in years 1 through 5, and ethical awareness rises after 6 years of service. Figure 6–1 compares means.

Table 6–4 Ethical Awareness and Years of Service: Nonsupervisors Only

	(1) Not Serious–(5) Very Serious			
	Conflict of Interest	Exploiting Authority	Abuse of Authority	Malfeasance
Less than 1 Year				
Not at all serious 1.5	20.9% (27)	0.8% (1)	0.8% (1)	0.8% (1)
Slightly serious 1.6–2.5	31.8% (41)*	0.8% (1)	9.3% (12)	0.8% (1)
Moderately serious 2.6–3.5	27.9% (36)	4.6% (6)	27.9% (36)	0.0% (0)
Serious 3.6–4.5	14.7% (19)	38.8% (50)	38.0% (49)*	5.4% (7)
Very serious 4.6–5	4.7% (6)	55.0% (71)*	24.0% (31)	93.0% (120)*
Means	2.72	4.45	3.94	4.87
1–2 Years				
Not at all serious 1.5	30.0% (72)	0.4% (1)	8.8% (21)	0.0% (0)
Slightly serious 1.6–2.5	34.1% (82)*	2.9% (7)	15.1% (36)	0.4% (1)
Moderately serious 2.6–3.5	22.1% (53)	13.4% (32)	30.1% (72)*	0.0% (0)
Serious 3.6–4.5	9.6% (23)	38.1% (91)	26.8% (64)	7.1% (17)
Very serious 4.6–5	4.2% (10)	45.2% (108)*	19.2% (46)	92.5% (222)*
Means	2.46	4.25	3.52	4.89
3–5 Years				
Not at all serious 1.5	31.6% (148)	0.2% (1)	9.6% (45)	0.0% (0)
Slightly serious 1.6–2.5	33.7% (158)*	4.5% (21)	15.3% (72)	0.2% (1)
Moderately serious 2.6–3.5	21.1% (99)	10.4% (49)	32.1% (151)*	1.3% (6)
Serious 3.6–4.5	8.7% (41)	38.3% (180)	27.5% (129)	6.0% (28)
Very serious 4.6–5	4.9% (23)	46.6% (219)*	15.5% (73)	92.5% (435)*
Means	2.40	4.25	3.45	4.88
6–10 Years				
Not at all serious 1.5	31.6% (222)*	1.0% (6)	8.7% (61)	0.0% (0)
Slightly serious 1.6–2.5	30.4% (214)	2.6% (18)	17.4% (122)	0.0% (0)
Moderately serious 2.6–3.5	22.5% (158)	9.3% (65)	31.0% (217)*	0.7% (5)
Serious 3.6–4.5	10.5% (74)	36.7% (258)	28.9% (203)	5.5% (39)
Very serious 4.6–5	5.0% (35)	50.4% (354)*	14.0% (98)	93.8% (659)*
Means	2.47	4.31	3.42	4.92
11–15 Years				
Not at all serious 1.5	25.4% (97)	0.2% (1)	12.1% (46)	0.2% (1)
Slightly serious 1.6–2.5	35.1% (134)*	2.9% (11)	17.0% (65)	0.0% (0)
Moderately serious 2.6–3.5	19.1% (73)	7.6% (29)	29.3% (112)*	0.5% (2)
Serious 3.6–4.5	12.0% (46)	30.9% (118)	28.5% (109)	3.9% (15)
Very serious 4.6–5	8.4% (32)	58.4% (223)*	13.1% (50)	95.3% (364)*
Means	2.62	4.39	3.35	4.93*

(continues)

Table 6–4 (continued)

	Conflict of Interest	Exploiting Authority	Abuse of Authority	Malfeasance
16–20 Years				
Not at all serious 1.5	27.9% (74)*	1.5% (4)	8.3% (22)	0.4% (1)
Slightly serious 1.6-2.5	27.2% (72)	2.3% (6)	18.1% (48)	0.7% (2)
Moderately serious 2.6-3.5	24.9% (66)	9.8% (26)	34.0% (90)*	0.0% (0)
Serious 3.6-4.5	13.6% (36)	30.9% (82)	24.5% (65)	5.7% (15)
Very serious 4.6-5	6.4% (17)	55.5% (147)*	15.1% (40)	93.2% (247)*
Means	2.60	4.34	3.39	4.89
Over 20 Years				
Not at all serious 1.5	18.7% (51)	0.7% (2)	6.6% (18)	0.7% (2)
Slightly serious 1.6-2.5	24.6% (67)	2.2% (6)	14.0% (38)	0.4% (1)
Moderately serious 2.6-3.5	25.4% (69)*	7.4% (20)	35.3% (96)*	0.7% (2)
Serious 3.6-4.5	19.5% (53)	28.7% (78)	29.8% (81)	4.1% (11)
Very serious 4.6-5	11.8% (32)	61.0% (166)*	14.3% (39)	94.1% (256)*
Means	2.99*	4.44*	3.51*	4.89
Gamma[1]	.079**	.074**	-.052**	.131**

[1]Gamma scores for supervisors are .174** for conflict of interest, .131** for exploiting authority, .112** for abuse of authority, and -.016 for malfeasance.

*largest percentage/(n)/mean

**p < .05

Within abuse of authority, the largest percentage of officers with less than 1 year of service rate abuse of authority as serious (38%), as compared with officers with 1 to 2 years of service (27%) and officers with 3 to 5 years of service (28%). These percentages, however, do not steadily increase until after the officer has been in service at least 15 years.

There is a modestly curvilinear relationship within conflict of interest. Officers with less than 1 year of service have the highest percentage of respondents (28%) that view conflict of interest as moderately serious. There is a slight decline in these percentages, which range from 19% to 22% with officers who have 1 to 15 years of service followed by a moderate increase of around 25% with officers who have more than 15 years of service.

Officers with less than 1 year of service have the highest overall means, whereas officers who have over 20 years of service hold the second largest overall means. The lowest overall means are with officers who have between

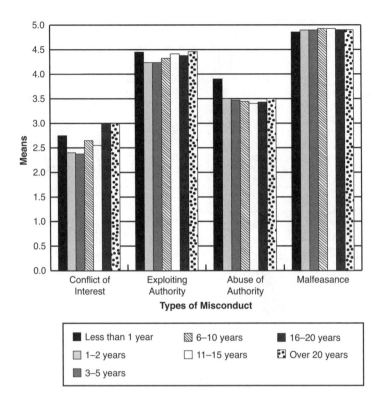

Types of Misconduct

■ Less than 1 year	▨ 6–10 years	■ 16–20 years
□ 1–2 years	□ 11–15 years	▣ Over 20 years
▨ 3–5 years		

FIGURE 6–1 Ethical awareness by years of service

3 to 5 years of service. As noted, the exception is abuse of authority, which continues to drop slightly through the 11- to 15-year group. The levels of awareness even among the highest two length of service categories are lower than for those with less than 2 years of service. There is an increase in means with officers who have more than 6 years of experience; however, there are large ranges between officers who have 6 to 10 years of service and officers who have 11 to 15 years of service. There is an even larger range between officers who have 16 to 20 years of service and officers who have over 20 years of experience. Regardless of years on the force, officers rate exploiting authority as more serious than abuse of authority.

Two interesting findings emerge from length of service means. First, there is a gap in means between officers who have been in service for less than 1 year and officers who have been in service for 1 to 2 years. Research indicates that officer's attitudes and behaviors are impacted during the first year of service in that new recruits come to service with high ideals. Second, there is a gap between officers who have been in service for 3 to 5 years and officers who have been in service for more than 20 years. Research shows that the average officer who is disciplined for misconduct has served approximately 7 years. It is possible that negative attitudes form prior to the seventh year and that officers engage in misconduct over a period of time before eventually being formally disciplined or even reported to superiors.

Gamma scores are substantially lower for length of service than for the previous two variables. This is to be expected when the relationship is more or less curvilinear. These results highlight the need to control for supervisory status when analyzing length of service as factoring in supervisors gives noticeably different results as footnote 1 in Table 6–4 indicates.

An organizational factor that is considered within this study is the size of agency. Respondents for this survey typically work in very large agencies with over 500 sworn officers, whereas more than half of the agencies that participated in this study are either small or very small. Table 6–5 shows percentages, number of respondents, and means for ethical awareness according to the size of agency.

Regardless of size of agency, a majority of respondents rate exploiting authority as more serious than abuse of authority, and exploiting authority is considered to be almost as serious as malfeasance. There are three different patterns of variation for the four awareness indices. There is little difference for exploiting authority, which 85% to 90% of the respondents in the department size categories viewed as at least a serious offense as malfeasance, which 92% to 95% of the respondents viewed as a very serious offense.

Regarding conflict of interest, there is no consistent difference related to size. A majority of respondents from small and very large see these behaviors as no more than slightly serious. In contrast, only 34% and 38%, respectively, from very small and large agencies offer a slightly serious rating. The medium-sized agencies are in the middle.

Abuse of authority, on the other hand, shows a size difference. Less than 3 in 10 respondents in smaller size agencies rate these behaviors at least serious, whereas 48% to 55% of the respondents in the medium-sizes and larger agencies take this view. These results suggest that the social bond among officers may be stronger in smaller organizations in which officers are likely to know each other personally, as well as sharing a professional/occupational association.

Large agencies have the highest overall means with medium agencies holding the second highest overall means. Small agencies have the lowest

Table 6–5   Ethical Awareness and Agency Size

(n, # of agencies)	(1) Not Serious–(5) Very Serious			
	Conflict of Interest	Exploiting Authority	Abuse of Authority	Malfeasance
Very Small, <25 officers (87, 8)				
Not at all serious 1.5	10.3% (9)	0.0% (0)	10.3% (9)	0.0% (0)
Slightly serious 1.6–2.5	24.1% (21)	1.2% (1)	21.8% (19)	1.1% (1)
Moderately serious 2.6–3.5	30.0% (26)*	12.6% (11)	39.2% (35)*	0.0% (0)
Serious 3.6–4.5	14.9% (13)	25.3% (22)	18.3% (16)	6.9% (6)
Very serious 4.6–5	20.7% (18)	60.9% (53)*	9.2% (8)	92.0% (80)*
Means	3.26*	4.43*	3.14	4.87
Small, 25–75 officers (212, 9)				
Not at all serious 1.5	22.6% (48)	0.5% (1)	15.7% (33)	0.0% (0)
Slightly serious 1.6–2.5	29.0% (61)	2.8% (6)	22.2% (47)	0.5% (1)
Moderately serious 2.6–3.5	31.1% (66)*	10.4% (22)	32.3% (68)*	0.9% (2)
Serious 3.6–4.5	10.0% (21)	33.0% (70)	22.7% (48)	6.1% (13)
Very serious 4.6–5	7.5% (16)	53.3% (113)*	7.1% (15)	92.5% (196)*
Means	2.72	4.35	3.05	4.90
Medium, 76–200 officers (344, 6)				
Not at all serious 1.5	15.4% (53)	1.2% (4)	6.1% (21)	0.0% (0)
Slightly serious 1.6–2.5	33.0% (113)*	3.2% (11)	12.5% (43)	0.3% (1)
Moderately serious 2.6–3.5	26.7% (92)	8.7% (30)	28.8% (99)*	0.6% (2)
Serious 3.6–4.5	15.7% (54)	25.0% (86)	28.5% (98)	6.4% (22)
Very serious 4.6–5	9.3% (32)	61.9% (213)*	24.1% (83)	92.7% (319)*
Means	2.91	4.41	3.72*	4.91
Large, 201–500 officers (235, 2)				
Not at all serious 1.5	15.7% (37)	0.0% (0)	7.6% (18)	0.4% (1)
Slightly serious 1.6–2.5	22.1% (52)	3.4% (8)	16.6% (39)	0.0% (0)
Moderately serious 2.6–3.5	19.1% (45)	11.5% (27)	20.8% (49)	0.9% (2)
Serious 3.6–4.5	27.0% (63)*	34.5% (81)	34.1% (80)*	5.1% (12)
Very serious 4.6–5	16.2% (38)	50.6% (119)*	20.9% (49)	93.6% (220)*
Means	3.25	4.34	3.60	4.89
Very large, >500 officers (2229, 5)				
Not at all serious 1.5	27.3% (609)	0.4% (11)	6.9% (153)	0.2% (5)
Slightly serious 1.6–2.5	29.9% (665)*	2.2% (48)	14.4% (320)	0.3% (6)
Moderately serious 2.6–3.5	23.0% (512)	7.2% (160)	30.8% (685)	0.5% (11)
Serious 3.6–4.5	13.1% (293)	32.9% (733)	31.4% (698)*	4.3% (96)
Very serious 4.6–5	6.7% (149)	57.3% (1273)*	16.5% (368)	94.7% (2108)*
Means	2.62	4.41	3.56	4.92*
Gamma	–.163**	.003	.063**	.111**

*largest percentage/(n)/mean
**$p < .05$

overall means. Size of agency shows some differences in ethical awareness amongst officers. Abuse of authority had the largest range in means with conflict of interest fairly close behind. No agency consistently had the highest means across the different types of misconduct. Very small agencies hold the highest means for conflict of interest and exploiting authority, whereas medium agencies have the highest means for abuse of authority. Small agencies had lower means overall than other agencies. Officers did rate exploiting authority as more serious than abuse of authority. The gamma scores for agency size are weak and show the lack of any clearly defined relationship between agency size and officer attitudes toward misconduct. The complete results regarding size of agency demonstrate the unclear and potentially shifting impact of this variable on the attitudes of police officers. The same uncertainty is reflected in the literature.

Some trends that coincide with previous results do emerge. Respondents rate exploiting authority and malfeasance as more serious than conflict of interest. Exploiting authority is rated as more serious than abuse of authority, and almost as serious as malfeasance. Although exploiting authority has a majority of officers rating it as very serious, the percentages are much lower than those rating malfeasance as very serious.

Two additional variables that have not been explored thus far deserve attention: first, the variable that measures an officer's perceptions of existing agency policy, and second, the variable that measures officer perceptions of peer attitudes toward misconduct. These two variables have the potential to influence officer awareness more so than any other variable explored in this study. There is a strong correlation, as indicated Table 6–6, between agency policy and an officer's attitude toward misconduct. This strong correlation suggests that at the very least an officer's awareness of existing policy does impact his or her attitudes toward misconduct.

There is an even higher correlation, as indicated in Table 6–7, between an officer's perception of peer attitudes toward misconduct and the officer's

Table 6–6 Correlations Between Agency Policy and Officer Attitudes

	Correlation
Conflict of Interest awareness and knowledge of policy	.569**
Exploiting Authority awareness and knowledge of policy	.577**
Abuse of Authority awareness and knowledge of policy	.488**
Malfeasance awareness and knowledge of policy	.763**

**p < .05

Table 6-7 Correlations Between Officer Attitudes and Perceptions of Peer Attitudes

	Correlation
Conflict of Interest awareness and peer attitudes	.844**
Exploiting Authority awareness and peer attitudes	.775**
Abuse of Authority awareness and peer attitudes	.815**
Malfeasance awareness and peer attitudes	.721**

$**p < .05$

attitude toward misconduct. This very high correlation could be attributed to solidarity among officers within an agency, or it could be an officer projecting his or her own views on peers. To some extent, the former may be true given the low standard deviations and variances for exploiting authority and malfeasance. Standard deviations and variances are much higher, however, for conflict of interest and abuse of authority suggesting officers may be projecting views.

FACTORS THAT HAVE THE BIGGEST IMPACT ON ETHICAL AWARENESS

Thus far, this chapter has explored the independent variables separately (with the exception of years of service which is controlled for supervisory position). Two new variables are included in the regression model: the officer's perception of peer attitudes and the officer's perception of existing agency policy. Regression permits assessing the combined and relative impact of the independent variables. The regression model in Table 6–8 explores the predictive nature of all of the variables coupled with the variables explored in the previous section.

According to the conflict of interest model, 75% of an officer's attitude toward the seriousness of this type of misconduct can be explained by the variables included in the model. The other types of misconduct had high percentages as well, with 65% of the exploiting authority model, 70% of the abuse of authority model, and 70% of the malfeasance model explained by the independent variables.

Table 6-8 Ethical Awareness Regression

Independent Variables	Conflict of Interest $\beta(t)$	Exploiting Authority $\beta(t)$	Abuse of Authority $\beta(t)$	Malfeasance $\beta(t)$
Others' seriousness	.741 (68.927)**	.643 (51.647)**	.750 (67.564)**	.423 (35.064)**
Policy	.160 (14.793)**	.235 (18.922)**	.152 (13.697)**	.520 (43.186)**
Rank	.122 (11.580)**	.101 (8.182)**	.126 (10.943)**	.034 (2.958)**
Length of service	.007 (.667)	.012 (1.006)	-.020 (-1.792)	.004 (.333)
Agency size	-.014 (-1.539)	.008 (.702)	-.007 (-.646)	-.005 (-.459)
Adjusted R^2	.748	.653	.700	.703
F	1816.754	1151.997	1427.034	1449.488
s.e.	.606	.429	.605	.185

*$p < .05$
**$p < .01$

Regardless of the nature of the misconduct, the factors that influence an officer's attitudes toward misconduct the most consistently are the officer's perception of peer attitudes toward misconduct, the officer's perception of whether a policy exists within their agency, and the officer's rank. The officer's perception of peer attitudes is the strongest predictor for conflict of interest (β = .741), exploiting authority (β = .643), and abuse of authority (β = .750). The officer's perception of whether a policy exists within their agency is the strongest predictor for malfeasance misconduct (β = .520) with peer attitudes (β = .423) a close second. As indicated in the earlier discussion, when controlling for rank and supervisory status, length of service is not related to awareness. Also, agency size appears to have little, if any, separate impact on an officer's ethical awareness across all types of misconduct. Nonstandardized coefficients yielded similar results. Using stepwise and hierarchical regression did not impact these results.

The regression model is presumably impacted by the high correlation between an officer's own attitudes regarding the misconduct and the officer's perception of the peer's attitudes toward misconduct. Although excessively high levels of collinearity ($R^2 \geq .80$) are not present, R^2 comes dangerously close to the threshold. None of the correlations between these variables exceeds .90 eliminating singularity or perfect multicollinearity

(Tabachnick & Fidell, 2001). Still, in considering future regressions, care will be taken to distinguish between what may be a tightly clustered set of mutually reinforcing attitudes, on the one hand, and other more objectively measurable characteristics on the other.[1]

CONCLUSIONS

Descriptive statistics in this section have shown officers consistently believe abuse of authority is less serious than exploiting authority misconduct regardless of years of service, rank, supervisory position, or size of agency. This contradicts hypothesis 1, which asserts that the more serious the misconduct, the higher the officer's ethical awareness. Support can be found for hypothesis 1 in that exploiting authority, abuses of authority, and malfeasance consistently have higher means than conflict of interest.

Also, malfeasance consistently has the highest means. Officers from medium and large agencies, who have been in service longer and who are administrators, detectives, or supervisors tend to rate misconduct more seriously than other officers. These results lend partial support to hypotheses 2 and 3.

An officer's ethical awareness is most impacted by the nature of the misconduct and whether the officer is a supervisor. Other factors that contribute include the size of the officer's agency, the length of service, and the officer's rank. The longer an officer has been in service, the higher that officer's rank and supervisory position will have higher ethical awareness.

Finally, the size of the police agency has a negative impact on conflict of interest, whereas the size of agency has a positive impact on attitudes toward abuse of authority; therefore, officers in smaller agencies may view conflict of interest more seriously, whereas officers in larger agencies view abuse of authority more seriously. Table 6–8 explores the ethical awareness regression model that takes into consideration the officer's perception of peer attitudes and agency policy, rank, length of service, and agency size.

---

[1] A regression model that excludes perceptions regarding peer attitudes influences the results yielding an adjusted R^2 of .347 for conflict of interest, .280 for exploiting authority, .250 for abuse of authority, and .583 for malfeasance.

Analysis of association and comparison of mean ratings of seriousness, comparison of officer perceptions with objective measures of seriousness, and the regression model lend partial support to the first six hypotheses. Hypothesis 1 asserts that the more serious the misconduct, the higher an officer's ethical awareness. Malfeasance consistently has higher means than the other types of misconduct. Exploiting authority, however, was consistently rated more seriously than abuse of authority, contradicting hypothesis 1 in part.

Hypothesis 2 asserts that officers who are supervisors (or higher rank) will have higher ethical awareness. Both supervisors and managers had higher levels of ethical awareness, although they shared the same tendency, as observed in the overall sample to rate abuse of authority lower than exploiting authority. In subsequent chapters, only supervisor status will be used in cross-tabulations, and rank, which separates nonsupervisors from supervisors, will be used in regression. Rank impacted ethical awareness according to the regression model.

Hypothesis 3 asserts that length of service controlling for rank and supervisory position will have a curvilinear relationship with ethical awareness. The results support hypothesis 3 in that officers with less than 1 year of service consistently had higher ethical awareness than officers with 1 to 10 years of service. Also, officers with 11 or more years of service generally increased in ethical awareness, creating the curvilinear relationship hypothesized in this study.

Hypothesis 4 asserts that size of police agency will not impact an officer's ethical awareness. This hypothesis is supported by the data. There were no clear trends across the four measures. Size does not have a significant effect in the regression model.

Hypothesis 5 asserts that policy will impact an officer's ethical awareness, and this is supported by the data. The regression model shows awareness of policy as the second strongest predictor of ethical awareness. Hypothesis 6 asserts that an officer's perceptions regarding peer ethical awareness will impact an officer's ethical awareness. The regression model showed this variable to be the strongest predictor of an officer's ethical awareness.

What impact does an officer's ethical awareness have on an officer's ethical standards? Do officers feel as strongly about punishment for police misconduct as they do about the behavior itself? The following chapter explores ethical standards.

DISCUSSION QUESTIONS

1. What situational, organizational, and individual factors impact ethical awareness? Can you think of others not mentioned in this chapter?
2. Do you agree with the way the data is interpreted in this chapter? Do you think that these data help explain an officer's ethical awareness?
3. Were you surprised by any of the findings? Identify what surprised you and why it was surprising.
4. Should abuse of authority be considered more serious than exploiting authority? For example, should misuse of force be considered more serious than an officer receiving a day off from work in exchange for working on a supervisor's car?
5. How serious do you think the behavior depicted in each scenario is? Does your opinion mirror that of the typical officer?

REFERENCE

Tabachnick, B. G., & Fidell, L. S. (2001). *Using Multivariate Statistics*. Needham Heights, MA: Allyn & Bacon.

CHAPTER 7

Ethical Standards

OBJECTIVES

- Distinguish ethical standards from ethical awareness and action
- Identify the situational, individual, and organizational factors that impact ethical standards of police officers
- Analyze the National Institute of Justice data, and apply it to the ethical standards hypotheses
- Recognize the findings that were most surprising from the data analysis, including supervisory impact and conflicting views on punishment regarding misuse of force

The National Institute of Justice (NIJ) study addresses ethical standards through questions regarding punishment. Officers are asked to assess what punishment should follow from the various misconduct scenarios, as well as what punishment would follow the misconduct described and whether their agency has an established policy regarding the misconduct. Standards were measured in this study according to six categories of possible punishment for officer misconduct rated on a scale from one to six. Punishments offered as responses in the NIJ instrument include and are coded as follows:

1. No punishment
2. Verbal reprimand
3. Written reprimand
4. Period of suspension without pay
5. Demotion in rank
6. Dismissal

These are not the only punishment options available to agencies. For example, officers can be transferred to undesirable units, or requested transfers can be denied. This chapter focuses on responses to what punishment officers believe should follow misconduct and what punishment would follow. This chapter begins by analyzing the descriptive statistics for ethical standards followed by a regression model for ethical standards.

WHAT ARE ETHICAL STANDARDS FOR POLICE OFFICERS?

Hypotheses 7 through 13 focus on the relationship between ethical standards and the nature of the misconduct, as well as individual and organizational factors. These individual and organizational factors include supervisory position, rank, years of service, agency size, policy, ethical awareness, and perceptions of peer attitudes.

H7: The more serious the misconduct, the higher that officer's ethical standards.

H8: Officers who are supervisors will have higher ethical standards.

H9: An officer's length of service controlling for rank and supervisory status will have a curvilinear relationship to an officer's ethical standards.

H10: The size of the police agency will have no relationship to an officer's ethical standards.

H11: An officer's awareness of existing policies regarding misconduct will positively impact that officer's ethical standards.

H12: An officer's perceptions regarding peer ethical awareness and standards will positively impact that officer's ethical standards.

H13: The higher an officer's ethical awareness, the higher that officer's ethical standards.

Ethical standards are measured according to what an officer believes should be the punishment for misconduct. The ethical standards measure was created averaging all of the scenario responses regarding punishment that should follow misconduct. The scenarios fall into four categories, which include conflict of interest, exploiting authority, abuse of authority, and malfeasance, and means were used for the scenarios falling into each category.

SITUATIONAL, INDIVIDUAL, AND ORGANIZATIONAL FACTORS THAT AFFECT ETHICAL STANDARDS

How do officer attitudes regarding discipline compare against objective measures regarding misconduct? Objective measures would indicate that conflict of interest misconduct should warrant a verbal or written reprimand. Exploiting authority should receive at least a suspension without pay or perhaps a demotion in rank. Abuse of authority and malfeasance warrant dismissal.

The dependent variables are a little different when analyzing ethical standards as opposed to ethical awareness. First, ethical standards are not rated on a Likert-type scale, but are actual categories of punishment. Second, ethical standards are measured on a scale from 1 to 6, which increases in severity. Table 7–1 uses the same four types of ethical awareness misconduct as dependent variables.

As with ethical awareness, respondents generally view exploiting authority as more serious than abuse of authority. A majority of respondents (69%) rate exploiting authority as deserving suspension without

---

Table 7–1 Ethical Standards Dependent Variable Summary

(1) no punishment (2) verbal reprimand (3) written reprimand
(4) period of suspension without pay (5) demotion in rank (6) dismissal

	Conflict of Interest	Exploiting Authority	Abuse of Authority	Malfeasance
No punishment 1.5	28.7% (889)	0.5% (17)	8.7% (270)	0.2% (7)
Verbal reprimand 1.6–2.5	42.2% (1310)*	4.6% (143)	23.1% (715)	0.3% (8)
Written reprimand 2.6–3.5	19.3% (598)	25.8% (800)	33.3% (1032)*	3.0% (92)
Suspension without pay 3.6–4.5	7.1% (220)	38.9% (1205)*	24.5% (759)	14.9% (464)
Demotion or dismissal 4.6–6	2.7% (83)	30.2% (935)	10.4% (323)	81.6% (2532)*
Means	2.33	4.00	3.29	5.22

*largest percentage/(n)

pay, demotion, or dismissal. Only half as many respondents (35%) rate abuse of authority as deserving the same disciplinary actions. These results contradict objective measures that rate abuse of authority as deserving demotion or dismissal. These results also contradict hypothesis 5, which posits that the more serious the misconduct, the higher the ethical standards for officers.

Unlike the ethical awareness results, in which respondents view exploiting authority as almost as serious as malfeasance, respondents do not view exploiting authority as deserving the same level of punishment as malfeasance. An overwhelming majority of respondents (82%) indicate malfeasance deserves demotion or dismissal, whereas only 30% indicate that exploiting authority deserves demotion or dismissal. This finding may suggest that attitude about discipline is a more demanding measure of ethical attitudes than awareness. In support of hypothesis 5, exploiting authority, abuse of authority, and malfeasance are all rated as deserving more punishment than conflict of interest, and malfeasance is rated as deserving the strongest punishment.

Objective measures would dictate a verbal or written reprimand for conflict of interest misconduct. Less than a majority of respondents (42%), however, believe that conflict of interest deserves a verbal reprimand, and even fewer (19%) would give a written reprimand.

Supervisors are the individuals responsible for determining, administering and enforcing the appropriate punishment for officer misconduct. This responsibility gives the supervisor a somewhat different perspective with respect to punishment. Table 7–2 explores the impact of supervisory position has on ethical standards.

There are important differences in attitudes between supervisors and nonsupervisors. A third of supervisors view abuse of authority as deserving suspension without pay (34%) compared with 22% of nonsupervisors. These results show support for hypothesis 8, which asserts that supervisors will have higher ethical standards than nonsupervisors.

Exploiting authority is viewed as deserving high levels of punishment by supervisors where 45% of supervisors would punish officers who exploit authority with either demotion or dismissal. Meanwhile, 27% of nonsupervisors rate exploitation of authority as deserving the same form of punishment. Regardless of supervisory position, respondents rate abuse of authority as deserving less punishment than exploiting authority. These results contradict hypothesis 7 in part as ethical standards did not increase steadily where

Table 7–2 Ethical Standards and Supervisory Position

(1) no punishment (2) verbal reprimand (3) written reprimand
(4) period of suspension without pay (5) demotion in rank (6) dismissal

	Conflict of Interest	Exploiting Authority	Abuse of Authority	Malfeasance
Supervisor				
No punishment 1.5	13.9% (85)	0.0% (0)	4.6% (28)	0.0% (0)
Verbal reprimand 1.6–2.5	39.6% (243)*	1.2% (7)	16.8% (103)	0.2% (1)
Written reprimand 2.6–3.5	27.7% (170)	15.8% (97)	32.2% (198)	0.8% (5)
Suspension without pay 3.6–4.5	13.1% (80)	37.9% (233)	33.9% (208)*	6.5% (40)
Demotion or dismissal 4.6–6	5.7% (35)	45.1% (277)*	12.5% (77)	92.5% (568)*
Means	2.78*	4.36*	3.55*	5.56*
Nonsupervisor				
No punishment 1.5	32.4% (801)	0.7% (17)	9.7% (240)	0.3% (7)
Verbal reprimand 1.6–2.5	42.9% (1059)*	5.5% (136)	24.8% (611)	0.3% (7)
Written reprimand 2.6–3.5	17.2% (425)	28.3% (700)	33.5% (828)*	3.5% (87)
Suspension without pay 3.6–4.5	5.6% (137)	39.0% (962)*	22.2% (547)	17.1% (422)
Demotion or dismissal 4.6–6	1.9% (48)	26.5% (654)	9.8% (242)	78.8% (1949)*
Means	2.22	3.91	3.21	5.13
Gamma	.363**	.303**	.221**	.411**

*largest percentage/(n)/mean
**p < .05

misconduct became more serious. There is partial support for hypothesis 7 in that malfeasance, abuse of authority, and exploiting authority all rated higher means for harsher punishment than conflict of interest.

Only two in five supervisors (40%) rate conflict of interest as deserving a verbal reprimand, and approximately the same percentage of nonsupervisors (43%) rate conflict of interest as deserving the same discipline. The difference between supervisors and nonsupervisors within conflict of interest can be seen in the percentage of supervisors (14%) and nonsupervisors (32%)

that believe no punishment is warranted for conflict of interest violations. These results lend further support to hypothesis 8, showing supervisors to be more ethically aware than nonsupervisors.

As was the case for ethical awareness, means for ethical standards are higher with supervisors than with nonsupervisors. The difference between means for supervisors and nonsupervisors is larger for conflict of interest than the other types of misconduct with the least difference in means with respect to malfeasance. This was also the case with ethical awareness, indicating more agreement among respondents with respect to malfeasance and less agreement with respect to conflict of interest.

As was the case within ethical awareness, gamma scores are moderately strong across all types of misconduct. Abuse of authority gamma weights are the lowest of the four scores, indicating the weakest relationship. These results support a positive relationship between supervisory position and an officer's attitude toward punishment for misconduct. As noted in Chapter 4, rank will be explored further in the regression model later in this chapter.

What relationship, if any, will there be between years of service and punishment? A curvilinear relationship appeared in Chapter 4 between ethical awareness and years of service. Ethical standards, however, are different as previously demonstrated. Years of service controlling for supervisory status are explored in Table 7–3.

Regardless of the number of years officers have served, respondents rate exploitation of authority as deserving more punishment than abuse of authority. These results contradict hypothesis 7 with respect to the nature of the misconduct coinciding with ethical standards. A third of officers with less than 1 year of service and a third of officers with more than 20 years of service rate exploitation of authority as deserving either demotion or dismissal as compared with about a quarter of officers with 1 to 10 years of service rate exploiting authority as deserving either a written reprimand or suspension without pay. Gamma scores are weak as was the case with ethical awareness, suggesting that a nonlinear relationship is possible. These results indicate a curvilinear relationship and support hypothesis 8.

There is no curvilinear relationship within conflict of interest or abuse of authority. There is, however, a fairly substantial gap between attitudes of officers with less than 1 year of service (48% verbal reprimand) and officers with 1 to 2 years of service (38% verbal reprimand) with respect

---

Table 7–3 Ethical Standards and Years of Service: Nonsupervisors Only

(1) no punishment (2) verbal reprimand (3) written reprimand
(4) period of suspension without pay (5) demotion in rank (6) dismissal

	Conflict of Interest	Exploiting Authority	Abuse of Authority	Malfeasance
Less than 1 Year				
No punishment				
1.5	29.5% (38)	0.8% (1)	2.3% (3)	0.8% (1)
Verbal reprimand				
1.6–2.5	48.1% (62)*	3.1% (4)	24.0% (31)	0.0% (0)
Written reprimand				
2.6–3.5	14.7% (19)	23.2% (30)	29.5% (38)*	1.6% (2)
Suspension without pay				
3.6–4.5	5.4% (7)	40.3% (52)*	22.5% (29)	20.9% (27)
Demotion or dismissal				
4.6–6	2.3% (3)	32.6% (42)	21.7% (28)	76.7% (99)*
Means	2.26	4.05	3.59*	5.11
1–2 Years				
No punishment				
1.5	38.8% (93)*	1.2% (3)	8.0% (19)	0.4% (1)
Verbal reprimand				
1.6–2.5	38.3% (92)	5.7% (14)	29.3% (70)	0.4% (1)
Written reprimand				
2.6–3.5	10.4% (25)	31.8% (76)	30.5% (73)*	5.4% (13)
Suspension without pay				
3.6–4.5	8.3% (20)	36.4% (87)*	19.2% (46)	22.9% (55)
Demotion or dismissal				
4.6–6	3.3% (10)	24.7% (59)	13.0% (31)	70.9% (170)*
Means	2.20	3.86	3.28	4.95
3–5 Years				
No punishment				
1.5	38.9% (182)	1.1% (5)	13.4% (63)	0.4% (2)
Verbal reprimand				
1.6–2.5	41.4% (194)*	7.4% (35)	24.9% (117)	0.4% (2)
Written reprimand				
2.6–3.5	15.6% (73)	33.4% (157)	31.3% (147)*	5.8% (27)
Suspension without pay				
3.6–4.5	2.4% (11)	34.3% (161)*	21.5% (101)	22.1% (104)
Demotion or dismissal				
4.6–6	1.7% (8)	23.8% (112)	8.9% (42)	71.3% (335)*
Means	2.05	3.77	3.12	4.94

(continues)

Table 7–3 Ethical Standards and Years of Service: Nonsupervisors Only (continued)

	Conflict of Interest	Exploiting Authority	Abuse of Authority	Malfeasance
6–10 Years				
No punishment 1.5	34.0% (239)	0.3% (2)	9.9% (69)	0.0% (0)
Verbal reprimand 1.6–2.5	45.5% (320)*	5.3% (37)	24.1% (169)	0.0% (0)
Written reprimand 2.6–3.5	15.7% (110)	30.0% (210)	35.7% (250)*	3.3% (23)
Suspension without pay 3.6–4.5	3.7% (26)	39.9% (280)*	22.3% (156)	13.8% (97)
Demotion or dismissal 4.6–6	1.1% (8)	24.5% (172)	8.0% (56)	82.9% (583)*
Means	2.12	3.88	3.18	5.19
11–15 Years				
No punishment 1.5	28.9% (110)	0.5% (2)	11.0% (42)	0.3% (1)
Verbal reprimand 1.6–2.5	44.1% (168)*	4.5% (17)	23.3% (89)	0.0% (0)
Written reprimand 2.6–3.5	17.8% (68)	26.7% (102)	35.6% (136)*	2.3% (9)
Suspension without pay 3.6–4.5	8.4% (32)	40.3% (154)*	21.2% (81)	17.8% (68)
Demotion or dismissal 4.6–6	0.8% (3)	28.0% (107)	8.9% (34)	79.6% (304)*
Means	2.26	3.99	3.17	5.17
16–20 Years				
No punishment 1.5	28.7% (76)	0.8% (2)	9.5% (25)	0.0% (0)
Verbal reprimand 1.6–2.5	41.9% (111)*	6.4% (17)	25.7% (68)	1.1% (3)
Written reprimand 2.6–3.5	20.8% (55)	23.5% (62)	32.6% (86)*	2.7% (7)
Suspension without pay 3.6–4.5	7.5% (20)	41.7% (110)*	23.1% (61)	14.8% (39)
Demotion or dismissal 4.6–6	1.1% (3)	27.6% (73)	9.1% (24)	81.4% (215)*
Means	2.31	3.93	3.23	5.25

(continues)

Table 7–3 (continued)

	Conflict of Interest	Exploiting Authority	Abuse of Authority	Malfeasance
Over 20 Years				
No punishment				
1.5	22.1% (60)	0.7% (2)	6.6% (18)	0.7% (2)
Verbal reprimand				
1.6–2.5	40.4% (110)*	4.4% (12)	24.3% (66)	0.4% (1)
Written reprimand				
2.6–3.5	25.7% (70)	21.7% (59)	35.3% (96)*	2.2% (6)
Suspension without pay				
3.6–4.5	7.0% (19)	41.6% (113)*	25.0% (68)	11.8% (32)
Demotion or dismissal				
4.6–6	4.8% (13)	31.6% (86)	8.8% (24)	84.9% (231)*
Means	2.56*	4.08*	3.29	5.32*
Gamma[1]	.116**	.064**	–.001	.133**

[1]Gamma scores for supervisors are .142** for conflict of interest, .096** for exploiting authority, .068 for abuse of authority, and .142** for malfeasance.

*largest percentage/(n)/mean

**$p < .05$

to conflict of interest. There is also a gap in attitudes between officers with 3 to 5 years of service (31% written reprimand) and 6 to 10 years of service (36% written reprimand) with respect to abuse of authority. These results, however, contradict hypothesis 9.

As for malfeasance, there is little variation in this category of misconduct. A majority of all officers, regardless of years of service, believe that this type of misconduct deserves demotion or dismissal. The variation occurs in the percentages of officers who believe that this type of misconduct warrants suspension without pay or some other lesser punishment. Officers with 1 to 5 years of service (71%) have the lowest percentages of officers that choose demotion or dismissal. Officers with less than 1 year of service (77%) and officers with over 6 years of service (80% to 85%) have higher percentages of respondents that recommend demotion or dismissal. These results show partial support for hypothesis 9 that there is a curvilinear relationship between ethical standards and years of service.

As was the case with ethical awareness, there is gap in means across all types of misconduct between officers who have been in service for less than 1 year and officers who have been in service for 1 to 2 years. Means continue to drop with officers who have 3 to 4 years of service and then rise steadily after 6 years of service. The differences in means are less pronounced here than with ethical awareness. Still, these results show some support for hypothesis 9.

There was no relationship between ethical awareness and agency size. It is hypothesized that the same will be true with ethical standards. Table 7–4 explores whether a relationship exists between agency size and an officer's ethical standards.

Regardless of agency size, the majority of respondents rate exploitation of authority as deserving more punishment than abuse of authority. A third of respondents from large agencies rate abuse of authority as deserving suspension without pay as compared with only 12% of respondents in very small and small agencies. Medium and very large agencies had comparable results with 27% and 25%, respectively. These results are still below an expected objective measure of demotion or dismissal and are in contradiction with hypothesis 7 that the more serious the misconduct, the higher the officer's ethical standards.

Exploiting authority results are similar, with 45% of respondents from large agencies rating exploiting authority as deserving demotion or dismissal. This is in comparison to 19% of respondents at small agencies and 25% of respondents at very small agencies. Respondents at medium-size agencies and very large agencies fared a little better, with 30% to 32% of respondents rating exploiting authority as deserving demotion or dismissal. The results for abuse of authority and exploiting authority show somewhat of a linear progression based on size of agency; however, this is the only trend that emerges from all of the results.

Conflict of interest results show no clear pattern. A majority of very small agencies (58%) and small agencies (51%) view conflict of interest as deserving a verbal reprimand. Meanwhile, respondents from medium to very large agencies had lower percentages ranging from 36% to 46% of respondents choosing verbal reprimand. Gamma scores are weak and somewhat mixed as with ethical awareness. These results support hypothesis 9 showing no clear pattern, particularly when compared with the results from the previous chapter on ethical awareness.

Table 7–4 Ethical Standards and Agency Size

(1) no punishment (2) verbal reprimand (3) written reprimand
(4) period of suspension without pay (5) demotion in rank (6) dismissal

(n, # of agencies)	Conflict of Interest	Exploiting Authority	Abuse of Authority	Malfeasance
Very Small, <25 officers (87, 8)				
No punishment 1.5	9.2% (8)	0.0% (0)	20.7% (18)	0.0% (0)
Verbal reprimand 1.6–2.5	57.5% (50)*	9.2% (8)	29.9% (26)	0.0% (0)
Written reprimand 2.6–3.5	24.1% (21)	28.7% (25)	33.3% (29)*	3.4% (3)
Suspension without pay 3.6–4.5	4.6% (4)	36.8% (32)*	11.5% (10)	23.0% (20)
Demotion or dismissal 4.6–6	4.6% (4)	25.3% (22)	4.6% (4)	73.6% (64)*
Means	2.59	3.81	2.68	4.96
Small, 25–75 officers (212, 9)				
No punishment 1.5	26.4% (56)	1.0% (2)	16.0% (34)	0.5% (1)
Verbal reprimand 1.6–2.5	51.4% (109)*	7.1% (15)	38.2% (81)*	0.9% (2)
Written reprimand 2.6–3.5	17.5% (37)	31.6% (67)	28.8% (61)	2.4% (5)
Suspension without pay 3.6–4.5	3.8% (8)	41.0% (87)*	12.3% (26)	21.2% (45)
Demotion or dismissal 4.6–6	0.9% (2)	19.3% (41)	4.7% (10)	75.0% (159)*
Means	2.22	3.74	2.75	4.99
Medium, 76–200 officers (344, 6)				
No punishment 1.5	22.7% (78)	0.3% (1)	5.3% (18)	0.0% (0)
Verbal reprimand 1.6–2.5	45.6% (157)*	2.6% (9)	21.9% (75)	0.0% (0)
Written reprimand 2.6–3.5	22.4% (77)	30.9% (106)	33.5% (115)*	2.9% (10)
Suspension without pay 3.6–4.5	7.0% (24)	33.8% (116)*	26.8% (92)	15.2% (52)
Demotion or dismissal 4.6–6	2.3% (8)	32.4% (111)	12.5% (43)	81.9% (281)*
Means	2.42	4.07	3.43	5.28

(continues)

Table 7-4 Ethical Standards and Agency Size (continued)

(n, # of agencies)	Conflict of Interest	Exploiting Authority	Abuse of Authority	Malfeasance
Large, 201–500 officers (235, 2)				
No punishment				
1.5	12.8% (30)	0.0% (0)	8.5% (20)	0.0% (0)
Verbal reprimand				
1.6–2.5	35.5% (83)*	4.7% (11)	18.7% (44)	0.0% (0)
Written reprimand				
2.6–3.5	20.5% (48)	24.2% (57)	24.7% (58)	4.3% (10)
Suspension without pay				
3.6–4.5	20.9% (49)	26.0% (61)	29.4% (69)*	13.2% (31)
Demotion or dismissal				
4.6–6	10.3% (24)	45.1% (106)*	18.7% (44)	82.5% (194)*
Means	3.02*	4.24*	3.56*	5.30*
Very Large, >500 officers (2229, 5)				
No punishment				
1.5	32.2% (717)	0.6% (14)	8.1% (180)	0.3% (6)
Verbal reprimand				
1.6–2.5	41.0% (911)*	4.5% (100)	22.0% (489)	0.3% (6)
Written reprimand				
2.6–3.5	18.7% (415)	24.5% (545)	34.6% (769)*	2.9% (64)
Suspension without pay				
3.6–4.5	6.1% (135)	40.9% (909)*	25.3% (562)	14.2% (316)
Demotion or dismissal				
4.6–6	2.0% (45)	29.5% (655)	10.0% (222)	82.3% (1834)*
Means	2.24	4.00	3.31	5.23
Gamma	−.147**	.030	.088**	.059**

*largest percentage/(n)/mean

**$p < .05$

As with ethical awareness, large agencies have the highest overall means, and medium agencies have the second highest overall means. Very small and small agencies hold the lowest overall means. These results were similar to ethical awareness overall. These results suggest there may be a relationship between agency size and ethical standards, which contradicts hypothesis 10.

The trends that do occur include respondents rating exploiting authority, abuse of authority, and malfeasance as deserving more punishment than conflict of interest. Exploiting authority is rated as deserving more punishment than abuse of authority and almost deserving as much punishment as malfeasance. Although exploiting authority has a majority of officers rating it as deserving high levels of punishment, the percentages are much lower than those rating malfeasance as deserving the most serious punishment.

Officer perceptions of existing agency policy and officer perceptions of peer attitudes toward punishment will be used in the regression model explored in the section that follows. Correlations between agency policy and an officer's attitude toward punishment are shown in Table 7–5. The strong correlations show that an officer's awareness of existing agency policies regarding punishment impacts the officer's attitudes toward punishment for misconduct.

Correlations are very high, as was the case with ethical awareness, between an officer's perception of peer attitudes toward punishment and the officer's attitude toward punishment, as shown in Table 7–6.

Table 7–5 Correlations Between Agency Policy and Officer Attitudes toward Punishment

	Conflict of Interest
Conflict of Interest and knowledge of policy	.549**
Exploiting Authority and knowledge of policy	.460**
Abuse of Authority and knowledge of policy	.477**
Malfeasance and knowledge of policy	.327**
**p < .05	

Table 7–6 Correlations Between Officer Attitudes and Perceptions of Peer Attitudes

	Conflict of Interest
Conflict of Interest and peer attitudes	.753**
Exploiting Authority and peer attitudes	.828**
Abuse of Authority and peer attitudes	.726**
Malfeasance and peer attitudes	.787**
**p < .05	

FACTORS THAT HAVE THE BIGGEST IMPACT ON ETHICAL STANDARDS

Thus far, this chapter has explored supervisory position, years of service, and agency size with respect to ethical standards. What impact does the officer's perception of peer attitudes toward punishment have on the officer's attitude toward punishment? What impact does the officer's perception of policy have on the officer's ethical standards? The regression model that follows in Table 7–7 explores the predictive nature of these variables coupled with the variables explored in the previous section.

As with the ethical awareness models, high percentages of an officer's attitude toward punishment can be explained by the variables included in the model. Regardless of the nature of the misconduct, the factors that influence an officer's attitudes toward misconduct the most consistently are the officer's perception of peer attitudes toward punishing misconduct, the officer's perception of the seriousness of the misconduct, the officer's perception of whether a policy exists within their agency (although it is

Table 7–7 Ethical Standards Regression

Independent Variables	Conflict of Interest $\beta(t)$	Exploiting Authority $\beta(t)$	Abuse of Authority $\beta(t)$	Malfeasance $\beta(t)$
Others' standards	.510 (40.604)**	.698 (65.149)**	.526 (41.135)**	.713 (60.162)**
Own seriousness	.481 (25.884)**	.349 (23.392)**	.440 (24.103)**	.211 (10.902)**
Others' seriousness	-.005 (-.280)	-.046 (-3.111)**	.027 (1.476)	-.005 (-.296)
Policy	-.033 (-2.623)**	-.034 (-3.099)**	-.036 (-2.919)**	-.047 (-2.870)**
Rank	.057 (5.157)**	.036 (3.479)**	.063 (5.298)**	.083 (6.758)**
Length of service	.015 (1.362)	.025 (2.480)*	.012 (1.065)	.034 (2.824)**
Agency size	.000 (.016)	.015 (1.650)	-.006 (-.620)	.027 (2.539)*
Adjusted R^2	.736	.765	.699	.660
F	1210.331	1420.297	1008.897	848.011
s.e.	.512	.463	.597	.494

*$p < .05$
**$p < .01$

weak and negative), and the officer's rank. These results lend partial support to hypotheses 12, 11, 8, and 9, respectively.

The officer's perception of peer attitudes regarding punishment is the strongest predictor regardless of the type of misconduct. The officer's perception of whether a policy exists within their agency is a much weaker predictor than was the case within the ethical awareness models. The officer's perception of peer seriousness of misconduct, the officer's length of service, and agency size have mixed results with some influence depending on the type of misconduct. Nonstandardized coefficients yielded similar results. Using stepwise and hierarchical regression did not impact these results.

The regression model may be impacted by the high correlation between an officer's own attitudes regarding punishment and the officer's perception of the peer's attitudes toward punishment.[1] Although high levels of collinearity ($R^2 \geq .80$) are not present, R^2 comes dangerously close to the threshold. None of the correlations between these variables exceeds .90 eliminating singularity or perfect multicollinearity (Tabachnick & Fidell, 2001).

CONCLUSIONS

Hypothesis 7 asserts that there is a relationship between types of misconduct and ethical standards. The more serious is the misconduct, the higher an officer's ethical standards. There is partial support for this hypothesis as was the case with ethical awareness. Again, consistently across all analysis, officers found exploiting authority should warrant higher punishment than abuse of authority. Exploiting authority, abuse of authority, and malfeasance all rated higher than conflict of interest and malfeasance always rated the highest; therefore, partial support could be found for hypothesis 7.

Hypothesis 8 asserts that supervisory position will affect an officer's ethical standards. Hypothesis 9 posits that an officer's ethical standards will have a curvilinear relationship to length of service. Partial support can

---

[1] A regression model that excludes perceptions regarding peer attitudes influences the results yielding an adjusted R^2 of .582 for conflict of interest, .417 for exploiting authority, .518 for abuse of authority, and .225 for malfeasance.

be found for these hypotheses. Supervisors were found to have higher means and percentages compared with objective measures. Managers recommended harsher punishments than regular officers lending support for hypothesis 8. Officers with less than 1 year of service showed the same results as with ethical awareness recommending harsher punishment than officers with 1 to 5 years of experience. Officers with 11 years of service and higher did consistently recommend harsher punishment than officers with less experience.

Hypothesis 10 asserts that there is no relationship between the size of agency and an officer's ethical standards. There is partial support for this hypothesis. There were some trends with ethical awareness and standards with respect to means, suggesting that hypothesis 10 is unsupported; however, analysis of percentages according to objective measures show only mixed results with no clear trends amongst percentages. The regression model also gives only mixed results showing little or no relationship between size of agency and ethical standards.

Hypothesis 10 asserts a relationship between an officer's ethical standards and that officer's awareness of existing agency policies. The regression model shows a weak link with only limited support for hypothesis 11; however, there is a strong relationship between an officer's ethical standards and an officer's perception of peer standards in support of hypothesis 12. There is also a strong relationship between an officer's ethical standards and the officer's ethical awareness in support of hypothesis 13.

Thus far Chapters 6 and 7 have analyzed individual and organizational factors in order to determine the effect on an officer's ethical awareness and standards. Knowing the attitudes of officers regarding the severity of misconduct, the punishment that should follow misconduct, and the punishment that would follow misconduct, what impact does this information have on an officer's willingness to report the misconduct in question?

DISCUSSION QUESTIONS

1. What situational, individual, and organizational factors impact ethical standards? Can you think of others not mentioned in this chapter?
2. Do you agree with the way the data is interpreted in this chapter? Do you think these data help explain an officer's ethical standards?
3. Were you surprised by any of the findings? Identify what surprised you and why it was surprising.

4. Should abuse of authority receive harsher punishment than exploiting authority?
5. What punishment do you think should follow each of the scenarios in the NIJ study? Are you in agreement with the typical officer?

REFERENCE

Tabachnick, B. G., & Fidell, L. S. (2001). *Using Multivariate Statistics*. Needham Heights, MA: Allyn & Bacon.

CHAPTER 8

Ethical Action

OBJECTIVES

- Distinguish ethical action from ethical awareness and standards
- Identify the situational, individual, and organizational factors that impact the ethical actions of police officers
- Analyze the National Institute of Justice data and apply it to the ethical action hypotheses
- Recognize the findings that were most surprising from the data analysis, including supervisory impact and conflicting views of a police officer's willingness to report misuse of force

This chapter theorizes that an officer's ethical action is shaped by attitudes toward misconduct and punishment. As mentioned in Chapter 5, an officer is more likely to break the code of silence if expected by his or her peers to do so and if it will be sustained by appropriate official disciplinary action. Thus far, this book has analyzed officer attitudes regarding seriousness of misconduct and punishment. The focus of this chapter now shifts to consider officer behavior, specifically, an officer's willingness to report peer misconduct.

Ethical action can take many forms. Officers could choose to counsel a fellow officer who has committed misconduct or seek help for the offending officer. Reporting misconduct is just one of many choices an officer can make under the circumstances. Within the context of this study, however, it is the only action available for analysis.

WHAT IS CONSIDERED ETHICAL FOR A POLICE OFFICER?

Ethical action is impacted by the nature of the misconduct, individual factors, situational factors, and organizational factors. These variables are explored in the following hypotheses:

H14: The more serious the misconduct, the greater the likelihood of an officer's ethical action.

H15: Officers who are supervisor are more likely to take ethical action.

H16: An officer's length of service controlling for rank and supervisory status will have a curvilinear relationship to the officer's ethical action.

H17: The size of the police agency will have no relationship to an officer's ethical action.

H18: An officer's awareness of existing policies regarding misconduct will positively impact that officer's willingness to take ethical action.

H19: An officer's ethical and perceptions regarding peer ethical awareness, standards, and action will positively impact that officer's willingness to take ethical action.

H20: The higher the officer's ethical awareness and standards, the greater the likelihood of an officer's ethical action.

The scenarios fall into four categories, which include conflict of interest, exploiting authority, abuse of authority, and malfeasance, and means were used for the scenarios falling into each category.

SITUATIONAL, INDIVIDUAL, AND ORGANIZATIONAL FACTORS THAT AFFECT WHETHER A POLICE OFFICER WILL TAKE ETHICAL ACTION

Ethical action is measured similarly to ethical awareness. Respondents were asked how willing they would be to report the misconduct based on a five-point Likert-type scale with one equaling definitely unwilling to report and five equaling definitely willing to report. Objective measures would suggest that any violation of office policy and any misconduct would warrant reporting that misconduct.

Believing that behavior is serious and deserves harsh punishment is much different from actually reporting misconduct. The same dependent variables are explored in this chapter as in the previous two chapters. The Likert-type scale used gives respondents an opportunity to rate their level of willingness to report peer misconduct. Table 8–1 reports ethical action results.

Respondents are more willing to report exploiting authority (35%) than abuse of authority (11%). This contradicts hypothesis 12, which asserts that the more serious the misconduct, the more likely an officer is willing to report it. In support of hypothesis 12, a majority of respondents (65%) are definitely willing to report malfeasance. Nearly a majority of respondents (49%) are definitely unwilling to report conflict of interest misconduct.

Results are somewhat mixed for exploiting authority and abuse of authority. A little less than one third of respondents (29%) would probably report exploiting authority misconduct as compared with 16% of respondents who would probably report abuse of authority. A little more than a third (35%) of respondents would definitely report exploiting authority misconduct as compared with 11% of respondents who would definitely report abuse of authority. As many as 24% of respondents are unwilling to report abuse of authority as compared with 8% of respondents who are unwilling to report exploiting authority. The largest percentage of respondents within abuse of authority (27%) might be willing to report, but are

Table 8–1 Ethical Action Dependent Variable Summary

	(1) Definitely would not report–(5) Definitely would report			
	Conflict of Interest	Exploiting Authority	Abuse of Authority	Malfeasance
Definitely would not report 1.5	48.5% (1503)*	8.2% (253)	24.2% (749)	5.0% (154)
Probably would not report 1.6–2.5	22.9% (710)	10.4% (324)	21.3% (659)	4.8% (150)
Might/might not report 2.6–3.5	15.3% (475)	17.9% (554)	27.2% (844)*	7.3% (226)
Probably would report 3.6–4.5	7.8% (243)	28.6% (888)	16.0% (497)	17.7% (551)
Definitely would report 4.6–5	5.5% (171)	34.9% (1082)*	11.3% (350)	65.2% (2023)*
Means	2.15	3.71	2.87	4.32

*largest percentage/(n)

not certain, as compared with 18% within the exploiting authority category. These results contradict objective measures that rate exploiting authority as serious and abuse of authority as very serious.

These results also contradict hypothesis 12, which posits that the more serious the misconduct, the more willing officers will be to report that misconduct. In support of hypothesis 12, respondents are most willing to report malfeasance and least willing to report conflict of interest. Also, respondents are more willing to report exploiting authority and abuse of authority than they are willing to report conflict of interest.

Reporting misconduct may be as difficult an action for supervisors as for officers. Supervisors ultimately are the persons responsible for carrying out punishment, as noted in Chapter 5. Whether supervisors are more willing than officers to take ethical action is explored in Table 8–2.

In support of hypothesis 15, there is a difference between supervisor and nonsupervisor ethical action. A majority of supervisors (64%) would definitely report exploiting authority as compared with less than a third (28%) of nonsupervisors. An overwhelming majority of supervisors (88%) would definitely report malfeasance, as opposed to 59% of nonsupervisors. As for conflict of interest, 34% of supervisors probably would or definitely would report, whereas only 8% of nonsupervisors feel the same way.

Means are consistent with results reported for ethical awareness and standards. Supervisors have higher means than nonsupervisors. Meanwhile, gamma scores are higher here than in any variables explored thus far. Gamma weights for abuse of authority remain the weakest. Regardless of supervisory position, respondents are more willing to report exploiting authority than abuse of authority, which contradicts hypothesis 14. These results are consistent with ethical awareness and standards.

Will new officers be willing to report misconduct? Considering that most, if not all, new officers are on probation during the first 6 months or so of their careers, it is unclear whether the curvilinear relationship will hold up within ethical action. Table 8–3 explores the impact years of service has on ethical action when controlling for supervisory position.

Analysis of years of service yields mixed results. Generally, regardless of years of service, respondents are more willing to report exploiting authority than abuse of authority in contradiction to hypothesis 14. A majority of respondents, regardless of years of service, would definitely report malfeasance. A majority of respondents with 1 to 15 years of service would definitely not report conflict of interest. Respondents are more

Table 8–2 Ethical Action and Supervisory Position

(1) Definitely would not report–(5) Definitely would report

	Conflict of Interest	Exploiting Authority	Abuse of Authority	Malfeasance
Supervisor				
Definitely would not report 1.5	22.1% (136)	1.5% (9)	12.4% (76)	1.0% (6)
Probably would not report 1.6–2.5	21.1% (129)	3.9% (24)	15.8% (97)	1.3% (8)
Might/might not report 2.6–3.5	22.4% (138)*	6.2% (38)	26.7% (164)*	2.1% (13)
Probably would report 3.6–4.5	17.1% (105)	24.6% (151)	22.8% (140)	7.2% (44)
Definitely would report 4.6–5	17.3% (106)	63.8% (392)*	22.3% (137)	88.4% (543)*
Means	3.03*	4.45*	3.45*	4.79*
Nonsupervisor				
Definitely would not report 1.5	55.1% (1363)*	9.9% (244)	27.2% (671)	6.0% (148)
Probably would not report 1.6–2.5	23.4% (577)	12.1% (299)	22.8% (561)	5.7% (142)
Might/might not report 2.6–3.5	13.4% (331)	20.8% (514)	27.3% (674)*	8.6% (212)
Probably would report 3.6–4.5	5.5% (136)	29.6% (732)*	14.3% (354)	20.4% (504)
Definitely would report 4.6–5	2.6% (64)	27.6% (681)	8.4% (208)	59.3% (1467)*
Means	1.93	3.53	2.72	4.20
Gamma	.529**	.548**	.362**	.604**

*largest percentage/(n)/mean
**$p < .05$

willing to report exploiting authority, abuse of authority, and malfeasance in support of hypothesis 14. These results are somewhat consistent with ethical awareness and standards results.

Results are less clear with respect to exploiting authority and abuse of authority. A majority of officers with 6 to 20 years of service probably would report or definitely would report exploiting authority misconduct, whereas a majority of respondents with more than 20 years of service would definitely report misconduct. The remaining respondents are split

Table 8–3 Ethical Action and Years of Service: Nonsupervisors Only

(1) Definitely would not report–(5) Definitely would report

	Conflict of Interest	Exploiting Authority	Abuse of Authority	Malfeasance
Less than 1 Year				
Definitely would not report 1.5	48.1% (62)	3.1% (4)	15.5% (20)	1.6% (2)
Probably would not report 1.6–2.5	33.3% (43)	8.5% (11)	22.5% (29)	2.3% (3)
Might/might not report 2.6–3.5	9.3% (12)	24.8% (32)	26.3% (34)*	10.8% (14)
Probably would report 3.6–4.5	8.5% (11)	35.7% (46)*	24.8% (32)	22.5% (29)
Definitely would report 4.6–5	0.8% (1)	27.9% (36)	10.9% (14)	62.8% (81)*
Means	1.97	3.74	3.11*	4.37
1–2 Years				
Definitely would not report 1.5	55.4% (133)*	11.3% (27)	27.6% (66)	7.1% (17)
Probably would not report 1.6–2.5	25.4% (61)	16.7% (40)	23.0% (55)	8.3% (20)
Might/might not report 2.6–3.5	11.7% (28)	21.8% (52)	28.5% (68)*	10.4% (25)
Probably would report 3.6–4.5	5.0% (12)	28.9% (69)*	13.0% (31)	24.2% (58)
Definitely would report 4.6–5	2.5% (6)	21.3% (51)	7.9% (19)	50.0% (120)*
Means	1.89	3.32	2.71	4.02
3–5 Years				
Definitely would not report 1.5	61.5% (288)*	13.8% (65)	34.2% (161)*	9.2% (43)
Probably would not report 1.6–2.5	20.7% (97)	13.6% (64)	19.6% (92)	8.5% (40)
Might/might not report 2.6–3.5	12.2% (57)	23.0% (108)	24.7% (116)	11.3% (53)
Probably would report 3.6–4.5	3.9% (18)	28.9% (136)*	13.0% (61)	24.0% (113)
Definitely would report 4.6–5	1.7% (8)	20.7% (97)	8.5% (40)	47.0% (221)*
Means	1.79	3.30	2.60	3.89

(continues)

Table 8–3 (continued)

	Conflict of Interest	Exploiting Authority	Abuse of Authority	Malfeasance
6–10 Years				
Definitely would not report 1.5	55.5% (390)*	9.0% (63)	27.2% (191)*	4.6% (32)
Probably would not report 1.6–2.5	24.7% (174)	12.4% (87)	25.7% (180)	4.7% (33)
Might/might not report 2.6–3.5	13.1% (92)	22.2% (156)	26.3% (184)	9.4% (66)
Probably would report 3.6–4.5	5.0% (35)	30.1% (211)*	13.4% (94)	22.0% (155)
Definitely would report 4.6–5	1.7% (12)	26.3% (185)	7.4% (52)	59.3% (417)*
Means	1.88	3.52	2.66	4.26
11–15 Years				
Definitely would not report 1.5	59.2% (226)*	11.0% (42)	28.6% (109)*	7.6% (29)
Probably would not report 1.6–2.5	22.5% (86)	11.5% (44)	21.8% (83)	5.2% (20)
Might/might not report 2.6–3.5	13.3% (51)	16.5% (63)	27.6% (105)	7.1% (27)
Probably would report 3.6–4.5	2.9% (11)	29.1% (111)	15.2% (58)	17.8% (68)
Definitely would report 4.6–5	2.1% (8)	31.9% (122)*	6.8% (26)	62.3% (238)*
Means	1.83	3.59	2.67	4.21
16–20 Years				
Definitely would not report 1.5	52.4% (139)*	8.7% (23)	27.3% (72)	4.9% (13)
Probably would not report 1.6–2.5	22.3% (59)	10.6% (28)	21.2% (56)	5.7% (15)
Might/might not report 2.6–3.5	15.5% (41)	20.1% (53)	29.9% (79)*	6.8% (18)
Probably would report 3.6–4.5	5.7% (15)	29.9% (79)	13.6% (36)	13.2% (35)
Definitely would report 4.6–5	4.1% (11)	30.7% (81)*	8.0% (21)	69.4% (184)*
Means	2.01	3.62	2.69	4.35

(continues)

Table 8-3 Ethical Action and Years of Service: Nonsupervisors Only (continued)

	Conflict of Interest	Exploiting Authority	Abuse of Authority	Malfeasance
Over 20 Years				
Definitely would not report 1.5	44.1% (120)*	7.3% (20)	18.8% (51)	4.4% (12)
Probably would not report 1.6–2.5	20.2% (55)	8.5% (23)	23.9% (65)	4.1% (11)
Might/might not report 2.6–3.5	18.0% (49)	17.6% (48)	30.5% (83)*	3.3% (9)
Probably would report 3.6–4.5	11.4% (31)	28.7% (78)	14.3% (39)	15.8% (43)
Definitely would report 4.6–5	6.3% (17)	37.9% (103)*	12.5% (34)	72.4% (197)*
Means	2.33*	3.82*	2.94	4.45*
Gamma[1]	.069**	.094**	.013	.161**

[1]Gamma scores for supervisors are .211** for conflict of interest, .216** for exploiting authority, .180** for abuse of authority, and .200** for malfeasance.
*largest percentage/(n)/mean
**p < .05

between might/might not report, probably would report, and definitely would report misconduct. These results contradict the curvilinear relationship predicted in hypothesis 14. Exploring means, however, support a curvilinear relationship within length of service with officers who have less than 1 year of service holding means consistent with officers who have more than 10 years of service.

Figure 8–1 shows the percentage of respondents who would definitely report misconduct by length of service.

The results are even more spread out within abuse of authority. Officers with less than 1 year of service are split between probably would not report (22%), might/might not report (26%), and probably would report (25%). Respondents with anywhere from 1 to 20 years of service are split between definitely would not report, probably would not report, and might/might not report. Meanwhile, officers with more than 20 years are spread across four categories with the highest percentage within might/might not report. Officers with less than 1 year of service are split between probably would not report, might/might not report, and probably would report. Abuse-of-authority results do not lend support to hypothesis 14.

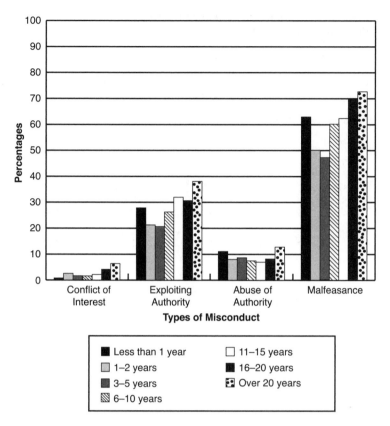

FIGURE 8-1   Percentage who would definitely report by length of service

Ethical awareness and standards found no relationship with agency size. This study hypothesizes that the same will be true for ethical action. Whether reporting behavior is impacted by agency size is explored in Table 8–4.

The results for agency size only partially support hypothesis 15, which asserts that there is no relationship between agency size and willingness to report misconduct. There are no clear trends, and many results show splits along different levels of willingness to report. For example, a majority of respondents from medium (65%), large (62%), and very large agencies (65%) would either probably or definitely report a peer who exploited authority as compared with 46% of respondents from small agencies and 56% respondents from very small agencies. Overall, the percentages indicate more willingness to report exploiting authority than abuse of authority regardless of size of agency. These results are consistent with ethical awareness and standards and contradict hypothesis 17.

Table 8-4 Ethical Action and Agency Size

(1) Definitely would not report–(5) Definitely would report

(n, # of agencies)	Conflict of Interest	Exploiting Authority	Abuse of Authority	Malfeasance
Very Small, <25 officers (87, 8)				
Definitely would not report 1.5	31.0% (27)*	11.5% (10)	42.5% (37)*	6.9% (6)
Probably would not report 1.6–2.5	26.4% (23)	13.8% (12)	31.0% (27)	5.7% (5)
Might/might not report 2.6–3.5	23.0% (20)	18.4% (16)	10.4% (9)	13.8% (12)
Probably would report 3.6–4.5	5.8% (5)	13.8% (12)	11.5% (10)	24.2% (21)
Definitely would report 4.6–5	13.8% (12)	42.5% (37)*	4.6% (4)	49.4% (43)*
Means	2.60	3.61	2.22	4.05
Small, 25–75 officers (212, 9)				
Definitely would not report 1.5	59.4% (126)*	15.1% (32)	49.6% (105)*	11.8% (25)
Probably would not report 1.6–2.5	17.5% (37)	17.0% (36)	21.3% (45)	7.6% (16)
Might/might not report 2.6–3.5	15.1% (32)	21.7% (46)	20.8% (44)	11.8% (25)
Probably would report 3.6–4.5	5.2% (11)	20.3% (43)	6.1% (13)	21.2% (45)
Definitely would report 4.6–5	2.8% (6)	25.9% (55)*	2.4% (5)	47.6% (101)*
Means	1.89	3.28	2.06	3.85
Medium, 76–200 officers (344, 6)				
Definitely would not report 1.5	41.6% (143)*	8.2% (28)	21.6% (74)	4.4% (15)
Probably would not report 1.6–2.5	22.4% (77)	10.8% (37)	21.3% (73)	4.9% (17)
Might/might not report 2.6–3.5	18.6% (64)	15.7% (54)	24.0% (82)*	8.4% (29)
Probably would report 3.6–4.5	8.7% (30)	25.4% (87)	19.3% (66)	16.3% (56)
Definitely would report 4.6–5	8.7% (30)	39.9% (137)*	14.0% (48)	66.0% (227)*
Means	2.38	3.76*	3.01*	4.32

(continues)

Table 8–4 (continued)

	Conflict of Interest	Exploiting Authority	Abuse of Authority	Malfeasance
Large, 201–500 officers (235, 2)				
Definitely would not report 1.5	32.7% (77)*	13.2% (31)	23.4% (55)	8.9% (21)
Probably would not report 1.6–2.5	21.7% (51)	8.5% (20)	17.0% (40)	5.1% (12)
Might/might not report 2.6–3.5	18.7% (44)	16.6% (39)	25.5% (60)*	8.5% (20)
Probably would report 3.6–4.5	17.5% (41)	26.4% (62)	19.2% (45)	16.2% (38)
Definitely would report 4.6–5	9.4% (22)	35.3% (83)*	14.9% (35)	61.3% (144)*
Means	2.66*	3.61	3.01*	4.15
Very large, >500 officers (2229, 5)				
Definitely would not report 1.5	50.8% (1130)*	6.8% (152)	21.5% (478)	3.9% (87)
Probably would not report 1.6–2.5	23.5% (522)	9.9% (219)	21.3% (474)	4.5% (100)
Might/might not report 2.6–3.5	14.2% (315)	17.9% (399)	29.2% (649)*	6.3% (140)
Probably would report 3.6–4.5	7.0% (156)	30.8% (684)	16.4% (363)	17.6% (391)
Definitely would report 4.6–5	4.5% (101)	34.6% (770)*	11.6% (258)	67.7% (1508)*
Means	2.07	3.76*	2.93	4.39*
Gamma	–.108**	.056**	.138**	.144**

*largest percentage/(n)/mean
**$p < .05$

There was more division in opinion regarding whether to report abuse of authority. Officers from medium and very large agencies were split between definitely would not report, probably would not report, and might/might not report for abuse of authority. Almost half of respondents from small agencies (50%) and very small agencies (43%) definitely would not report abuse of authority. Respondents from large agencies were split between definitely not reporting abuse of authority (23%) and maybe reporting abuse of authority (26%). These results are consistent with previous results found in this chapter, less agreement among respondents regarding whether to report abuse of authority. These results offer the clearest relationship between size and the dependent variables. Small and very small departments appear to have more solidarity with respect to an unwillingness to report misconduct.

As with previous results for ethical awareness and standards, a majority of officers from medium (66%), large (61%), and very large agencies (68%) would definitely report malfeasance. Almost a majority of respondents from very small (49%) and small agencies (48%) would definitely report malfeasance. These differences between agencies are much greater than those found within ethical awareness and standards; however, these results do lend support for hypothesis 14 in that officers are more willing to report malfeasance than the other types of misconduct.

Conflict of interest results also lend support to hypothesis 12 in that respondents are less likely to report it than the other types of misconduct. There is one interesting exception within very small agencies where a higher percentage of respondents definitely would not report abuse of authority (43%) than conflict of interest (31%). Again, no clear pattern emerges within conflict of interest, lending further support for hypothesis 15 that there is no relationship between an officer's ethical action and the size of the agency.

The regression model explored later in this chapter includes two important variables explored previously in Chapters 4 and 5. These variables include (1) officer perceptions of existing agency policy and officer perceptions of peer attitudes toward reporting misconduct and (2) officer willingness to report misconduct and officer perception of peer willingness to report misconduct. Correlations between agency policy and an officer's attitude toward reporting are shown in Table 8–5. The strong correlations show that an officer's awareness of existing agency policies impacts the officer's attitudes toward reporting misconduct.

Correlations between an officer's willingness to take action and perceptions of peer action are explored in Table 8–6. These correlations are the highest of all such variables explored thus far. Multicollinearity issues arise with the extremely high correlations, and this condition will be

Table 8–5 Correlations Between Agency Policy and Ethical Action

	Conflict of Interest
Conflict of Interest and knowledge of policy	.435**
Exploiting Authority and knowledge of policy	.417**
Abuse of Authority and knowledge of policy	.357**
Malfeasance and knowledge of policy	.252**
**p < .05	

Table 8-6 Correlations Between Officer Action and Perceptions of Peer Action

	Correlation
Conflict of Interest and peer attitudes	.931**
Exploiting Authority and peer attitudes	.818**
Abuse of Authority and peer attitudes	.757**
Malfeasance and peer attitudes	.825**
**p < .05	

considered when interpreting the regression model is presented later in this chapter.

These very high correlations may reflect conformity within an agency. It is also possible that respondents were attempting to justify their responses regarding willingness to report by responding that others would do the same. Police literature suggests that these high correlations reflect conformity or solidarity amongst officers (Klockars et al., 2006; Trautman, 1997).

FACTORS THAT HAVE THE BIGGEST IMPACT ON AN OFFICER'S ETHICAL ACTION

Thus far, this chapter has explored supervisory position, rank, years of service, promotion, and agency size with respect to ethical awareness. We have seen that the officer's perception of peer attitudes very closely matches his or her own willingness to report misconduct. What additional impact does the officer's perception of policy, his or her attitudes, and his or her personal and organizational characteristics have on the officer's ethical action? The regression model that follows in Table 8–7 explores the predictive nature of these variables.

Comparing regression results in Table 8–8 from the Standards model in the previous chapter shows that how serious the respondent believes the misconduct (own seriousness) still has roughly the same impact on how much punishment should follow and the officer's willingness to report that misconduct. The officer's perception of peer standards (others standards) drops substantially and changes from a positive to a negative impact on an officer's willingness to report misconduct. Meanwhile, the

Table 8–7 Ethical Action Regression

Independent Variables	Conflict of Interest β(t)	Exploiting Authority β(t)	Abuse of Authority β(t)	Malfeasance β(t)
Others' reporting	.841 (93.085)**	.709 (58.204)**	.617 (49.893)**	.784 (67.809)**
Own standards	.069 (6.159)**	.199 (11.589)**	.166 (11.149)**	.236 (14.738)**
Others' standards	−.049 (−5.184)**	−.103 (−6.498)**	−.044 (−3.434)**	−.139 (−9.014)**
Own seriousness	.257 (20.441)**	.386 (25.276)**	.563 (34.804)**	.219 (12.654)**
Others' seriousness	−.186 (−16.243)**	−.276 (−18.107)**	−.324 (−19.289)**	−.185 (−12.613)**
Policy	−.002 (−.306)	.002 (.218)	−.047 (−4.651)**	−.028 (−1.933)
Rank	.086 (12.677)**	.100 (10.160)**	.094 (9.816)**	.071 (6.562)**
Length of service	.002 (.300)	.023 (2.380)*	.016 (1.702)	.013 (1.259)
Agency size	.020 (3.537)**	.038 (4.457)**	.044 (5.260)**	.046 (4.868)**
Adjusted R^2	.903	.791	.804	.741
F	3147.851	1285.068	1383.336	969.702
s.e.	.377	.566	.572	.559

*p < .05
**p < .01

Table 8–8 Ethical Standards Regression Comparison

Others' standards	.510 (40.604)**	.698 (65.149)**	.526 (41.135)**	.713 (60.162)**
Own seriousness	.481 (25.884)**	.349 (23.392)**	.440 (24.103)**	.211 (10.902)**
Others' seriousness	−.005 (−.280)	−.046 (-3.111)**	.027 (1.476)	−.005 (−.296)

**p < .05

officer's perception of peer awareness (others seriousness) becomes strongly negative with respect to willingness to report as compared with only marginally negative with respect to standards.[1]

---

[1] A regression model that excludes perceptions regarding peer attitudes influences the results yielding an adjusted R^2 of .611 for conflict of interest, .548 for exploiting authority, .635 for abuse of authority, and .334 for malfeasance.

These results highlight the difference in factors that affect attitudes versus behavior. The officer's ethical awareness affects the officer's willingness to report misconduct more so than the officer's perceptions of peer attitudes. This suggests that impacting the officer's attitudes toward the seriousness of misconduct may impact the officer's willingness to report that misconduct.

According to the conflict of interest model, 90% of an officer's attitude toward the seriousness of this type of misconduct can be explained by the variables included in the model. This is the only regression model with variables that exceed multicollinearity limits. There is collinearity between an officer's willingness to report conflict of interest and the officer's perception of whether others would report conflict of interest misconduct ($\beta = .841$). Nonstandardized coefficients yielded similar results.

The other types of misconduct had high percentages as well, but no multicollinearity issues. The regression model may be impacted by the high correlation between an officer's own attitudes regarding the misconduct and the officer's perception of the peer's willingness to report misconduct. This is the case within conflict of interest; however, high levels of collinearity ($R^2 \geq .80$) are not present within the remaining types of misconduct. None of the correlations between these variables exceeds .90 for the remaining types of misconduct eliminating singularity or perfect multicollinearity (Tabachnick & Fidell, 2001).

Regardless of the nature of the misconduct, all of the independent variables influence an officer's attitudes toward misconduct with the exception of policy and length of service. As was apparent in the correlation analysis, the officer's perception of whether peers would report misconduct is the strongest predictor for conflict of interest ($\beta = .841$), exploiting authority ($\beta = .709$), abuse of authority ($\beta = .617$), and malfeasance ($\beta = .784$). Rank continues to have a consistent and modest impact on willingness to report. The officer's own standards also have a modest impact on willingness to report. Length of service and the officer's awareness of agency policy appear to have little, if any, impact on an officer's ethical action. When it comes to reporting, agency size does make some difference. Nonstandardized coefficients yielded similar results. Using stepwise and hierarchical regression did not impact these results.

CONCLUSIONS

This chapter has found partial support for hypotheses 14 through 20. Hypothesis 14 asserts that the more serious the misconduct, the more likely the officer will be willing to take ethical action. Partial support for this hypothesis was found in each of the analysis within this chapter. Officers are more willing to report exploiting authority, abuse of authority, and malfeasance than conflict of interest. Officers are more willing to report malfeasance than any other type of misconduct. The one contradiction that consistently showed up in the analysis was that officers are less willing to report abuse of authority than exploiting authority misconduct.

Hypothesis 15 asserts that officers who are supervisor are more likely to take ethical action. These results proved to be true across the different types of misconduct. There is partial support for hypothesis 16 that posits a curvilinear relationship between ethical action and years of service. Overall, officers with less than 1 year of service were more likely to report misconduct than officers with 1 to 5 years of service. As officers remain in service after 6 years, they become more willing to report misconduct.

Hypothesis 17 asserts that there is no relationship between the size of agency and an officer's willingness to report misconduct. There is partial support for this hypothesis. Very few patterns emerge when analyzing means and percentages for agency size. For example, there is no linear relationship or even curvilinear relationship. In addition, agency size did not prove important in the regression model. Still, in contrast to the lack of consistency in the relationship between size and the other dependent variables, officers in smaller agencies are less likely to report the most serious forms of ethical misconduct.

According to hypothesis 18, an officer's awareness of existing policies regarding misconduct will positively impact that officer's willingness to take ethical action. Unlike ethical awareness and standards, however, policy did not appear to impact an officer's willingness to take action. Hypothesis 19 asserts that an officer's perceptions regarding peer ethical awareness, standards, and action will positively impact that officer's willingness to take action and the regression model shows some support for this hypothesis.

Hypothesis 20 theorizes that the higher the officer's ethical awareness and standards, the greater the likelihood of an officer's ethical action.

The regression model offers support for this hypothesis. The officer's own attitudes toward misconduct appear to impact the officer's willingness to report misconduct. Awareness is, however, almost always a stronger factor than standards.

DISCUSSION QUESTIONS

1. What situational, individual, and organizational factors impact an officer's ethical actions? Can you think of others not mentioned in this chapter?
2. Do you agree with the way the data are interpreted in this chapter? Do you think these data help explain an officer's willingness to report fellow officers for misconduct?
3. Were you surprised by any of the findings? Identify what surprised you and why it was surprising.
4. Should an officer be more willing to report abuse of authority than exploiting authority?
5. Which of the types of behavior would you be willing to report within the scenarios in the National Institute of Justice study? Are you in agreement with the typical officer?

REFERENCES

Klockars, C. B., Ivkovic, S. K., & Haberfeld, M. (2006). *Enhancing Police Integrity*. New York: Springer Publishing.

Tabachnick, B. G., & Fidell, L. S. (2001). *Using Multivariate Statistics*. Needham Heights, MA: Allyn & Bacon.

Trautman, N. E. (1997). *The National Law Enforcement Officer Disciplinary Research Project*. National Discipline Research Summary II.

CHAPTER 9

In Law Enforcement We Trust: Ethical Attitudes and Behaviors of Law Enforcement Officers and Supervisors

Steven Klingaman

OBJECTIVES

- Investigate the differences in ethical behaviors among different levels of management and their impact on officers' attitudes
- Discuss Pollock's two perceptions of law enforcement officers— crime fighter and public servant
- Present the role of the supervisor within the organization, a supervisor's ethical decision making within the organization, and the various levels of supervisory position within an organization
- Review organizational culture literature as it relates to the role of the supervisor within police agencies
- Analyze National Institute of Justice data with respect to supervisors in law enforcement

INTRODUCTION

The ethical values that law enforcement agencies exhibit can affect public perceptions of the agency's ability to protect and serve. The general public's perception is a result of the agency's ability to demonstrate that the ethical values they possess are a reflection of those possessed by the citizens. As public servants, all law enforcement personnel are obligated to fulfill their duties in the best interest of the public to which they serve. This obligation includes ethical responsibilities to both the agency and the people. To the public, police officers must demonstrate a higher level of ethical behavior due to their position of authority and power (Johnson & Cox, 2005). The organizational values of an agency are instilled in its management, which in turn ingrains it into subordinates. Any discrepancy between the values and beliefs of a manager and those of the agency could have detrimental effects on the subordinate. The focus of this chapter is to investigate the differences in ethical behaviors among different levels of management and its impact on officer's attitudes. By analyzing the responses to a National Institute of Justice survey of law enforcement agencies, a better understanding of the ethical attitudes and behaviors of law enforcement personnel can be achieved. The results will illustrate the relationships, if any, that exist between the ethical attitudes and behaviors of different levels of management and those exhibited by other law enforcement personnel.

The ethical values of an agency can most readily be observed in those who have the most contact with the general public. While the agency may have a strong ethical responsibility to the public, the actual ethical values and behaviors exercised by its personnel determine the perceptions of those they serve. Conflicting views by superiors regarding what is right and wrong behavior can lead to confusion and misinterpretation by subordinates. This in turn can lead to substandard performance and lack of trust by the public.

By studying the relationships between the ethical attitudes of different levels of management and officer attitudes, we will be able to identify whether or not a difference of behaviors exists between these classifications of law enforcement officers. It will also help to determine if the level of management is related to a person's ethical behavior. A difference of behaviors can be an indicator of possible conflicts and potential abuses by both management and the subordinates who follow their orders. These differences also can have a considerable impact on the organizational culture of an agency. Since the organizational culture of a law enforcement agency is comprised of the inter-actions between administration, supervisors, and line officers, any significant difference in the values and behaviors that exists between these members of the same organization can result in internal conflicts, corruption, and loss of public support. The literature review that follows will help to understand the consequences and problems that are related to the ethical differences that occur between levels of management and line officers and the impact it can have on the culture of the organization.

RESEARCH AND LITERATURE REVIEWS

The perspective of law enforcement personnel can be viewed differently. Pollock (1998) describes two perceptions of law enforcement officers. The first being the "crime fighter responsibilities," which can be characterized as an enforcer of the law above all other, and that criminals are the enemy of the public. The public should understand that the decisions made by law enforcement are for the good of the community. The priority of law enforcement is crime control and order. The second perspective Pollock (1998) describes is law enforcement as the "public servant." As a public servant, law enforcement serves everyone. They are to protect all citizens and carry out their duties without prejudice. Unlike the "crime fighter," there are no enemies unless one considers society as an enemy (Pollock, 1998).

The understanding of these two perspectives is important when assessing ethical issues. The two perspectives may have different ethical values that are employed in the decision-making process while on the job. It is this decision-making process that makes the ethical training of all law enforcement officers so important. The outcome of any situation is dependent upon the ethics, beliefs, attitudes, and training of the officers responding. The ability to make the necessary decisions that produce positive results comes from not only the officer but from the agency he or she represents.

It is the view of "public servant" that will be taken within the context of this paper. As a public servant, law enforcement personnel are committed to the varying behavioral expectations that the general public demands from this profession. These expectations are higher than those of any other profession due to the power and authority a law enforcement officer pos-sesses (Johnson & Cox, 2005). This behavior is affected by different levels of authority as well as the culture of the organization. Administrators, supervisors, and line officers all contribute to the ethical behaviors of each other. The intensity of these contributions varies depending upon the organization and situation. Collectively, the ethical contributions of all personnel comprise the culture and environment in which law enforcement is conducted.

The different ethical considerations that are contributed are a product of the duties that each line officer, supervisor, and administrator must fulfill. Line officers are exposed to confrontations with criminals and the public. Their values and behaviors are most readily seen and tested on a daily basis. They must deal with many problems and situations that require them to use the combination of the ethical values learned in training, those derived from personal values, those influenced by peers, and those that are expected by the public. They use their discretion to handle ethical dilemmas that occur while on duty. Discretion, as defined by Pollock (1998), is "the ability to choose between two or more courses of behavior" (p. 151). This discretion is influenced by an officer's ethical values and plays a more important role in decision making than rules and regulations (Pollock, 1998). As members of a law enforcement organization, the attitudes and behaviors that affect a line officer's discretion are incorporated into the contributions to the culture within the organization.

The contributions of administrative ethics help to set the tone of the organizational culture of a law enforcement agency. This is where the policies and procedures for the values of the organization must begin. Administrators are responsible for developing the goals and guidelines that subordinate officers are to follow (IACP, 2001). Administrators must consider the reputation of the organization and public trust it must uphold. Unlike line-officers, administrators are not faced with the daily street level decision-making that occurs. But, they are still responsible for the influences on those decisions. This is why such an importance is placed on the ethical values that administrators must possess. An administrator's personal ethical values should not interfere with the administrator's duty to the goals of the organization (Burke, 1989; Thompson, 1992). Although these values can still influence ethical standards, it is the combination of organizational responsibility, public perception, and political influence that administrators often use to shape the organizational culture that exists within a law enforcement agency.

Supervisors are the one classification that is caught in the middle. Their ethical contributions to the organizational culture of the law enforcement agency are derived from their personal beliefs as well a mixture of line officer and administrative ethics. The supervisor's duties are to ensure that the policies and procedures implemented by administrators are carried out by subordinates and that subordinates adhere to these policies and procedures while fulfilling their duties to the public and to the organization. Supervisory responsibility also extends to playing the main role in the development and utilization of ethical values by line officers (Peak et al., 1999; IACP, 2001). Some supervisors, such as sergeants, have more of a connection with line officers, which can affect their attitudes toward ethical values. Paoline (2001) found that street supervisors often have the same attitudes toward organizational environments as line officers. The contributions of supervisors to organizational culture helps to bring together the organizational values of the agency as set forth by administrators and the day to day ethical values that are exercised by line officers. This is an important role due to its "mediation" between labor and management so that the organization runs smoothly (Peak et al., 1999).

The classifications of officers used here are formed by levels of authority within an organization. The levels of authority used in this study are line officers, first-line managers, mid-level managers, and senior-level managers. These levels can influence the attitudes and behaviors of other officers. The next sections will discuss what shapes these different levels of authority and what role organizational culture plays in shaping law enforcement agencies.

LEVEL OF AUTHORITY AND ITS INFLUENCE

As "street-level bureaucrats," line officers must subscribe to a higher level of behaviors just as other public officials (Lipsky, 1980; Raines, 2005). Since line officers are the public representatives of a law enforcement agency, their behaviors and decisions are under the most scrutiny. It is here that the ethical behavior and reputation of the organization begins. It is important that officer recruits receive the best possible ethical training so they may carry it with them not only through out their careers but out to the streets where it will be put to the test. Police training often focuses on following rules and regulations and the conduct of officers based upon these tenets. Control by policy, not by human behavior is usually the approach taken to train recruits. Concentration on policy over behavior can lead to officers doing what is right out of fear of being caught rather than knowing what is right or wrong (Johnson & Cox, 2005). Behavior that is not consistent with that of the citizenry can result in eroding public confidence and lack of community support.

It is the responsibility of the supervisors, as well as administrators, to ensure that line officers who confront the public on a daily basis are trained in not only the duties they perform, but also the moral and ethics reasons behind what they do (Peak et al., 1999; IACP, 2001). It is at this level that a distinction of ethical behaviors can exist within an organization. Supervisors who may believe that certain actions can be justified or can be kept from upper management may cross the line of unethical behavior. The position of supervisor, whether it is for a small or large group, is a position that can be described as line work while also being administrative.

First-line managers, such as sergeants and some corporals and lieutenants, are viewed as a rank caught between management and line officer. Officers see them as still tied to the street side of policing. Anything above this level is viewed as out-of-touch with the streets. Higher ranks are considered to be more interested in political and economic interests than the safety of officers (Barker, 1999). Line supervisors are caught in the middle of being told how things will be done according to administrators and how things really are on the streets. From this difference a supervisor must use his or her judgment when making decisions involving line officers and the public. Supervisors must win the respect of their subordinates by not forgetting what it is like in the real world yet also adhere to the management duties set forth by administrators.

Mid-level manager positions are considered to be more administrative and less policing. Ranks such as captains and lieutenants can be considered mid-level managers. These managers are responsible for carrying out the policies set forth by senior-level managers. At this level, officers have begun to lose their "street cop" attitudes and adopt the administrative view. Career mobility is a focus and greater loyalty and commitment to the organization increases (Barker, 1999). They may build their reputations upon the reputation of the organization. Subordinate to senior-level managers, it is the duty of the mid-manager to make sure the policies set forth by their superiors is carried out and that the agency runs smoothly. After all, their careers depend on it.

Good ethical training begins at the top. According to Thompson (1985), "Administrative ethics involves the application of moral principles to the conduct of officials in organizations." An administrator, or senior-level manager, must carry out the policies of their superiors who are usually people in political positions. Senior-level managers often include ranks such as majors and colonels. To do otherwise would not be ethical because this is the profession that a person has chosen by free will (Thompson, 1985). Administrators, although bound by their duties of carrying out the policies set forth by their superiors, should make every attempt to establish highest of ethical guidelines for their personnel to follow. Upper-management must take a leadership role in conveying the agency's overall quality of ethics to its officers. An ethical culture must start with upper-management's commitment to setting the ethical standard for the agency then making sure it is carried out (O'Mally, 1997).

As those responsible for setting the standard for organizational culture in a law enforcement organization, recruiting the right administrators is the first step to a fulfilling this goal. Needless to say that law enforcement agencies strive to attract highly qualified, ethical administrators. Still, applicants to high level administrative positions often can display traits that impress interviewers but do not illustrate the true core values that comprise their integrity. A careful examination into what a candidate believes and the values he or she holds should be done. The programs of a leader who has strong beliefs and values gain better support from the public, are more effective, and last longer. Ethics and integrity can help determine how a person will behave and perform. The future leaders of police agencies need to possess the ethical qualities that will help to reshape policing and the public problems it faces (Plummer, 1995). Official obligations and moral duties are dependent upon each other. It can become problematic to place individuals into administrative positions that must choose between personal morals and organizational responsibility. These positions may require the incumbent to choose between their morals and values and the institutional obligations (Burke, 1989). This is why a greater importance should be placed on selecting the right administrator. To retain the trust of the people, the administration should not be in conflict with the mission and goals of a public organization. The administration should then be able to convey these goals and ethical concerns to all personnel.

Promoting good ethical culture requires good ethical officers in those management positions that have the greatest influence. This is done through the promotion process. The promotional process can be a barrier to change in an organization. As an officer advances through the ranks of an agency, their attitudes and organizational beliefs are molded by their experience and environment. Their commitment to the organization can be affected by the promotional opportunities available (Jaramillo et al., 2005). The practice of promoting those who would make the best managers is often wrought with favoritism and partiality. Barker (1999) suggests that many officers believe that the process is not by merit but by political grounds that encourage minority and female promotions. Bolton's (2003) qualitative analysis rejects the idea that minorities are favored over whites. From a minority's perspective, promotion in an organization is made more difficult. Whetstone (2001) also concludes that the promotional system itself eliminates many from upward mobility. His study showed that minorities and women were encouraged more than white males but even this was minimal. Whetstone (2001) also found that unfair testing process, biased administration, and lack of openings were organizational reasons for individuals not to participate in the promotional process. Conflicting feelings about the promotional process and lack of encouragement from management can create problems and an unhealthy organizational culture. Suspicions of the intentions of managers and loss of confidence by subordinates can result in lower morale and distrust in management. These feelings can then affect an officer's attitudes and behaviors.

The promotion process is used to select those officers that will ultimately establish the goals of the agency. Those who seek promotion should be in it for the work itself, not just the economic gain (Scarborough et al., 1999). Those who attempt to promote, whether line officer or manager, do it for certain reasons. Studies have shown that personal reasons account for attempting to promote and that increased pay does not play a major role (Whetstone, 2001; Scarborough et al., 1999). Management's role in the selection may be biased in that those who are promoted most likely share the same personal views and opinions of the managers responsible for the promotion. This may result in a command structure with the same attitudes and behaviors that leave very little room for diversity of thought.

When this occurs, having the wrong type of officers in administrative positions can have detrimental affect on the organization.

CULTURAL INFLUENCE

Organizational culture plays an important role in the development of new officers. Wilson (1989) defines organizational culture as "a persistent, patterned way of thinking about the central tasks of and human relationships within an organization." It is a combination of factors such as environment, attitudes, feelings, beliefs, morals, and values that exist within the people and the organization. This "culture" that exists has been cited as a cause of problems that can occur within an organization (Johnson & Cox, 2005; Klockars et al., 2000; Bolton, 2003; Trautman, 2000). Organizations can often encourage unethical behavior by introducing the behavior that it expects from its new recruits. Even the paramilitary methods used in training can influence a new officer to accept the ethical views of the organization over his or her own (Johnson & Cox, 2005).

Organizational culture works upon a person's behavior by pressuring human emotions such as acceptance, fear, pride, and ambition. Through formal and informal groups, the behaviors of new officers can often be altered to "fit in" in a new environment. If this environment is corrupt or unstable, the effect on the new officer could result in unacceptable performance and difficulty in decision making. The lines between what is right and wrong can become distorted. Right and wrong may now be defined as what is good or bad for the organization as opposed to what is good or bad for the public.

According to Klockars et al. (2000), "Corruption is the abuse of police authority for gain." Until recently police agencies handled corruption through the administration/individual approach or "bad apple" approach. This approach views corruption as a moral defect in an individual, not the system or agency. The ethical dilemmas faced by law enforcement officers can be influenced by not only the officer but by the environment in which the officer operates. By minimizing the role of the organization in ethics places the responsibility on the individual. This does little to solve the problems associated with ethical behaviors and agency integrity. The administrative/individual approach views police integrity as a system that expels and prevents "bad apples" from polluting the system (Klockars et al., 2000). Stopping corrupt individuals from entering the system prevents corruption from occurring.

Today a different approach focuses on the environment and culture of the organization and its relationship to the training and behaviors of law enforcement officers. An organizational/occupational approach views police integrity as a system in which an organizational culture does not tolerate unethical behaviors. Klockars et al. (2000) concluded that the integrity of police agencies varies within the United States. Officers must know their agency's policy for behavior as well as the penalties of breaking such policy. Officers must also know the seriousness of misconduct, the level of punishment, as well as the agency's intolerance of the code of silence (Klockars et al., 2000).

Organizational culture that can lead to corruption is influenced by the separation from the public, a strong dependence upon each other, and the resistance to change. A lack of training in ethics and a stronger focus on the organization and its beliefs influences ones thinking (Johnson & Cox, 2005). Within law enforcement agencies, a difference in cultures between line officers and management can create an untrusting atmosphere.

Wilson (1989) describes the street cop/management cop cultures that often pit line officers against management. Line officers want the assurance that management will support them at any cost. Management must protect the entire agency at any cost. This may mean disciplining officers and setting examples of those who do misdeeds. Line officers can form distrust toward management when they believe that management has "sold out" to the political side (Wilson, 1989). This division between street work and administrative work can result in an agency that is susceptible to problems or corruption from either side.

Organizational culture that tolerates corruption can lead to an atmosphere in which a "code of silence" thrives and is used to cover up unethical actions by both line officers and the organization. This code of silence is one of the four dimensions that lead to corruption according to Klockars et al. (2000). Trautman (2000) found that 79% of police academy recruits surveyed acknowledged that a code of silence exists and is fairly common. This code, often denied by administrators and officers, is a direct result of unethical organizational culture. Combating the code of silence includes ethics training, consistent accountability, open communication between officers and leaders, an anonymous reporting system, and whistleblower protection. Field training officers and line supervisors have the most ability to prevent a code of silence (Trautman, 2000). The use of such a code casts doubts by the public on the integrity and truthfulness of the organization. Not only does this damage the reputation of the agency, but it damages the reputation of the profession.

The practice of law enforcement suffers as a result of unethical behaviors by individuals and organizations. According to Cooper (1987), organizations can corrupt a practice by pursuing external goods such as power, status, money, or prestige. An organization must possess virtues that support the ethical principles of the organization and the citizens it serves. The virtues of the administrators or officers must be consistent with the internal goods of the practice. No virtues set forth by the practice and supported by the organization should ever be violated to advance the well-being of that organization. Individuals have a duty to their colleagues to abstain from subverting the virtues held by their practice. Each colleague then expects the same from each other. It is this expectation that keeps the practice respectable. Lack of virtues by an individual damages the entire practice (Cooper, 1987).

It is the organizational approach that must be addressed and changed so that the problem of corruption can be fixed. The old transactional style of leadership in which one leader controls the organization needs to be replaced with a transformational style in which changes are made through the cooperation and input of all the members of an organization. Therefore, if positive changes are to be made, it will take the consensus of the entire organization from the bottom to the top (Johnson & Cox, 2005).

The overall results of law enforcement organizations lacking ethical behaviors that are expected by the public are mistrust and the loss of support. As governmental organizations, law enforcement agencies must demonstrate their ability to retain the trust of the citizens they protect. Gaining public trust requires the process of an organization and public administrators to possess trustworthy behaviors. Ethical behaviors that lead to public trust include integrity, openness, loyalty, ethical competence, and consistency. The more ethical a government is, the more public trust it gains. The more a government does to improve its ethical state, the more support and trust it receives. The behaviors of individuals within a government can strongly influence public trust. Management must act as role models to subordinates; this helps to create a more ethical environment that increases public trust. Openness by employees should be encouraged. Increased openness among employees leads to increased public trust (Feldheim & Wang, 2004).

ANALYSIS AND METHODOLOGY OF THE SURVEY QUESTIONS

The National Institute of Justice (NIJ) conducted a study into the integrity of 30 law enforcement agencies. This study consisted of 11 hypothetical scenarios used to measure police misconduct and corruption. The scenarios varied in seriousness and were rated by the participants. Less serious scenarios included running a security business during off hours, accepting unsolicited meals and small value items from merchants on a beat, receiving holiday gifts of food and liquor, and covering up an officer involved in a DUI. Moderately serious scenarios included excessive force after a foot pursuit, a supervisor giving a subordinate time off in return for mechanical work on the supervisor's personal car, exchange of free drinks for ignoring a bar that is open too late, and receipt of a kickback from a towing company. The most serious of scenarios involved stealing a watch from a crime scene, taking money from a found wallet, and accepting a bribe in exchange for not issuing a traffic citation. The responses to the questions about each scenario suggest the ethical attitudes and behaviors exhibited by the participants and, collectively, the agency they represent (Klockars et al., 2000).

The responses to the survey were used to measure officers' knowledge of their own policies regarding the actions, their opinions of the seriousness of the offense, how others view the seriousness of the offense, the level of discipline that should be invoked, the level of discipline that would probably be invoke, if the officer would report another officer engaged in the behavior, and if other officers would report others engaged in the behavior (Klockars et al., 2000).

The behaviors suggested by the NIJ survey give an indication of the organizational culture that exists within each agency. This culture, as mentioned earlier, is a culmination of all the attitudes and beliefs of all personnel as well as the policies and views of the organization. To investigate this further, the focus of this chapter will be on just one scenario. Scenario number seven of the survey, a supervisor allows a subordinate time off during a holiday in return for mechanical work on the supervisor's personal car, will be examined to determine if there is a significant difference in the responses of line officers and supervisors. This scenario is the only one of the eleven that was designed to evaluate the ethical behaviors of supervisors. By using this scenario, one can investigate the ethical behaviors of officers and different levels of management. This will be done by analyzing the responses of those who indicated which rank they hold. An "unknown" or "other" response to this question of rank resulted in the respondent's answers to be excluded from this study.

Analyzing scenario seven can illustrate ethical disparities that could exist between different levels of management and its impact on officers. By examining this, one may be able to determine the ethical attitudes and even predict the ethical behaviors that exist within a law enforcement organization. It is hypothesized that:

H1: Officer attitudes toward supervisor misconduct is positively associated with the officer's attitude regarding peer attitudes toward supervisor misconduct, the officer's awareness of policies prohibiting the supervisor misconduct, supervisor position, length of service, and the size of the agency.

H2: Officer attitudes toward punishing supervisor misconduct is positively associated with the officer's attitude regarding peer attitudes toward supervisor misconduct, the officer's awareness of policies prohibiting the supervisor misconduct, actual punishment, supervisory position, length of service, and the size of the agency.

H3: An officer's willingness to report supervisor misconduct is positively associated with the officer's attitude regarding peer willingness to report misconduct, the officer's attitude regarding peer attitudes toward supervisor misconduct, the officer's attitude regarding punishing supervisor misconduct, the officer's awareness of policies prohibiting the supervisor misconduct, actual punishment, supervisory position, length of service, and the size of the agency.

This study will focus on the attitudes of officers and managers toward scenario seven of the NIJ survey. The responses to three questions concerning scenario seven will be analyzed to determine any inconsistencies between the three different levels of management and the attitudes and behaviors of officers toward supervisor misconduct. The first question, "How serious do you consider this behavior to be?" is answered using a five-point Likert scale ranging from "Not at all serious" to "Very serious."

The second question, "If an officer in your agency engaged in this behavior and was discovered doing so, what if any discipline do you think should follow?" uses the ordinal list of choices: "None," "Verbal reprimand," "Written reprimand," "Period of suspension without pay," "Demotion in rank," and "Dismissal." The third question, "Do you think you would report a fellow police officer who engaged in this behavior?" again uses a five-point Likert scale ranging from "Definitely not" to "Definitely yes." The first and second questions reveal attitudes one would have toward the situation, whereas the third question is an indication of behavioral action. These particular questions are used to investigate the different levels of management and officer's attitudes.

The different ranks of officers used in this survey are constructed by combining the indicated ranks the officers provided when answering a survey question regarding their rank. For this analysis, five ranks of officers are used. These ranks are officers that include recruits, line officers, deputies, and corporals who are not supervisors; detectives; first-line supervisors comprised of sergeants and corporals who are supervisors; mid-level managers that include lieutenants and captains; and senior-level managers consisting of majors, colonels, and chiefs.

The three levels of management, first-line, mid-level, and senior-level, and officer attitudes are the focus of this study. By separating these levels of management, we are able to acquire a better understanding of how management views certain ethical situations and its impact on officer attitudes.

VALIDITY

Thirty police agencies were contacted in which 3,235 officers from all of the contacted agencies responded. This resulted in an overall response rate of 55.5%. Due to confidentiality, the exact types of police agencies contacted were not revealed; however, the types of agencies did not include any State agencies and only one Sheriff's agency (Klockars et al., 2000). There is also selection bias of the surveyed agencies as they were not randomly chosen. The sample taken from law enforcement agencies was done as a convenience sample, hence there is an increased threat to external validity. Therefore the conclusions of this chapter are only representative of the agencies who participated in the NIJ study.

RESULTS

Analysis of the data collected by the NIJ survey regarding scenario seven has been compiled into the following tables. Table 9–1 illustrates basic statistics of the groups that were analyzed while the other three are regression models that could be used to address the attitudes and behaviors of officers and management. The regression models are based upon the independent variables listed in the tables while the dependent variable is the responses of officers. Using these different variables in each situation provide indicators for determining what factors influence an officer's decision-making process.

Table 9–1 Means, Standard Deviations, and Variances of the Three Levels of Management

Level of Management		Seriousness of Supervisor Misconduct	Discipline of Supervisor Misconduct	Willingness to Report Supervisor Misconduct
		1 = Not at all serious 2 3 4 5 = Very serious	1 = None 2 = Verbal reprimand 3 = Written reprimand 4 = Suspension w/out pay 5 = Demotion 6 = Dismissal	1 = Definitely no 2 3 4 5 = Definitely yes
Officers	Mean	4.06	3.47	3.19
	Std. Deviation	1.100	1.246	1.467
	Variance	1.210	1.553	2.152
	N	2085	2082	2080
First-line managers	Mean	4.53	3.90	4.22
	Std. Deviation	.762	1.055	1.072
	Variance	.581	1.113	1.149
	N	376	376	377
Mid-level managers	Mean	4.61	3.90	4.33
	Std. Deviation	.619	.949	1.057
	Variance	.384	.900	1.118
	N	167	166	166
Senior-level managers	Mean	4.63	4.20	4.46
	Std. Deviation	.771	1.135	1.087
	Variance	.594	1.288	1.181
	N	57	56	57

Table 9-1 presents the means, standard deviations, and variances of officers and the three levels of management studied in regards to the three questions of the scenario. These responses were based upon the individual's attitudes and behaviors toward the misconduct. One noteworthy item of interest here is that there is a slight increase in the mean scores of the three levels of management as rank increases. While there is a slight increase, the difference in means among management levels is very small in comparison to the difference in means between officers and managers. Also, standard deviations and variances are higher for discipline and willingness to report. These results suggest that managers have similar responses in attitudes toward the seriousness of the misconduct, but are not as cohesive in their attitudes toward how to punish and whether or not to report supervisory misconduct.

Table 9–2 represents the regression analysis observed from the attitudes of the respondents toward the seriousness of a supervisor's misconduct in the scenario. The results show that although all three levels of management are significant, no level of management has much of an impact on an officer's attitude toward the seriousness of supervisor misconduct (β =.061, .067, .017, respectively). Of all three levels, mid-level managers have the highest beta weights. The same is true for length of service (β =.029) and the size of the agency (β =.010). The results partially support hypothesis one, which states that officer attitudes toward supervisor misconduct is positively associated with the officer's attitude regarding peer attitudes

Table 9–2 Results of Regression Analysis of Officer's Own Attitudes Toward the Seriousness of Supervisor Misconduct

Independent variables	Attitudes Toward Seriousness		
	B	**Std. Error**	**Beta**
First-line managers	.194**	.037	.061
Mid-level managers	.306**	.053	.067
Senior-level managers	.132**	.084	.017
Length of service	.018*	.007	.029
Size of agency	.009	.010	.010
Violation of policy	.222**	.014	.206
Others' views of seriousness	.627**	.012	.661

R^2 = .648   *p < .05
F = 791.747   **p < .001

toward supervisor misconduct, the officer's awareness of policies prohibiting the supervisor misconduct, supervisor position, length of service, and the size of the agency. The impact of supervisory position, although small, does lend some support to this hypothesis while the size of the agency, which is not significant, does not.

What does have a much stronger impact is an officer's attitudes about the way others view the seriousness of the misconduct (β = .661) and to a lesser extent the possibility of it being a violation of policy (β = .206). This supports hypothesis one that the attitudes of others toward the seriousness of supervisor misconduct does affect an officer's attitude and is partially supported by whether the offense is a violation of policy. An officer's attitude can be influenced by peer pressure or doing wrong in the eyes of fellow officers.

Policy violation could affect this attitude because if an officer feels that this type of violation is overlooked or does not know if such a policy exists then the officer may not view this as serious. This model demonstrates that a major influence on the attitudes an officer has toward the seriousness of misconduct can be from how he or she believes others will feel about the seriousness of the misconduct.

The second regression model, Table 9–3, illustrates an officer's opinion of what discipline should be dealt supervisors who engage in misconduct. Here again we find that the level of management does not have a crucial impact on

Table 9–3 Regression Analysis of an Officer's Opinion of What Discipline Should Follow Supervisor Misconduct

Independent variables	Attitudes Toward Seriousness		
	B	Std. Error	Beta
First-line managers	–.094*	.042	–.026
Mid-level managers	–.085	.061	–.016
Senior-level managers	.090	.097	.010
Length of service	.041**	.008	.058
Size of agency	.018	.012	.017
Violation of policy	.079**	.017	.064
Others' views of seriousness	–.048*	.019	-.044
Discipline that would follow	.585**	.012	.598
Own attitude toward seriousness	.389**	.021	.337

R^2 = .660   *p < .05
F = 646.290   **p < .001

attitudes toward discipline (β = $-.026$, $-.016$, .010, respectively). The negative beta weights indicate that first-line and mid-level managers actually have a negative impact on an officer's attitude toward discipline. The strongest negative beta weights are exhibited by first-line managers while senior-level managers demonstrate the strongest positive beta weights among the levels of managers. Length of service (β = .058) and agency size (β = .017) do not a have an effective role in officer's attitudes. Even violation of policy (β = .064) and other's views of the seriousness of the conduct (β = $-.044$) has little to do with influencing an officer's views of punishment. Length of service and an officer's awareness of a violation of policy only partially support hypothesis two which states that officer attitudes toward punishing supervisor misconduct is positively associated with the officer's attitude regarding peer attitudes toward supervisor misconduct, the officer's awareness of policies prohibiting the supervisor misconduct, actual punishment, supervisory position, length of service, and the size of the agency. Supervisory position, agency size, and peer attitudes toward supervisor misconduct are either insignificant or demonstrate a negative impact toward an officer's attitude toward punishment.

What an officer expects the punishment will be (β = .598) and his or her own attitude toward the seriousness of the offense (β = .337) does impact an officer's opinion about punishment. These two factors support hypothesis two. They both strongly influence the attitudes of officers.

The regression model suggests that the level of punishment an officer feels is justifiable can be regulated by what he or she believes the real punishment to be. This effects an officer's opinion in that the officer knows the possible "range limits" set by the agency. Punishment cannot be too strict or too lenient. The officer's own feelings of how serious the misconduct is will also dictate how much punishment should be bestowed.

The last regression model, Table 9–4, shows the willingness of to report supervisor misconduct. Although the three levels of management are significant, they are still not very strong predictors of reporting supervisor misconduct (β = .080, .074, .035, respectively). First-line managers have the strongest impact with mid-level managers close behind. This third regression model also demonstrates the trend of senior-level managers to have the weakest impact out of all the levels of management. Senior-level managers tend to show the weakest beta weights throughout the three models compared to the other levels of management.

Table 9–4 Regression Analysis of Officer's Own Willingness to Report Supervisor Misconduct

Independent Variables	Willingness to Report Misconduct		
	B	Std. Error	Beta
First-line managers	.352**	.045	.080
Mid-level managers	.475**	.065	.074
Senior-level managers	.374**	.103	.035
Length of service	.028*	.009	.033
Size of agency	.060**	.013	.045
Discipline that would follow	.048**	.014	.041
Own attitude toward seriousness	.484**	.022	.346
Others' attitudes toward seriousness	–.269**	.022	–.203
Violation of policy	.034	.018	.022
Other officers reporting	.765**	.014	.705

$R^2 = .734$ * $p < .05$

$F = 827.696$ ** $p < .001$

As with the other two models, the length of service ($\beta = .033$) and the size of an agency ($\beta = .045$), even though they are significant, still do not impact an officer's decision to report supervisor misconduct. Violation of policy ($\beta = .022$) and the possible discipline that is expected ($\beta = .041$) showed no indication of being a strong influence on decision making. Hypothesis three which states that an officer's willingness to report supervisor misconduct is positively associated with the officer's attitude regarding peer willingness to report misconduct, the officer's attitude regarding peer attitudes toward supervisor misconduct, the officer's attitude regarding punishing supervisor misconduct, the officer's awareness of policies prohibiting the supervisor misconduct, actual punishment, supervisory position, length of service, and the size of the agency is partially supported by these results. All variables lend support to hypothesis three, except for an officer's awareness of policy violation, due to its insignificance, and an officer's attitude regarding peer attitudes toward supervisor misconduct because it impacts one's willingness to report in a negative way. How serious an officer believes others think the misconduct is ($\beta = -.203$) has a slightly negative impact on an officer reporting the misconduct. This indicates that the more serious the officer thinks their peers view the misconduct the less likely they are to report it. The perception of peer attitudes toward such behavior can thus result in making decisions based upon peer pressure rather than on ethical awareness. This is where the possibility of corruption and unethical behaviors can begin.

The biggest determining factor of whether an officer is willing to report misconduct is the officer's perception of whether or not other officers would report this misconduct (β = .705). The officer's attitude toward the seriousness of misconduct also influences the decision to report misconduct (β = .346). Hypothesis 3 is supported by the influence of other's willingness to report misconduct. It is also partially support by one's own attitude toward the seriousness of the misconduct. This behavior of whether to report an incident or not relies deeply on the actions of others.

No one wants to be a whistleblower and face the possibility of reprisal from fellow officers or management. But, this may also be opposed by a person's own feelings of how serious the misconduct is. It is in these situations when the internal pressure of what to do is eclipsed by the pressures of others. This model illustrates what can be expected when informal organizations and peer pressures have more influence than rules and regulations. This can lead to unreported acts of unethical behaviors. A strong indicator of a person's willing to report unethical conduct is how they might perceive other's willingness to report the same conduct. This could be helpful in identifying and correcting problems with the "code of silence" within an organization.

The results of the correlations of attitudes and behaviors is shown in Table 9–5 help to support all three hypotheses in that the highest correlation in each of the three categories of own attitude toward seriousness, own attitude toward punishment, and own willingness to report misconduct is an officer's perception of what he or she believes others feel. The presumption of other's attitude toward seriousness by an officer shows a very strong positive relationship to an officer's own attitude toward seriousness of supervisor misconduct. This again indicates that an officer's own feelings and attitudes are influenced by what he or she believes other officer's attitudes are. One's own feelings toward punishment that should follow and seriousness of the offense also show a moderate positive relationship which can influence officer's decisions.

Attitudes toward punishment that should follow and punishment that would follow exhibit a strong positive relationship. An officer's beliefs about

Table 9–5 Correlations of Attitudes and Behaviors

	Correlations		
	Own Attitude Toward Seriousness	Own Attitude Toward Punishment	Own Willingness to Report
Own attitude toward seriousness	1	.586**	.589**
N	3083	3074	3075
Others' attitudes toward seriousness	.778**	.522**	.522**
N	3077	3071	3072
Punishment that should follow	.586**	1	.590**
N	3074	3077	3072
Punishment that would follow	.408**	.748**	.482**
N	3072	3070	3070
Own willingness to report misconduct	.589**	.590**	1
N	3075	3072	3078
Others' willingness to report misconduct	.492**	.532**	.807**
N	3074	3071	3074
Length of service	.138**	.139**	.218**
N	3062	3056	3058
Size of agency	-.021	.021	.012
N	3083	3077	3078
Violation of policy	.554**	.509**	.424**
N	3071	3066	3067
First-line managers	.126**	.098**	.201**
N	3054	3049	3049
Mid-level managers	.100**	.063**	.146**
N	3054	3049	3049
Senior-level managers	.060**	.069**	.096**
N	3054	3049	3049

**Significant at the .01 level (2-tailed)

how others feel toward punishment of supervisor misconduct play a large role in their own attitudes toward punishment. Not wanting to be too harsh or too lenient on punishment, officers may develop a consensus of the punishment misconduct deserves from other co-workers. There is also a moderate relationship to one's own attitude toward seriousness and willing to report that may affect the level of punishment for this misconduct.

Moderate positive relationships exist between an officer's own attitude and other's attitudes toward the seriousness of the offense and an officer's attitude toward punishment and the willingness to report. Other's willingness to report misconduct shows a very high positive correlation to the willingness of one's own reporting of such incidents. This is very important because it illustrates and supports the idea of the "code of silence" and the informal police subculture that can lead to corruption (Klockars et al., 2000; Trautman, 2000; Pollock, 1998).

There seems to be almost no relationship between level of management and the three categories examined. Ranging from .060 to .201, these relationships are significant but show little in regards to strength. The first-line manager although does show a stronger relationship than the mid-level or senior-level managers.

CONCLUSIONS

This study explored the ethical attitudes and behaviors between law enforcement personnel and the different relationships that exist. This study demonstrated through correlation and regression analysis that strong relationships do exist between an officer's own attitudes and behaviors and those he or she believes that others exhibit. The results show that attitudes and behaviors are influenced by fellow officers.

The findings indicate that level of management has no major affect on the attitudes and behaviors that are exhibited by officers. There are slight differences in responses between first-line, mid-level, and senior-level managers but these were found to be insignificant. Even though these management levels do not play an important role, what was found was that the dependence upon the perceived notion of what other officers thought does.

An officer's attitude toward the seriousness of supervisor misconduct is affected by how he or she feels about other officer's attitudes toward this misconduct. The officer's knowledge of the conduct as being a violation of policy or not also influences their decision on seriousness. This demonstrates how an officer's judgment toward ethical behavior is molded. The level of management has very little effect on this ethical decision. The length of service or size of agency also plays a very small part in the officer's views. Dependency upon what an officer thinks other's attitudes are puts more importance on making sure that all officers in an organization conform to high ethical standards.

Punishment that an officer feels should follow the supervisor misconduct is affected by not only his or her attitude toward the seriousness of
the offense but more importantly what punishment would be received by
the department. This indicates that officers will judge the punishments
for such violations based upon the organization's view. This can be advantageous if the agency has a record of appropriate and consistent penalties
for this type of misconduct.

The most important aspect of this study is the examination of an officer's willingness to report supervisor misconduct. Level of management,
length of service, agency size, punishment that would follow, and other's
attitudes toward seriousness play no significant role in the decision to
report, but the willingness of others to report does. This is illustrated by the
major dependence upon the willingness of others to report such misconduct and the smaller influence of one's own attitude toward seriousness.
With such a strong influence by others on reporting ethical misconduct, an
officer surrenders his or her own beliefs and values to his or her co-workers.
This behavior is then controlled by the "group" or to a larger extent, the
organization. This can also be advantageous to the organization if it main-
tains a culture of high expectations of ethical standards. By preserving these
standards throughout the organization, officers will adhere to them better if
they believe others are doing the same. This is why continued ethics training is so important to the integrity of an organization.

Level of management, in this study, did not seem to have much of an
influence on officer attitudes or behaviors. The limits of this study do not
allow for an in depth analysis of the varying levels of management. Using
only one scenario in which supervisor misconduct was evaluated limits
the findings to this particular type of misconduct. Other variables that
were not considered in this study could contribute to the inconsistent
managerial views and influence of different levels of management on the
attitudes and behaviors of law enforcement officers. The affects of differences among levels of management on different peer attitudes and behaviors could be the subject of future analyses.

As indicated by the regression models, the influence of others has a
great power over those making ethical decisions. This power can often
lead to a subverted culture that can exist within an organization. The peer
pressure and perceptions of what others may think can lead an officer to
"go along with the crowd" or "watch each other's backs." This can then
develop into lack of integrity or even corruption (Klockars et al., 2000;

Johnson & Cox, 2005). Corrupt or dishonest organizations are then at risk of losing public trust. Loss of trust in turn results in loss of support (Feldheim & Wang, 2004).

The correlations found between the questions of attitude and behavior also help to sustain the hypotheses which indicate that the influence of others can influence one's own decision-making process. This demonstrates not only that a relationship exists between the supposed views of others and one's own views, but it shows that there is a strong relationship. The strength of this relationship is so strong that it has been known to corrupt officers and ruin careers. The work of Weisburd et al. (2000) supports the idea that going against another officer can result in social isolation. This work also reports that most officers agree that not reporting misconduct is not uncommon (Weisburd et al., 2000). This "code of silence" may often lead officers and management to step over that boundary of breaking ethical rules and into corruption (Klockars et al., 2000; Trautman, 2000).

This helps to provide a starting point to determine what ethical problems can exist within the law enforcement community and what areas need to be addressed during ethics training. Ethics training needs to be a balance of theoretical and practical applications. This training needs to address critical thinking, reasoning skills, and problem solving abilities. Identifying and defining the virtues that comprise integrity is the first step in developing officers of integrity (Vicchio, 1997). Ethics training should not end after the usual short four-hour courses taught in most police training academies (IACP, 2001). Instead it should continue throughout an officer's career and into management. The use of ethics in a law enforcement agency is something that just cannot be taught, it must be integrated into the organizational culture (Vicchio, 1997).

DISCUSSION QUESTIONS

1. How can an officer balance his/her role as a crime fighter versus his/her role as a public servant?
2. What do you think is the role of a law enforcement supervisor within the context of community policing? Does this change within the context of a Homeland Security era? Is this role significantly different depending upon the level of supervisory position?

3. What impact does organizational culture have on supervisors in law enforcement?

4. Were you surprised by any of the results (regression or correlation) regarding the relationship between supervisor and officer attitudes toward misconduct? What about the punishment that should follow results—any surprises there? How about willingness to report?

REFERENCES

Barker, J. (1999). *Danger, Duty, and Disillusion: The Worldview of Los Angeles Police Officers.* Prospect Heights, IL: Waveland.

Bolton Jr., K. (2003). Shared perceptions: black officers discuss continuing barriers in policing. *International Journal of Police Strategies and Management, 26*(3), 386–399.

Burke, J. (1989). Reconciling public administration and democracy: the role of the responsible administrator. *Public Administration Review, 49*(2), 180–186.

Cooper, T. (1987). Hierarchy, virtue, and the practice of public administration: a perspective for normative ethics. *Public Administration Review, 47*(4), 320–328.

Feldheim, M., & Wang, X. (2004). Ethics and public trust: results from a national survey. *Public Integrity, 6*(1), 63–75.

IACP. (2001). Ethics Training in Law Enforcement, International Association of Chiefs of Police. Retrieved on February 2, 2006, from http://www.theiacp.org/documents/index.cfm?fuseaction=document&document_id=99.

Jaramillo, F., Nixon, R., & Sams, D. (2005). The effect of law enforcement stress on organizational commitment. *International Journal of Police Strategies and Management, 28*(2), 321–336.

Johnson, T., & Cox III, R. (2005). Police ethics: organizational implications. *Public Integrity, 7*(1), 67–79.

Klockars, C., Ivkovich, S., Harver, W., & Haberfeld, M. (2000). *The Measurement of Police Integrity.* Washington, D.C.: National Institute of Justice.

Lipsky, M. (1980). *Street Level Bureaucracy: Dilemmas of the Individual in Public Services.* New York: Russell Sage Foundation.

O'Mally, T. (1997). Managing for ethics: a mandate for administrators, *FBI Law Enforcement Bulletin.*

Paoline III, E. (2001). *Rethinking Police Culture: Officer's Occupational Attitudes.* New York: LRB.

Peak, K., Glensor, R., & Gaines, L. (1999). Supervising the police. In K. Dennis & R. McNamara (Eds.), *Police and Policing: Contemporary Issues* (pp. 37–56). Westport, CT: Praeger.

Plummer, L. (1995). In pursuit of honest leadership. *FBI Law Enforcement Bulletin, 64*(4), 16.

Pollock, J. (1998). *Ethics in Crime and Justice: Dilemmas and Decisions,* 3rd ed. Belmont, CA: Wadsworth.

Raines, J. (2005). Ethics, Integrity, and Police Misconduct: Analyzing Ethical Awareness, Standards and Action of Law Enforcement in the United States. Unpublished doctoral dissertation, North Carolina State University.

Scarborough, K., Tubergen, G., Gaine, L., & Whitlow, S. (1999). An examination of police officers' motivation to participate in the promotional process. *Police Quarterly, 2*(3), 302–320.

Thompson, D. (1985). The possibility of administrative ethics. *Public Administration Review, 45*(5), 555–561.

Thompson, D. (1992). Paradoxes of government ethics. *Public Administration Review, 52*(3), 254–259.

Trautman, N. (2000). Police Code of Silence Facts Revealed, Legal Officers Section of the International Association of Chiefs of Police, 2000 Conference. Retrieved November 27, 2005, from http://www.aele.org/loscode2000.html.

Vicchio, S. (1997). Ethics and police integrity. *FBI Law Enforcement Bulletin, 66*(7), 8.

Weisburd, D., Hamilton, E., Williams, H., Bryant, K., & Greenspan, R. (2000). Police Attitudes Toward Abuse of Authority: Findings from a National Study, National Institute of Justice. Retrieved February 10, 2006, from http://www.ncjrs.gov/pdffiles1/nij/181312.pdf.

Whetstone, T. (2001). Copping out: why police officers decline to participate in the sergeant's promotional process. *American Journal of Criminal Justice, 25*(2), 147–159.

Wilson, J. (1989). *Bureaucracy: What Government Agencies Do and Why They Do It.* New York: Basic Books.

CHAPTER 10

Law Enforcement Policy:
Use of Force

OBJECTIVES

- Explain misuse of force policy in the United States by focusing on three federal cases, which include *Tennessee v. Garner*, *Graham v. Connor*, and *Straw v. Stroud*
- Identify factors that impact a police officer's decision to use force
- Analyze some of the factors impacting a police officer's decision to use force using the National Institute of Justice study
- Discuss the implications of these factors that impact use of force policy

This chapter analyzes law enforcement policy in the United States regarding the use of force on the job. The focus will be on existing case law for law enforcement officers. Finally, this chapter will incorporate police officer perceptions regarding the unnecessary use of force from the NIJ study discussed in previous chapters. There are many important cases that address police officer use of force; however, this chapter focuses on three cases, which include *Tennessee v. Garner*, *Graham v. Connor*, and *Shaw v. Stroud*. These cases outline an officer's responsibility with respect to deadly force, force in general, and supervisory responsibilities in controlling unnecessary use of force.

The first case, *Tennessee v. Garner*, analyzes whether the use of deadly force to prevent the escape of an unarmed suspected felon is constitutional. The Court in *Graham v. Connor* addresses the constitutional standard that governs a citizen's claim that law enforcement used excessive force in the course of making an arrest, investigatory stop, or other "seizure" of his person.

Finally, *Shaw v. Stroud* focused on supervisor liability for officer use of force. Combined, these cases sketch the environment within which officers operate when making decisions regarding the use of force on the job.

TENNESSEE V. GARNER

At the time this case came to the U.S. Supreme Court, the state of Tennessee and the Memphis police department allowed for the use of deadly force against suspects fleeing the scene of a felony or resisting arrest. Officers responding to a burglary came upon a fleeing suspect who continued to run after an officer called out "police, halt." The officer was reasonably sure the suspect was unarmed, but would escape without immediate action. The suspect was fatally shot by the officer. The decedent's family brought this action alleging violations of the suspect's 4th, 5th, 6th, 8th, and 14th Amendment rights (*Garner* at 6).

The District Court held for the defendants, dismissed claims against the Mayor and Director of the Police Department for lack of evidence, and upheld the constitutionality of the state statute. The Court of Appeals affirmed the District Court's ruling with respect to the officer's actions, but remanded to have the District Court reconsider the city's liability and the constitutionality of allowing deadly force and hollow point bullets under the circumstances. The District Court did not change its initial decision. The Court of Appeals reversed and remanded with respect to the issue of the statute and department policy as a violation of the 4th Amendment (*Garner* at 6).

The U.S. Supreme Court, however, focused on the 4th Amendment claim and whether or not the use of deadly force is a "seizure" under the Constitution. The 4th Amendment provides for

> The right of the people to be secure in their persons, houses, papers, and effects against unreasonable searches and seizures, shall not be violated, and no warrants shall issue but upon probably cause, supported by oath or affirmation, and particularly describing the place to be searched, and the persons or things to be seized.

U.S. Const., Amend. 4. The Supreme Court found that the use of deadly force is a seizure and, therefore, invokes the requirements of the 4th Amendment. The 4th Amendment is a reasonableness test requiring a balancing of the nature and quality of the 4th Amendment intrusion against the importance of the governmental interest in intruding. According to the Court, where a suspect poses no immediate threat to the officer and/or others, then the use of deadly force is not reasonable (*Garner* at 10–13).

The Tennessee statute in question was found unconstitutional in authorizing deadly force against unarmed, non-dangerous suspects, but constitutional in allowing officers to use deadly force against suspects that pose a threat of serious physical harm either to the officers or to others. The Court chose not to rely on the common law rule supporting the statute as the common law rule arose when virtually all felonies were punishable by death (*Garner* at 10–13). The trend for states and law enforcement is a move away from the common law rule allowing deadly force to a more restrictive rule curtailing the use of deadly force in most situations.

GRAHAM V. CONNOR

This case examines the constitutional standard that governs a citizen's claim that law enforcement used excessive force in the course of making an arrest, investigatory stop, or other "seizure" of his person. Graham was suffering from an insulin reaction and asked a friend to drive him to a convenience store to purchase some orange juice. The store was crowded so Graham entered and left quickly. Officer Connor made an investigatory stop, called for backup, and arrested Graham who was behaving strangely. As a result of the arrest, Graham sustained a broken foot, cuts on his wrists, a bruised forehead, an injured shoulder, and a loud ringing in his ear. The District Court granted Defendants' motion for directed verdict at the close of Plaintiff's case. The District Court applied a 4 part substantive due process standard in granting a directed verdict that included a requirement that the Plaintiff show the excessive force was malicious and sadistically applied for the purpose of causing harm. The Court of Appeals affirmed (*Graham* at 389–91).

The U.S. Supreme Court, however, held that the proper standard to apply in excessive force cases is an objective reasonableness standard under the 4th Amendment. The two primary sources of constitutional protection against physically abusive governmental conduct are the 4th and 8th Amendments. Excessive force claims that arise from investigatory stops and/or arrests invoke the protection of the 4th Amendment. The 4th

Amendment is a reasonableness test requiring a balancing of the nature and quality of the 4th Amendment intrusion against the importance of the governmental interest in intruding. The reasonableness test requires judging objectively the actions of the officer from the perspective of a reasonable officer under the circumstances.

The Court did not apply the balancing test in this case, but remanded the case to the lower court for reconsideration under the proper test. This case essentially requires officers to objectively judge their own actions. An officer must consider the perspective of a reasonable officer under the circumstances when considering whether or not to use force on the job. However, whether an officer is acting reasonably is extremely subjective, making this difficult for officers to apply in their daily duties.

SHAW V. STROUD

This case analyzes supervisory responsibilities in controlling unnecessary use of force. Officer Morris pulled into Bowen's driveway suspecting Bowen of driving while impaired. Bowen ran from the car when Morris reached for his ticket book and Morris pursued him. Bowen's wife, Nancy, and daughter, Kimberly, heard Bowen say he would cooperate with the officer. Morris claims that Bowen fell and Morris held him around the collar. Bowen yelled out that he was going to jail and told Kimberly to get help because the law was trying to kill him. Kimberly ran to a nearby relative's house while Nancy watched from their front porch (*Shaw* at 794).

Morris requested backup and Bowen jerked away from Morris who then began hitting Bowen with his flashlight. Bowen and Morris struggled for the flashlight until Morris pulled out his gun and shot Bowen who continued to swing at Morris. Eventually, Morris fatally shot Bowen five times. This fatal confrontation transpired within 93 seconds from Morris' call for backup (*Shaw* at 794).

Stroud was Morris' supervisor for the first 5 years of his 7 year career. Stroud received multiple reports from various sources regarding Morris' use of excessive force over the years. Morris did receive counseling from a line sergeant regarding insulting the public. Morris was responsible for nearly half of the assault charges against arrestees for the entire department and 13 people accused Morris of using excessive force (*Shaw* at 795).

Judge Gore spoke to a Line Sergeant, White, about Morris' conduct and White filled out a complaint form and left it with Stroud's replacement,

Smith. Stroud did not take any action against Morris. Smith, however, monitored Morris' job performance and accompanied Morris on patrol on at least two occasions. White also advised Morris to be more courteous (*Shaw* at 795).

The District Court granted Morris summary judgment on the 14th Amendment due process claim, the negligent and intentional infliction of emotional distress claims only related to the minor son of Bowen. The District Court denied Stroud summary judgment on the 4th Amendment violation, the wrongful death claim, however, granted summary judgment on the intentional and negligent infliction of emotional distress claims and the 4th Amendment violation. Summary judgment was granted on all claims against Smith (*Shaw* at 797).

There are three elements to establishing a supervisory liability claim, which include:

1. the supervisor had actual or constructive knowledge that his subordinate engaged in conduct that posed a pervasive and unreasonable risk of constitutional injury to citizens,
2. the supervisor's response to that knowledge was so inadequate as to show deliberate indifference to or tacit authorization of the alleged offensive practices, and
3. there was a causal link between the supervisor's inaction and the particular constitutional injury suffered by the plaintiff.

While Stroud was Morris' supervisor, Morris was responsible for approximately half of the assault charges on law enforcement officers and resisting/delaying/obstructing an officer. Stroud did not take any action; therefore, Stroud is liable for the natural consequences of his actions. Bowen's death was a foreseeable consequence. Smith, on the other hand, took supervisory action in response to Morris' conduct. Smith's actions need not have been effective in order to be deemed adequate (*Shaw* at 798–799).

Both Smith and Stroud argued they were entitled to qualified immunity so long as their conduct did not violate clearly established statutory or constitutional rights of which a reasonable person would have known. Qualified immunity "shields officials from liability for discretionary acts only insofar as they do not violate clearly established constitutional rights" (Schwartz, 2003). Stroud argued that the law regarding supervisory liability and excessive force were not clearly established, however, the court did not agree based on established case law. Therefore, Stroud was not entitled to qualified immunity. Smith, however, was entitled to qualified immunity as Smith responded to Morris' misconduct, while Stroud ignored Morris' behavioral problems (*Shaw* at 799–805).

Essentially, *Shaw* established that supervisors will be held liable for the misuse of force by their line officers unless they take reasonable steps in response to potential misconduct. The trend in all three of these cases is a move away from unrestricted police use of force, as has been historically the case, to a more conservative, restrictive perspective governing police use of force.

FACTORS THAT IMPACT POLICE OFFICER USE OF FORCE

The excessive force question included in the NIJ instrument reads as follows:

> Two police officers on foot patrol surprise a man who is attempting to break into an automobile. The man flees. They chase him for about two blocks before apprehending him by tackling him and wrestling him to the ground. After he is under control both officers punch him a couple of times in the stomach as punishment for fleeing and resisting.

Surprisingly, officers did not find this behavior as serious as theft by an officer from a crime scene. In fact, this scenario was considered only moderately serious behavior by officer respondents in comparison to the other scenarios (Klockers et al., 2000). This paper analyzes the predictive value, as well as the relationship between several variables such as type of assignment, rank, and length of service and whether or not an officer perceives the use of force in this scenario as serious and whether or not they would report the misuse of force under the circumstances.

Multiple regression is a statistical tool used to determine whether certain variables can predict outcomes. Correlation is a statistical tool used to determine whether there is a relationship between variables. In order to use either tools for analysis, certain assumptions must be met (Tabachnick & Fidell, 2001). After screening the data in order to meet the requirements of these statistical tools, there remained 2,689 cases.[1]

---

[1] Multiple regression and correlation assume lack of multicollinearity or singularity, linearity, and an absence of outliers. Missing values were also deleted as were responses from officers who indicated they were not truthful on the survey.

Three dependent variables were analyzed to see whether several independent variables could be considered predictors of each dependent variable. The three dependent variables were the officer's perception of the seriousness of the misuse of force, whether the officer would report the misuse of force, and what discipline the officer thought should follow as a result of the misuse of force. The independent variables chosen were those that most closely operationalize the characteristics of the paramilitary organization. The independent variables that were tested as predictors included the type of police agency, type of assignment, rank in the police department, the length of service in general, the police department within which the officer served, and whether the officer is a supervisor.

Some independent variables were not significant and were removed one at a time in an attempt to strengthen the predictive value of the independents. Unfortunately, the independent variables predictive strength ranged from 8% to 8.4%. Essentially the independent variables only explain about 8.4% of the officer's perceptions regarding the misuse of force. The independent variables predictive strength ranged from 6.4% to 6.7% with respect to what discipline the officers felt should follow as a result of the misuse of force. The strongest predictive relationship existed between the independent variables and whether the officer would report the misuse of force. The independent variables explained approximately 12.9% of the officer's willingness to report.

Analyzing the individual relationships between each independent variable and each dependent variable yielded significant results. Each independent variable is significantly related to each dependent variable. Correlation values can be found in Table 10–1 below.

Table 10-1 Correlations: Misuse of Force

	Seriousness of Behavior	Discipline Should Follow	Reporting Misconduct
Police department	−.233	−.207	−.273
Length of service	.077	.084	.162
Rank	.092	.086	.143
Type of assignment	.083	.077	.108
Supervisor	.119	.121	.195
Type of agency	.154	.117	.142

The strongest relationship had a negative impact on all three dependent variables. The strongest positive relationships involved the independent variables supervisor and type of police agency. Therefore, an officer's police department has a negative impact on how serious an officer views misconduct and whether the officer will report that misconduct. Also, the officer will feel that less stringent discipline should follow depending upon their police department.

Meanwhile, supervisors view misuse of force more seriously than non-supervisors, are more likely to report such misconduct, and feel stronger discipline is warranted. As for type of agency, this variable was measured by size of agency. These correlations suggest that the smaller the agency, the more serious the officer views the misuse of force, the more likely the officer is to report the misconduct, and the more likely the officer feels stronger discipline is warranted. Finally, an officer's willingness to report is impacted the most significantly by the independent variables.

Looking at the responses of all officers in the survey, only slightly more than 50% of officers believe the misuse of force very serious. Over 25% view the misuse of force as moderate to not at all serious. Slightly less than 50% believe an officer should be suspended while over a third of officers believe a written or verbal reprimand or no action at all is warranted. Only slightly more than a third of officers would report the misuse of force at all and over 20% would not report the misuse of force.

Of the 11 case scenarios, the misuse of force was ranked 5th overall for seriousness, 6th overall for discipline, and 5th overall for willingness to report. Scenarios such as ignoring a bar closing late in exchange for a few drinks, accepting a kickback for auto repair referrals, and a supervisor exchanging a tune up on his car for an officer having a holiday off were all ranked more seriously and more likely to report.

These results are surprising given that the law has gradually become more and more restrictive regarding police use of force. Unfortunately, the data are unclear regarding the predictive strength of such factors as size of an agency, rank, police department, supervisory position and length of service. All that can be said from the data is that some factors have a strong influence over whether an officer views misuse of force as serious, is willing to report that misconduct, and deems the misconduct worthy of serious consequences.

DISCUSSION QUESTIONS

1. Do you agree with the outcomes in each of the three cases? Why or why not?
2. What factor do you think is most critical in determining whether or not an officer will use force? Explain why.
3. Can you think of other factors not mentioned in this chapter that might affect whether or not an officer uses force?
4. Based on all of these factors affecting use of force, those in this chapter and those you have come up with, how can policy be changed to improve officer decision making in use of force on the front lines?
5. What impact do you think training has, if any, on an officer's decision to use force?

REFERENCES

Graham v. Connor, 490 U.S. 386 (1989).

Klockars, C. B., Ivkovich, S. K., Harver, W. E., & Haberfeld, M. R. (2000, May). *The Measurement of Police Integrity.* Washington, D.C.: National Institute of Justice.

Shaw v. Stroud, 13 F.3d 791 (1994).

Tabachnick, B. G., & Fidell, L. S. (2001). *Using Multivariate Statistics.* Needham Heights, MA: Allyn & Bacon.

Tennessee v. Garner, 471 U.S. 1 (1985).

CHAPTER 11

Fostering Integrity in Police Agencies

OBJECTIVES

- Provide an improved understanding of police integrity in the United States
- Explain the impact of the National Institute of Justice study on police agencies
- Recommend changes in police culture
- Suggest future research necessary in police integrity

WHAT DO THE RESULTS FROM THE NATIONAL INSTITUTE OF JUSTICE STUDY MEAN FOR POLICE INTEGRITY?

This study explores an officer's ethical awareness, standards, and action to determine what type of officer has above-mean attitudes, mean, or below-mean attitudes regarding misconduct. This study also explores what type of agency has officers who have above-mean, mean, and below-mean attitudes toward misconduct. Findings support the conclusion that an officer's ethical awareness, or attitude toward the seriousness of misconduct, impacts that officer's standards and action.

This places a great deal of importance on an officer's ethical awareness. Attitudes toward misconduct have the potential to affect not just the officer, but the entire agency. Given that people generally resist reporting illegal and/or immoral behavior, ethical awareness is the foundation that determines to some degree whether a person, specifically an officer, will be willing to take ethical action.

Although the size of the agency appears to have no impact on how officers view misconduct, an officer's supervisory position does appear to impact how serious that officer views misconduct. Supervisors view misconduct as more serious than nonsupervisors, which is not surprising considering that supervisors have been on the job longer and may be the individuals responsible for administering punishment for officer misconduct. Being on the job longer does not necessarily mean officers view misconduct more seriously as their careers progress. There is a curvilinear relationship between an officer's attitudes toward misconduct and years of service controlling for supervisory position. The findings highlight a socialization process and/or negative experiences during the first 6 years of service that undercut the ideals of new recruits.

Particularly disturbing were the results with respect to abuse of authority, where all respondents viewed this type of misconduct as less serious than exploiting authority. These findings show a systematic unwillingness to recognize the severity of this type of misconduct. These results indicate a failure to provide the solid ethical foundation necessary to promote an officer's willingness to take ethical action.

Ethical standards are another important factor impacting an officer's willingness to report misconduct. Ethical awareness helps to shape the officer's attitude toward the seriousness of the misconduct. The ethical awareness attitude in turn helps shape the officer's attitude toward what punishment is appropriate. There is slippage between an officer's attitude regarding the seriousness of peer misconduct and the appropriate level of punishment. The officer's peers and supervisors, as well as the officer's agency, help shape both the officer's ethical awareness and ethical standards.

Ethical standards show similar results as those explored in ethical awareness. There is no relationship between size of agency and ethical standards, but there is a relationship between an officer's supervisory position and ethical standards. The curvilinear relationship between years of service and ethical standards is also present, although less pronounced than with ethical awareness. There is a strong reluctance by nonsupervisors with 1 to 5 years of service to administer the harshest punishments of demotion and dismissal for even the worst type of misconduct, malfeasance. The across-the-board unwillingness to administer harsher punishment for abuse of authority misconduct further erodes the strong ethical foundation necessary to promote peer reporting of misconduct.

Ultimately an officer's willingness to report misconduct is a key issue explored in this study. The same factors that affect an officer's ethical action are the same factors that affect an officer's ethical awareness and ethical standards. These factors affect an officer's ethical action in much the same way they affect the officer's ethical awareness and standards, but with further slippage. For example, supervisors believe the misconduct in question is more serious than nonsupervisors. They believe that harsher punishment is required than nonsupervisors, and they are more willing to report misconduct than nonsupervisors. Again, this emphasizes the importance of attitudes—attitudes toward seriousness of the offense and appropriate punishment—and the impact those attitudes have on actual behavior—an officer's willingness to report misconduct.

One finding that is different from results found with awareness and standards occurs in the regression model. There is clearly a greater reluctance to report abuse of authority and malfeasance in very small and small agencies as compared with larger ones. Very small and small agencies may attribute these results to a greater solidarity among peers coupled with less willingness to use formal discipline.

The most compelling findings are with respect to the nature of the misconduct and promotion. Regardless of rank, years in service, supervisory position, or size of agency, abuse of authority is rated as less serious and deserving less punishment, and officers were less willing to report. Equally alarming are the nonreporting patterns: 10 out of 11 officers would definitely not report abuse of authority; 2 out of 5 officers would not report malfeasance, and 3 out of 4 supervisors would not report abuse of authority. The implications of these findings are explored more fully in the section that follows.

All of the officer characteristics explored in this study impacted attitudes and behavior. The individual characteristics studied herein include whether an officer is a supervisor, the officer's rank, and length of service. The organizational factor examined in this study is the size of the agency. These variables unfortunately do not include age, race, and gender. The National Institute of Justice (NIJ) survey did not include questions regarding age, race or gender. This study has focused on individual and organizational characteristics that clearly deserve more attention in the literature.

HOW DO THE RESULTS FROM THE NIJ STUDY IMPACT POLICE AGENCIES?

The two variables that had the biggest impact on officer attitudes overall were officer perceptions of peer attitudes and an officer's knowledge of existing agency policy. The results of this study show that respondents tend to view others as being like themselves whatever their level of awareness, standards, and willingness to report. This is evidenced by the extremely high correlations between the respondent's attitudes toward misconduct, punishment, and reporting and the corresponding officer perceptions of peer responses. These findings show the importance of peer relationships within an agency. The second most important variable was an officer's knowledge of existing policy. This finding emphasizes the need for increased officer training with respect to agency policy.

The findings also suggest critical points on which police managers should focus attention during the career of their officers. First, the transition from new recruit to an officer who has more than 1 year of service coincides with the end of probation for new officers and is one critical point in an officer's career. A second critical point occurs when an officer has between 3 and 5 years of service. Here, one of several events potentially takes place for those officers that fall below the mean. An officer may commit misconduct, get caught, be fired or quit, or the officer might change his or her attitude toward misconduct. Also, officers who are passed on promotion after 6 years of service reach a critical point in their careers, whereas officers who are above the mean are more likely to have the opportunity to accept promotions. Ethics training for officers strategically placed at these critical junctures could impact officer attitudes and behavior with respect to police misconduct. All officers need training regarding misuse of force and professional courtesy.

Lipsky's (1980) work regarding street-level bureaucrats depicts officers as agents facing limited resources, nonvoluntary clients, ambiguous goals, inadequate performance measures, and faced with alienated work. As a consequence of this tumultuous environment, police officers are likely to encounter some level of misconduct at some point during their careers. The results of this research at least partially support the conclusion that officers are reluctant to report misconduct regardless of rank and length of service. Although there is variation associated with these characteristics, one could argue that the proportions that will not report misconduct are unacceptably high.

The type of alienated work depicted by Lipsky does appear within the case scenarios that depict the police taking actions that deny clients their humanity. The police brutality scenario, stealing money, accepting bribes, and theft of property are all examples of officers who are less concerned with their clients and professional or legal standards than with benefiting personally or collectively.

The impact socialization or sustained exposure to the factors that Lipsky (1980) describes appears to affect ethical awareness, standards, and action. Recruits generally had higher means than officers within rank comparisons. Also, officers with less than 1 year of service generally had higher means than officers with 1 to 2 years of experience. Officers with 3 to 5 years of experience tended to have the lowest means across ethical awareness, standards, and action.

Research discussed in Chapter 2 points out that officers enter the force with low levels of cynicism, but it steadily increases over the first 10 years of service. Other research indicates that the typical officers prosecuted for misconduct has approximately 5 to 10 years of service. The results of this study see a sharp decline in nonsupervisor attitudes toward misconduct when an officer has 3 to 5 years of service. These results combined with previous research indicate that officers are most vulnerable to misconduct during the early stages of their careers.

Controlling for supervisory position reveals that promotion may be the variable directly impacting these results. Officers who have been in service for 5 or more years and who are not promoted dramatically depart from their promoted counterparts with respect to attitudes toward misconduct, punishment, and reporting.

Future research analyzing officer stages of moral development controlling for promotion and years of service could lend further support to the results found herein. Kohlberg's stages of moral development (1984) may shed some light on these results regarding promotion and supervisory position. The findings suggest that promotion may impact how and whether an officer progresses from a conventional to a postconventional stage of moral development.

Sutherland might agree with the possibility of socialization effects as described previously here. Sutherland would argue that peers shape officer attitudes. This is how below mean officers are created within the socialization process. The results of this study seem to support Sutherland's theory as opposed to Hirschi's (2002) theory. Hirschi's (2002) theory would suggest that officers come to the force corrupt, and lack of controls allow these officers to commit misconduct. The literature, however, does not provide any evidence supporting this view of the police. One alternative would be that the new officer is corrupt before entering the force, but there have been adequate controls his or her entire life. After entering the force, these controls become inadequate, allowing some officers to commit misconduct. This explanation seems less likely and contradicts the findings with respect to new officers having higher means.

One way to combat these negative socialization effects is through officer training. Currently, all officers undergo a basic set of training courses when they enter police service. Not all training courses include ethics training and many devote only an hour or two at most to ethics. Continual ethics training throughout the officer's career is virtually nonexistent for police officers.

As for Paoline's (2001) five types of police officers, which include Tough-Cops, Clean-Beat Crime-Fighters, Avoiders, Problem-Solvers, and Professionals, these findings suggest either some changes to the five types or the creation of some other types of officers. Paoline's (2001) five types of officers do not consider officer attitudes toward misconduct, punishment, or willingness to report officer misconduct. His types do not consider the important role promotion plays in shaping officer attitudes, nor do the types include the impact of situational variables (nature of the misconduct). Each of the five types needs to consider the officer's attitude toward misconduct, punishment, and willingness to report. The five types should be expanded to include the Agency Custodians. These are the supervisors and higher ranked officers who are removed from the front-line conditions of the first four types. As the five types point out potential shortcomings in officers, identifying where officers fall within these categories would be an important tool for shaping officer ethics training.

Given the four types of misconduct within this study, abuse of authority showed the most consequential results. The scenarios themselves are unique in that officers who engage in abuse of authority like the scenarios within this study do more than commit misconduct. Both scenarios involve conspiratorial behavior that at least partially supports Klockars et al.'s (2004) idea of police solidarity. Both scenarios involve officers engaged in illegal behavior. Neither scenario involves an officer receiving economic benefit highlighting the importance of the psychic benefits the officer receives. This combination—conspiratorial behavior, police solidarity, illegal behavior, psychic benefits—distinguishes abuse of authority from the other types of misconduct.

The results for abuse of authority also distinguish abuse of authority from the other types of misconduct. The results for abuse of authority are important given that all officers, regardless of rank, years of service, and size of agency ranked exploiting authority misconduct as more serious, deserving of stronger discipline, and ultimately more worthy or reporting to authorities. Nevertheless, abuse of authority is more serious given the nature of the illegal behavior depicted in each of the two scenarios. Within abuse of authority for nonsupervisors according to length of service, solidarity overrides the normal curvilinear effect. This result reinforces the interpretation of these cases as tests of how officers feel about taking action that upholds the authority of the badge or protects a fellow officer. This sense gets stronger with greater length of service through moderately long periods of time and only slightly declines after that point. It is the one area in which the most experienced nonsupervisory officers have levels of awareness that are lower than new and recent recruits.

It is unclear whether other types of abuse of authority would find the same results. Consider an officer who coerces sexual favors from a prostitute in exchange for avoiding arrest or an officer who extends professional courtesy to an officer caught molesting a child. These types of abuse of authority might not evoke the same level of sympathy or willingness to shield the abusing officer from peers. Future research needs to explore other abuse of authority scenarios in order to determine the limits of officer solidarity.

Size-of-agency results were somewhat perplexing. The results do not show a linear or even a curvilinear relationship for officer attitudes according to size of agency. Generally, small agencies consistently showed low means across awareness, standards, and action, whereas large agencies showed consistently high means across awareness, standards, and action. The results for the remaining agencies were inconsistent revealing no pattern. The importance of these results is that the size of agency does not appear to impact greatly officer attitudes and behavior regarding misconduct.

This study has strong implications for new recruit and continual ethics training within law enforcement. There are many other issues other than those raised in this section that deserve further attention. The section that follows explores these issues.

RECOMMENDATIONS FOR CHANGING POLICE CULTURE AND FOR FUTURE RESEARCH

With respect to training, this study highlights specific areas of need within law enforcement. The results of this study show that patrol officers and officers with 3 to 5 years of service are in the greatest need of ethics training. Senior managers may need some ethics training specific to their needs because they are in a position to impact all officers in their agencies, to lead by example, to impact policy changes, and to implement necessary ethics training. All officers need counseling with respect to abuse of authority. This study is a good tool for surveying officers within an agency before assessing that agency's ethics training needs. Future research could focus on existing ethics training for law enforcement and use the survey instrument within agencies as an ethics assessment tool. It is important to explore other ethical issues through expansion of the list of scenarios used in the NIJ study in order to continually update and improve training efforts recommended here. For example, officers who are tempted to misrepresent information on official reports or to commit perjury.

Ethical standards for the purposes of this study have focused on formal punishments, as these were the only punishments utilized by the survey instrument. Other formal forms of punishment excluded from the survey include transferring officers, fines, counseling, and delays in promotion. Informal forms of punishment for misconduct include ostracizing officers socially and on the job. Future research could analyze the impact other forms of punishment, both formal and informal, have on an officer's attitude toward misconduct.

Ethical action within the context of this study focused on an officer's willingness to report misconduct. Future research could look into other ethical actions officers might take with respect to misconduct. For example, instead of reporting an officer for misconduct, an officer could offer counsel or seek counseling for the officer in question. The officer also could be given an opportunity to turn himself or herself in to supervisors.

Wilson's (1968) three styles of policing—the watchman, legalistic and service styles—is another source of future research. How does the officer incorporate the attitudes and behavior explored in this study into his or her daily job activities? Do Wilson's (1968) styles of policing each have an ethics profile depicting the officer's ethical attitude and behavior? How would an officer in an agency that employs the watchman style of policing respond to the survey instrument? A future study identifying agencies that use Wilson's (1968) style of policing could be asked to complete the survey instrument to create the appropriate ethics profile with the corresponding style of policing.

Paoline's (2001) five types of police officers—Tough-Cops, Clean-Beat Crime-Fighters, Avoiders, Problem-Solvers, and Professionals, as well as the suggested new type Agency Custodians—are another source of future research. How do each of Paoline's (2001) types of police officers respond to the survey instrument? Can an ethics profile be developed for each of Paoline's (2001) types of police officers? It is expected that Tough-Cops and Avoiders would have the lowest ethical awareness, standards, and action, whereas Professionals and Agency Custodians would have the highest levels of ethical awareness, standards, and action. Future research identifying officers within Paoline's (2001) five types of police officers could then administer the survey instrument to those officers and create an ethics profile with the corresponding type of police officer.

Kohlberg's (1984) stages of moral development—preconventional, conventional, and postconventional—are another source of future research. What are the ethical characteristics of officers at each level of moral development? Officers could complete the DIT 2 test followed by the survey instrument to determine whether a connection exists between moral development and ethical development.

It has been over a decade since the NIJ survey was first conducted. Since that time, policing has changed given the events of 9/11. The scenarios need to be updated to reflect these changes and to include different aspects of each type of misconduct. Independent variables left out in the first study should be included in future studies such as age, race, gender, and marital status. These controls are important factors, and their impact should be considered in future research.

The future research possible from this study is limitless. The NIJ research that is the subject of this study has not been fully exhausted itself.

CONCLUSION

The questions analyzed by this study are fundamental to administrative ethics. What causes differences in ethical attitudes and behaviors in street-level bureaucrats? For police officers several factors impact their ethical decision making. An officer's perceptions regarding peer attitudes impact that officer's attitudes and behaviors. What do my peers think? What would my peers do? These results show how important the role that solidarity plays in a law enforcement agency.

An officer's knowledge of existing policy impacts that officer's attitudes and behavior. These results show the important role training plays in an agency. Just knowing a policy exists and the punishment that will follow has an effect on the foundation—an officer's attitude toward that misconduct—and the action—an officer's willingness to report the misconduct.

Length of service has some impact on officer attitudes and behavior. New officers with less than 1 year of service have high ethical awareness and standards but are reluctant to report misconduct. This is understandable considering new recruits are on probation and may not be familiar with what happens to officers who report misconduct. Nonsupervisory officers with 1 to 6 years of service are less likely to report misconduct than officers who have been in service longer. These officers, nonsupervisors with 0 to 6 years of service, are the officers who are in the best position to report misconduct as they are the street-level bureaucrat witnessing misconduct first hand. These results suggest focusing attention on reporting behavior in nonsupervisory officers in the early stages of their careers.

The nature of the misconduct itself is an important factor to consider. Officers' responses to misconduct are situation dependent. Whether an officer makes an arrest, uses force, or reports peer misconduct is very much dependent upon the nature of the misconduct itself. All of the scenarios explored in this study are violations of office policy; however, the respondents were most impacted by the type of misconduct when considering whether to report. The more serious the misconduct did not equal an increase in the willingness to report given the results with respect to abuse of authority.

The focus of this study has been ethical decision making in the areas of misconduct, corruption, ethics, and moral reasoning within government, in particular, police ethics. Understanding the police officer's attitudes toward misconduct is an important step toward understanding ethical and unethical behavior within their ranks. Misconduct is hard to investigate because of unwillingness on the part of public officials to admit wrongdoing. That is why this study is so important to reaching an understanding of police ethics.

DISCUSSION QUESTIONS

1. Do you agree that results from the NIJ data analysis indicate a failure to provide the solid ethical foundation necessary to promote an officer's willingness to take ethical action? Why or why not?
2. Do you think that the unwillingness to administer harsher punishment for abuse of authority misconduct further erodes the strong ethical foundation necessary to promote peer reporting of misconduct? Why or why not?
3. This chapter discusses critical points in an officer's career when ethics training might be most effective. Do you agree or disagree with these points? What training should be given at these critical junctures? How would you structure such training?
4. Do you have suggestions for future research? Of the suggestions made in this chapter, which struck you as most interesting and why? What do you think would be the outcome if the research were conducted?

REFERENCES

Hirschi, T. (2002). *Causes of Delinquency*. Berkeley, CA: University of California Press.

Klockars, C. B., Ivkovic, S. K., & Haberfeld, M. (2004). *The Contours of Police Integrity*. Thousand Oaks, CA: Sage Publications.

Kohlberg, L. (1984). *The Psychology of Moral Development: The Nature and Validity of Moral Stages*. San Francisco: Harper & Row.

Lipsky, M. (1980). *Street-Level Bureaucracy: Dilemmas of the Individual in Public Services*. New York: Russell Sage Foundation.

Paoline III, E. A. (2001). *Rethinking Police Culture: Officers' Occupational Attitudes*. New York: LFB Scholarly Publishing LLC.

Wilson, J. Q. (1968). *Varieties of Police Behavior*. New York: Antheneum.

Index

Note: Italicized page number indicate figures; t *indicates tables.*

A

Absenteeism, alienated workers and, 16
Abuse of authority
  case scenarios
    categorizing of, 97
    ethical awareness for police officers and,
      110, 111
    by nature of misconduct, 99t
  correlations
    between agency policy and officer
      attitudes, 123, 123t
    between ethical action and agency
      policy, 158t
    between officer attitudes and
      perceptions of peer attitudes,
      123–124, 124t
  counseling with respect to, 208
  ethical action
    agency size and, 155, 156–157t, 157–158
    correlations between officer action and
      perceptions of peer action, 159t
    length of service and, 150, 151, 154
      nonsupervisors only, 152–154t
    regression, 160t
    respondent reporting for, 149, 150
    summary, 149t, 162
    supervisory position and, 151t
  ethical awareness
    agency size and, 121, 122t, 123
    descriptive statistics summary and,
      126, 127
    rank and, 115t, 116

    regression, 124, 125t
    respondent rating for, 111, 112
    summary, 112t
    supervisory position and, 113–114, 113t
    by years of service, *120*
      nonsupervisory only, 117,
      118–119t, 119
  ethical standards
    agency size and, 138, 139–140t, 140
    correlations between agency policy and
      officer attitudes toward
      punishment, 141t
    correlations between officer attitudes and
      perceptions of peer attitudes, 141t
    length of service: nonsupervisors only,
      135–137t
    regression, 142t
    summary, 131t
    summary of officer rating for, 143
    supervisory position and, 133t, 134
  Kolthoff's typology and, 96
  National Institute of Justice study
    consequential results for, 206–207
    data analysis and, 97
  officer length of service and, 134, 137
  percentage of who would definitely report,
    by length of service, *155*
  rank, gamma score and, 117
  systematic unwillingness to recognize
    severity of, 202, 203
Accreditation, 24
Adaptive cultures, 27

213